VISUAL COMPOSING

VISUAL COMPOSING
DOCUMENT DESIGN FOR PRINT AND DIGITAL MEDIA

Kathryn Riley

Jo Mackiewicz

Prentice Hall

Boston   Columbus   Indianapolis   New York   San Francisco   Upper Saddle River   Amsterdam
Cape Town   Dubai   London   Madrid   Milan   Munich   Paris   Montreal   Toronto   Delhi
Mexico City   Sao Paulo   Sydney   Hong Kong   Seoul   Singapore   Taipei   Tokyo

Editor in Chief: Vernon Anthony
Senior Acquisitions Editor: Gary Bauer
Editorial Assistant: Megan Heintz
Director of Marketing: David Gesell
Marketing Manager: Leigh Ann Sims
Marketing Assistant: Les Roberts
Senior Managing Editor: Central Publishing
Project Manager: Laura Messerly
Operations Specialist: Central Publishing
Senior Art Director: Jayne Conte
Text Designer: Pearson Central Design

Cover Designer: Suzanne Behnke
Manager, Rights and Permissions,
   Image Resource Center: Zina Arabia
Cover Art: Design and photography by Allen Hori
Full-Service Project Management: Mohinder Singh,
   Aptara®, Inc.
Composition: Aptara®, Inc.
Printer/Binder: Edwards Brothers
Cover Printer: Lehigh-Phoenix Color/Hagerstown
Text Font: Palatino

Credits and acknowledgments borrowed from other sources and reproduced, with permission, in this textbook appear on appropriate page within text.

Microsoft® and Windows® are registered trademarks of the Microsoft Corporation in the U.S.A. and other countries. Screen shots and icons reprinted with permission from the Microsoft Corporation. This book is not sponsored or endorsed by or affiliated with the Microsoft Corporation.

Many of the designations by manufacturers and seller to distinguish their products are claimed as trademarks. Where those designations appear in this book, and the publisher was aware of a trademark claim, the designations have been printed in initial caps or all caps.

Library of Congress Cataloging-in-Publication Data

Riley, Kathryn Louise
   Visual composing : document design for print and digital media / Kathryn Riley, Jo Mackiewicz.
      p. cm.
   Includes bibliographical references and index.
   ISBN-13: 978-0-13-170674-3 (alk. paper)
   ISBN-10: 0-13-170674-8 (alk. paper)
   1. Visual communication.   2. Digital media.   I. Mackiewicz, Jo.   II. Title.
   P93.5.R55 2011
   686.2'25–dc22   2010009680

10 9 8 7 6 5 4 3 2 1

Prentice Hall
is an imprint of

www.pearsonhighered.com

ISBN 13: 978-0-13-170674-3
ISBN 10:   0-13-170674-8

*To Frank, for his unfailing patience and support,
and to Miranda, Chex, and Remy.*

—KR

*To my grandmothers: Rose Teckla Collins
and Frances Marie Mackiewicz.*

—JM

BRIEF CONTENTS

CONTENTS

INTRODUCTION

Visual Composing: Document Design for Print and Digital Media is for readers, especially students of technical and professional communication, who want to learn the fundamentals of effective document design: how to present text in a way that is both visually attractive and usable, and how to use visual elements to complement or even replace text. As such, *Visual Composing* focuses on the rhetorical considerations, principles of document design, and practical skills needed to effectively present information in academic, workplace, and organizational settings.

Professional document designers certainly still play a key role in the publication process, especially for high-stakes projects and those intended for large-scale distribution. At the same time, the tools for everyday document design are now widely available, thanks to sophisticated software for producing and editing printed texts, Web sites, graphics, and photography. For example, widely used word processing programs such as Microsoft Word now have fairly advanced desktop publishing capabilities, allowing easy integration of visual components into print documents. Most businesses and organizations have (or need) a Web presence, and Web authoring is increasingly easy with user-friendly programs such as Dreamweaver. At the production end, printing (even in color) from digital sources is increasingly accessible and affordable. Contemporary college students, far from being technophobes, are willing and able to learn these print and digital media tools.

When it comes to visual composing, though, simply knowing the practical or technical side—how to use a tool—is not enough. We have all encountered cluttered newsletters, confusing forms, hard-to-interpret graphs, and poorly designed Web sites—in fact, there are several books and a Web site dedicated to "Web pages that suck" (Flanders & Willis, 1998; Flanders & Peters, 2002). The creators of those Web pages had the technical expertise to produce them. What they lacked was an understanding of the relevant principles for making the documents attractive and usable.

Visual Composing brings principles and practice together. Each chapter addresses the "what, why, and how" of integrating verbal and visual content, providing both a theoretical and practical framework. Claims about what does and does not work in document design are supported by references to classic and current research. This research-based approach enables more sophisticated and complex treatments of document design principles, rather than asking readers to settle for simplistic advice, personal opinion, or folk wisdom. It also provides principles that can be applied to new situations or design questions, not just to those covered in this book.

Beyond the specific principles covered in each chapter, we return throughout the book to a set of general criteria for effective visual composing:

- *Clarity:* Do visual elements contribute to the audience's understanding of the document?
- *Unity:* Are visual elements prepared consistently within the document and with respect to other related documents?
- *Usability:* Do visual elements enhance the utility of the document, and do they take into account the environment in which the document will be used?
- *Tone:* Are visual elements appropriate for the intended audience, the content, and for the image that the writer wants to convey?
- *Aesthetics:* Do visual elements enhance the document's appeal, making it stand out (in a positive way) from other similar documents that the reader might encounter?

The following sections expand on each of these criteria.

CLARITY

Because this book is aimed primarily at students of technical and professional writing, clarity is first and foremost among the criteria by which a document design must be judged effective or ineffective. Just as a fundamental precept of medical practice is "First, do no harm," so a fundamental precept of technical communication is, above all, to convey information in a clear and accurate way and in a way that is understandable by the intended audience. In fact, the code of ethics of the Society for Technical Communication stresses truthfulness, accuracy, and clarity of expression as key responsibilities of the technical communicator. The attractiveness of a document is irrelevant if readers do not understand the information in it or, worse, if the document design inadvertently or intentionally impedes understanding.

The primacy of clarity as a criterion for judging good design becomes especially apparent when you consider the types of information that technical and professional communicators are responsible for conveying in the documents that they design or collaborate in designing. Many of these documents are intended to help people find information (e.g., How do I contact Customer Service?), perform tasks (e.g., How do I changes the blades on my lawnmower?), or understand processes (e.g., How does this surgical procedure work?). Design that impedes understanding can lead to miscommunication, inefficiency, wasted money, dissatisfied customers, or, more seriously, to injury or death, in the case of poorly designed documents that convey instructions or warnings.

This raises an obvious question, of course: How do you know when something is "clear"? After all, we've all been in situations in which we said or wrote something that seemed perfectly clear to us, only to be misunderstood by someone else. For this reason, we have drawn, when possible, on research that uses observational and experimental evidence that one particular document design strategy enhances understanding when compared with an alternative one.

UNITY

As mentioned before, the property of unity refers to the consistency of visual elements, both within a document and with respect to other related documents. Many of the documents that technical and professional communicators prepare are either relatively lengthy (e.g., instruction manuals, employee handbooks) or part of a document set (e.g., a series of promotional brochures prepared by the same company). In both these situations, effective document design requires conscious, advance planning so that the document is internally unified as well as coherent with other related documents. For example, the use of the same font, or typeface, for major headings within a document will help people find their way through the document more easily. In other words, unified design can enhance the functional qualities of a document.

In a somewhat different way, having the same "look and feel" for related documents will help readers associate them with a particular organization and create a professional presence, since it will be apparent that there is a master plan for visual design within the organization. For example, if you are enrolled at a university, there is probably an office on campus called something like Communications and Marketing or Public Relations, and that office is likely to publish a style guide that dictates (or at least suggests) a number of design criteria to be used in university publications. These may range from acceptable and unacceptable uses of the university's logo, to preferred colors to be used in university newsletters and magazines, right down to preferred typefaces to be used in publications. The purpose of such standardization is to help the public recognize the university's publications immediately and to build the university's identity through this visual standardization. So, for example, when alumni receive the university magazine, they will immediately recognize it as being from their alma mater.

USABILITY

As the term implies, usability has to do with whether people can use a document—either a print document or a digital document, such as a Web site—for the purposes that they can reasonably expect the document to fulfill. The notion of usability testing and evaluation is associated today with Web design in particular, and many qualitative and quantitative research strategies exist for evaluating prototyped or existing Web sites. However, print documents and physical objects such as consumer products can, and should, also be evaluated for their usability. A document is said to be usable when people can find the information they are looking for in a reasonably straightforward way, in a reasonable amount of time, and with a minimum of frustration and false starts. As you can imagine, some of these characteristics can be objectively measured during a usability test. However, usability testing may also probe more subjective components, such as the user's sense of satisfaction with the document or whether the user would want to be a customer of the business that produced the document.

The usability of a print or digital document cannot be evaluated without considering the rhetorical situation in which it will be used—the people who will use it, their purpose for using it, and even the physical environment in which they will use it. Probably the most important thing to remember about usability testing and evaluation is the need to do it early and often in the design process. Fundamental design decisions such as whether to make a document available in print, how to bind it, what size paper to use, and so on, demand (at minimum) thoughtful analysis ahead of the fact and (ideally) actually working with representative users in representative environments so that modifications to the design can be made before the project is complete and certainly before it is put into production. For example, an instruction manual designed to be used in an automotive repair shop will call for different design decisions from the instructions for installing a piece of software. The process of prototyping, testing with representative users, and modifying the design in successive cycles is known as iterative design.

The second-most important thing to remember about usability testing is that it requires a sample of representative users. This might seem obvious, but too often a document's usability is assumed by the designer rather than being a quality that has actually been demonstrated by working with representative users. This evaluation process can be carried out using relatively structured, formal procedures or, less formally, by having representative members of the intended audience review the document during its developmental stage. That said, some principles of usability are sufficiently well established by former research that they do not need to be tested and confirmed every time you create a new document. For example, usability research within the field of Web design has established that usability is enhanced when navigation menus appear in a consistent location within the various pages of a Web site. One responsibility of the document designer is, therefore, being familiar enough with research to know which design features are considered "best practices" and which features should be given special attention during usability testing and evaluation.

TONE

Unlike clarity and unity, which can to some extent be objectively measured or at least identified, the criterion of tone is somewhat more ephemeral. As defined previously, gauging whether a particular document design creates an appropriate tone demands taking into consideration for the intended audience, the content, and the image that the writer wants to convey. You may hear your instructor refer to the rhetorical situation for a particular document; this has to do (in part) with complex questions such as the audience, the document's subject matter and purpose, the writer's relationship with the audience, and the writer's role within his or her organization.

Very often, tone is spoken of in binary terms such as formal/informal, personal/ impersonal, modern/traditional, and so on. These are useful starting points and can be applied somewhat objectively to certain design elements (e.g., we will see that specific features cause people to classify certain typefaces as more professional, while other features cause them to classify other typefaces as friendlier). That said, the difficult decision is sometimes which typeface to use for a particular rhetorical situation. For example, if you are called upon to create a series of informational brochures about medical conditions to be made available to patients in a doctor's office, what tone would you want to impart? On one hand, just about any medical condition is a serious matter for the person who has it (though obviously some conditions are more serious than others). On the other hand, part of your goal may be to make sure that patients are not unduly alarmed or "put off" by an overly serious-looking brochure, especially if it is designed to be read by people of varying ages, educational backgrounds, ethnicities, and genders. However, the goal of putting readers at ease may lead to a design whose lighthearted "look and feel" is incompatible with the serious nature of the content.

You can start to see how iterative design, including evaluation by representative audience members during the design process, might help you determine whether you are on the right track in terms of tone.

AESTHETICS

As briefly defined previously, a document's aesthetic qualities have to do with how visually appealing it is to the audience and with how well the document stands out (in a positive way) from other similar documents that the reader might encounter. You have probably heard the expression, "First impressions are last impressions," meaning that the initial impressions that people form (often quickly and unconsciously) are very difficult to change. If you think about your own reaction to print documents and Web sites, you can remember times when you have developed an initial impression based strictly on appearance rather than on content. Perhaps you have leafed through a textbook and thought, This is going to be a chore to read, or you have visited a company's Web site and thought, These people don't look as if they know what they are doing. On the other hand, perhaps you have picked out a CD by a musical group you were unfamiliar with, based at least partly on the fact that the cover design looked interesting and made you want to learn more. Or perhaps you have been reassured by the professional look of a Web site for a company that you were considering doing business with.

If pressed, it might be difficult for you to pinpoint exactly what made one document look off-putting or boring and another document look inviting or interesting, even though you may have had a strong reaction in one other direction or the other. This is the kind of response that we hear from people who say, "I don't know much about art, but I know what I like." Indeed, identifying the specific design elements that make one document more aesthetically appealing than another can be very challenging, especially in the absence of formal training in design and a specific vocabulary for talking about design features. One of the purposes of this book is to give you such a vocabulary as well as to help you understand, predict, and use some of the specific design features that have been identified by research as leading to a positive viewer response—for example, qualities such as symmetry and alignment or the use of certain color combinations and the avoidance of others.

One of the challenges of visual composing is maintaining a balancing act among these five criteria. For example, enhancing a document's usability often means adhering to the conventions of the genre being created. On the other hand, making a document more interesting—for example, creating a flyer that "stands out from the pack" so that viewers notice and respond to it—might mean breaking one or two conventions.

Rather than treating visual elements as divorced from written content, *Visual Composing* explores the way that design decisions must take into account both the written context and the audience for the document. Within each chapter and in end-of-chapter exercises, you as the student are invited to explore various types of content and rhetorical concerns, especially those typically encountered in professional situations.

ORGANIZATION AND APPROACH

The overall organization of *Visual Composing* follows a structure that makes sense pedagogically: It starts with relatively familiar and simple document design tasks and then leads to increasingly complex ones. The chapters in this book fall informally into six parts, each of which addresses similar tasks so that students are working on related concepts and skills.

- *Chapters 1–3:* Strategies for **modifying the appearance** of text for functional and rhetorical purposes.
- *Chapters 4–6:* Strategies for **laying out text** on different parts of the page or into different layouts, beyond the one-column 8.5 × 11 page.
- *Chapters 7–8:* Strategies for **visually representing detailed information**—including verbal, numerical, and technical information—through tables, graphs, and charts, to reinforce or replace written text.
- *Chapters 9–11:* Strategies for **using photography and color** in documents and for understanding the technical and production-related dimension of these elements.
- *Chapters 12–13:* Strategies for **moving from one medium to another**—for example, from print to digital media—and for creating a unified set of documents across several different types of media.
- *Chapter 14:* Strategies for **moving beyond conventional design** through techniques such as trompe l'oeil and three-dimensional designs.

One decision faced by anyone writing a book like this is how to balance general principles about document design with instruction in specific programs. Certainly anyone preparing for a career as a professional document designer will eventually need to master dedicated publishing software such as Adobe InDesign. However, we assume that most readers of this book are either just beginning to learn document design or are learning it to supplement their work in another field, such as technical and professional communication. We also recognize that, since Microsoft Office is the most widely used office suite in the world, students and faculty are much more likely to have access to Word and PowerPoint, on both their personal and university computers, than to dedicated publishing software. Even technical communication students who learn dedicated publishing software may find themselves interning or eventually working at a company equipped only with Microsoft Office. And we recognize that many students will want, or need, to practice and apply their document design skills right away; they need immediate access to programs and equipment that will allow them to do that.

For these reasons, we have designed many of the exercises so that they can be completed in Microsoft Office programs—in particular, Word, PowerPoint, and Excel. Likewise, most of the sample documents and design elements throughout the book were prepared using these programs. In addition, we have designed many of the exercises so that students can complete them with equipment and materials they are likely to have on hand for other purposes: a black-and-white printer stocked with 8.5 × 11 paper.

Of course, some topics demand more specialized equipment and software. For example, you will need access to a color printer to produce the exercises that rely on color. Likewise, when dealing with photography, you may want to explore dedicated software such as Adobe Photoshop or something similar. When working with Web design, you will benefit from access to Adobe Dreamweaver (formerly Macromedia Dreamweaver) or equivalent Web development software.

We also readily acknowledge that many of the topics in *Visual Composing*—for example, information display, photography, and Web design—could easily form the foundation for a freestanding course. Rather than attempting to replace such a course, *Visual Composing* is designed to introduce students to the fundamentals of theory and practice, as well as the working vocabulary, associated with design decisions in these areas. We encourage you to take further specialized coursework that will allow you to study and practice individual elements of document design in more depth.

In short, *Visual Composing* provides students and faculty with a pedagogically coherent, research-based textbook, one that addresses both principles and practical concerns and allows students to move immediately into the world of document design.

STUDENT RESOURCES

Many of the images in *Visual Composing* can be viewed in more detail or in color at the companion Web site www.pearsonhighered.com/riley. There you will also find links, keyed to each chapter, to additional Web resources such as software tutorials, document design tools, and online discussions of document design topics.

INSTRUCTOR RESOURCES

An **Instructor's Manual** and **PowerPoint Lecture Package** are available for instructors to download from the Instructor's Resource Center. To access supplementary materials online, instructors need to request an instructor access code. Go to www.pearsonhighered.com/irc, where you can register for an instructor access code. Within 48 hours of registering, you will receive a confirming e-mail including an instructor access code. Once you have received your code, locate your text in the online catalog and click on the Instructor Resources button on the left side of the catalog product page. Select a supplement, and a log-in page will appear. Once you have logged in, you can access instructor material for all Prentice Hall textbooks.

ACKNOWLEDGMENTS

We thank the reviewers of this book for their thoughtful feedback and insights: Danielle Nicole DeVoss, Michigan State University; John Rothfork, Northern Arizona University; Jennifer Sheppard, New Mexico State University; Karl Stolley, Illinois Institute of Technology; and Thomas R. Williams, University of Washington.

Pearson Education provided invaluable professional support throughout this project. We especially benefited from the help and patience of Gary Bauer, Executive Editor; Megan Heintz, Editorial Assistant; Laura Messerly, Project Manager; and Christina Taylor, Project Manager. Linda Thompson provided us with thorough but unobtrusive copyediting. Mohinder Singh of Aptara, Inc., worked carefully with us through numerous production details.

More locally, we also thank our colleagues, friends, and students at Illinois Institute of Technology and Auburn University: in particular, IIT staff and graduate students Susan Mallgrave, Shimoni Sheth, and Jing Gao for their help with manuscript preparation; Chelsea Kalberloh Jackson, Denise Moriarty, and Nancy Schoon of IIT's Communications department for their help in supplying art files; and James Maciukenas, an IIT doctoral student and design professional whose work so gracefully illustrates many of the principles discussed in this book. We are grateful to the many students who used drafts of this book while it was under development and whose enthusiasm about document design makes it a pleasure to teach the subject.

Let's get started!

Modifying Typography for Functional Purposes

This chapter focuses on choosing and modifying typefaces—such as the popular typeface Times New Roman—so that people can read and use your documents with greater ease. By the end of this chapter, you should be able to do the following:

- Differentiate between typeface legibility and readability
- Identify and use serif and sans serif typefaces
- Differentiate textual elements using typeface weight, shape, and size

OVERVIEW OF RELEVANT DESIGN CONCEPTS AND PRINCIPLES

Decisions about typography—the typefaces used to convey a verbal message—are some of the most important decisions that you will make as you create a document. Typography creates impressions not just in a literal sense but also in a metaphorical sense, by shaping the reader's attitude toward the document. Indeed, *typo* comes to English from a Greek word meaning "impression."

This chapter shows you how to choose and modify typefaces for functional purposes—to make your document clearer to readers and easier for them to use. For example, we look at how you can modify a typeface's weight, shape, and size to serve different functions and to differentiate specific verbal elements from the surrounding text. These functional purposes stand in contrast to typeface choices that relate to the tone, or personality, of your document (discussed in Chapter 2).

We will focus on variations on Times New Roman, since it is one of the most common typefaces used today and is often the default typeface in word processing and document design software.

WHY THESE PRINCIPLES ARE IMPORTANT

As discussed in the book's introduction, clarity and usability are essential properties of document design. These qualities, in turn, are promoted by the use of typefaces that are legible and readable. Legibility and readability are functional properties of typefaces, in that they contribute to your document's usability. The following sections discuss these properties in more detail.

Legibility

Legibility is the quality of being "decipherable and recognizable" (Tracy, 1995, p. 170). As such, it is especially relevant to words and phrases, as opposed to longer stretches of text. Legibility is especially important "in situations where people are scanning pages, reading signs, or skimming through catalogs or lists—wherever they need to instantly recognize words without having to spend extra seconds to read them" (Williams, 2008, p. 43). Figure 1.1 shows the difference between some extremely legible typefaces and some far less legible typefaces.

Typefaces that grab attention because they are ornamental (e.g., Script MT Bold) make recognizing words more difficult (Strizver, 2001, p. 45). In fact, some typefaces, called *display typefaces*, are designed to be printed in large sizes and used only in short stretches of text. A typical use for a display typeface might be a magazine ad or a billboard. In contrast, typefaces like Times New Roman and Arial, called *text typefaces*, are designed to be legible in smaller sizes. Obviously, text typefaces are far more common in professional and technical writing. Look, for example, at the title, headings, and body text in Figure 1.2, which shows instructions for installing a printer cartridge. The instructions for installing the printer cartridge display two different typefaces (not counting the Staples logo) in three colors, but all the typeface-color combinations are legible.

One of your goals as a visual composer is to understand when your readers will require legibility and to be able to select typefaces with this property. Let's say, for instance, that you want to use a table to organize a set of data. You want your reader to be able to single out the content of any given cell of the table, meaning that you want the data in the cells to be maximally legible. As Figure 1.3 illustrates, the Isabella font would not be an effective choice for conveying such information because recognizing its numerals is difficult.

In Figure 1.3, it is difficult to identify the numerals because they display ornamentation that makes them difficult to recognize. Because its numerals lack legibility, Isabella is clearly a poor choice for displaying tabular information. You should think about the legibility of your typefaces as you design other document elements that are composed of words or short stretches of text, such as headings, captions, and labels. The letterforms of the typefaces that you use should be easily recognizable.

Readability

Related to legibility is the functional property of *readability*. Readability is the quality of giving "visual comfort," which is especially important in long stretches of text

More legible	The Quick Brown Fox	Times New Roman
	The Quick Brown Fox	Cantoria MT
	The Quick Brown Fox	Spumoni LP
	The Quick Brown Fox	Onyx MT
Less legible	*The Quick Brown Fox*	Script MT Bold

FIGURE 1.1 Varying legibility of five typefaces.

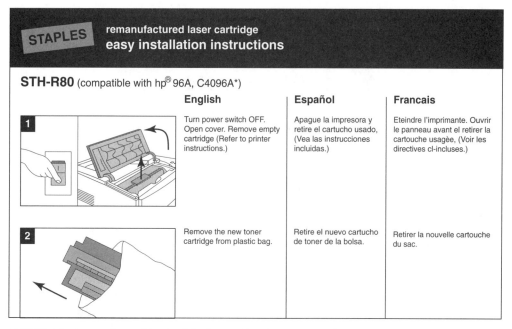

FIGURE 1.2   Instructions with a legible title and headings. Copyright Staples, Inc. Used by permission. (Visit www.pearsonhighered.com/riley to view this figure in color.)

Item	Cost
Airfare	2598.35
Hotel	645.67
Total	3244.02

FIGURE 1.3   Typeface with poor legibility (Isabella) used in a table.

(Tracy, 1995, p. 171; Williams, 2008, p. 33). Figure 1.4 shows the difference between a readable stretch of text, printed in Times New Roman, and a less readable stretch of text, printed in Impact.

As Figure 1.4 illustrates, not all typefaces make reading comfortable, even if those typefaces are legible. When used in a heading, Impact is a fairly legible typeface. However, the readability of Impact is relatively poor: The vertical strokes of its letterforms

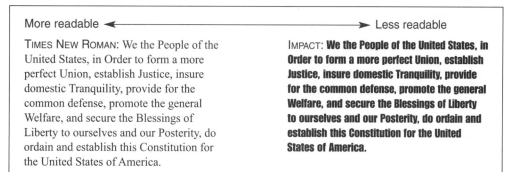

More readable ◄─────────────────────────► Less readable

TIMES NEW ROMAN: We the People of the United States, in Order to form a more perfect Union, establish Justice, insure domestic Tranquility, provide for the common defense, promote the general Welfare, and secure the Blessings of Liberty to ourselves and our Posterity, do ordain and establish this Constitution for the United States of America.

IMPACT: We the People of the United States, in Order to form a more perfect Union, establish Justice, insure domestic Tranquility, provide for the common defense, promote the general Welfare, and secure the Blessings of Liberty to ourselves and our Posterity, do ordain and establish this Constitution for the United States of America.

FIGURE 1.4   Comparative readability of Times New Roman and Impact.

> ● **The Dairy Stewardship Alliance,** a Ben & Jerry's collaborative initiative to develop a sustainability self-assessment tool kit for dairy farmers, marked Year One of successful implementation. Our thanks to the St. Albans Cooperative Creamery of Vermont and the University of Vermont for their support in a commitment we believe can help improve the environmental and social impacts of dairy farming.
>
> ● **We reached and exceeded** every one of the environmental performance goals at our Vermont manufacturing plants, from waste reduction to greenhouse gas emissions. Our own management initiatives and efficiencies gained from significant production increases drove these remarkable results.

FIGURE 1.5   Legible versus readable type in a Ben & Jerry's brochure. Ben & Jerry's Thoughts on 2005 Social & Environmental Performance. Copyright Ben & Jerry's. Used by permission. (Visit www. pearsonhighered.com/riley to view this figure in color.)

are thick, while the horizontal strokes of its letterforms are thinner, creating what look like black stretches of text. Typefaces like this make readers strain after reading a few lines. Note how the ice cream company Ben & Jerry's reserves a legible but not terribly readable typeface for bullet-point headings in its brochure (Figure 1.5). The company uses a readable typeface for the body text, that is, for content presented in larger units of prose such as paragraphs.

You will want to choose readable typefaces for the body text of your documents, but in your titles, headings, and other short lines of text, you can certainly experiment with typefaces that are less readable, as long as they are legible.

Exercise A

Answer the following questions based on your examination of the following typefaces (a–e).

1. Rank the typefaces from least legible to most legible. Then, state a reason for your assessments.
2. Rank the typefaces from least readable to most readable. Then, state a reason for your assessments.
3. Which of these typefaces would you classify as a display typeface? State a reason for your assessment.
4. Which of the typefaces would you classify as a text typeface? State a reason for your assessment.
   a. Belwe Lt: We hold these truths to be self-evident, that all men are created equal, that they are endowed by their Creator with certain unalienable Rights, that among these are Life, Liberty and the pursuit of Happiness.
   b. Nueva: We hold these truths to be self-evident, that all men are created equal, that they are endowed by their Creator with certain unalienable Rights, that among these are Life, Liberty and the pursuit of Happiness.
   c. Pepperwood: WE HOLD THESE TRUTHS TO BE SELF-EVIDENT, THAT ALL MEN ARE CREATED EQUAL, THAT THEY ARE ENDOWED BY THEIR CREATOR WITH CERTAIN UNALIENABLE RIGHTS, THAT AMONG THESE ARE LIFE, LIBERTY AND THE PURSUIT OF HAPPINESS.
   d. Bembo: We hold these truths to be self-evident, that all men are created equal, that they are endowed by their Creator with certain unalienable Rights, that among these are Life, Liberty and the pursuit of Happiness.
   e. Memphis: We hold these truths to be self-evident, that all men are created equal, that they are endowed by their Creator with certain unalienable Rights, that among these are Life, Liberty and the pursuit of Happiness.

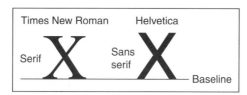

FIGURE 1.6   Serif and sans serif typefaces.

Serif and Sans Serif Typefaces

One way to avoid making your readers strain to read the body text of your documents is make appropriate use of *serif* and *sans serif* typefaces. Serif typefaces, such as Times New Roman, have "finishing strokes that project from the main stroke of a letter" (Craig & Bevington, 1999, p. 14). In Figure 1.6, you can see how the *x* letterform of Times New Roman has "feet" at each end of its main strokes. Contrast Times New Roman with Helvetica, a commonly used sans serif typeface; its *x* letterform does not have feet.

Traditionally, serif typefaces have been used for the body text of print documents (as opposed to online documents) because they seem to be more readable across stretches of printed text. Some document designers have postulated that serifs lead a reader's gaze along the *baseline*, the invisible line on which the letters sit. Under this theory, serifs guide the reader's gaze from one letterform and one word to another (e.g., Williams, 2008, p. 35), and this guidance of the reader's eye generates readability. For this reason, sans serif typefaces have traditionally been relegated to the display elements of print documents, such as headings, diagrams, and tables. However, the role of serifs in enhancing the readability of body text in printed documents has not been supported conclusively by empirical research, and you should remember that the practice of using serif typefaces for the body text of print documents is no longer set in stone. Many sans serif typefaces, such as Gill Sans and Optima, are also quite readable over extended text.

Another guideline for choosing among serif typefaces or among sans serif typefaces is the prescription to use sans serif typefaces in the body text of documents that audiences will read on a computer screen (e.g., documents such as Web pages) or projected onto a screen (documents such as PowerPoint presentation slides). This guideline stems from an assumption—as opposed to research findings—that a sans serif typeface is more readable than a serif typeface for body text in these media. Following this prescription is usually a safe choice, especially because some popular sans serif typefaces, like Verdana, were designed specifically to be read on a screen. In fact, research indicates that readers prefer sans serif typefaces for online reading (Bernard & Mills, 2000; Bernard, Mills, Peterson, & Storrer, 2001).

Exercise B

Answer the following questions based on your examination of the following typefaces (a–f).

1. Which are serif typefaces?
2. Which are sans serif typefaces?
3. Which letterforms help you to tell the difference between serif and sans serif typefaces?
   a. Minion: The quick brown fox jumps over the lazy dog.
   b. Stempel Garamond: The quick brown fox jumps over the lazy dog.
   c. Bell Gothic: The quick brown fox jumps over the lazy dog.
   d. Antique Olive: **The quick brown fox jumps over the lazy dog.**
   e. Perpetua: The quick brown fox jumps over the lazy dog.
   f. Bell Centennial: The quick brown fox jumps over the lazy dog.

Fixed and Variable Pitch

Pitch refers to the width of the horizontal space used for each letterform character. The width of letterforms (and the width of a space) in *fixed-pitch* typefaces does not vary. In a fixed-pitch typeface, a wide letterform such as *m* and a thin letterform such as *i* are assigned the same amount of space in a line of text. Traditional typewriters produce text in a fixed pitch. In contrast, the letterforms of *variable-pitch* typefaces take up varying amounts of space. For example, wide letterforms such as *m* and thin letterforms such as *i* take up different amounts of space. As a result, the amount of white space between letters—called *kerning*—is adjusted in a way that enhances legibility and readability. (You can adjust kerning in Microsoft Word under Font > Character Spacing; you will need to choose either "expanded" or "condensed" under Spacing and indicate the amount of space you want between letters.)

Fixed-pitch typefaces are not appropriate for long stretches of text in a document. The spaces between the letterforms and words of type set in a fixed-pitch typeface create "rivers" of white space in a block of text, especially when the line lengths are short. The following example shows how rivers of white space flow vertically in text that is set in a fixed-pitch typeface such as Orator, detracting from its readability.

```
We the People of the United States, in Order to form a
more perfect Union, establish Justice, insure domestic
Tranquility, provide for the common defense, promote the
general Welfare, and secure the Blessings of Liberty to
ourselves and our Posterity, do ordain and establish this
Constitution for the United States of America.
```

Exercise C

Label the following typefaces (a–e) as either (1) fixed pitch or (2) variable pitch.

- **a.** The quick brown fox jumps over the lazy dog.
- **b.** The quick brown fox jumps over the lazy dog.
- **c.** The quick brown fox jumps over the lazy dog.
- **d.** The quick brown fox jumps over the lazy dog.
- **e.** The quick brown fox jumps over the lazy dog.

MODIFYING TYPEFACES TO DIFFERENTIATE TEXTUAL ELEMENTS

After you have decided on a typeface that is legible and readable enough to suit your purpose, you may find that you need to differentiate textual elements from one another. For example, you may want to set off a heading or highlight a term that you are defining or emphasizing. In the following sections, we will investigate which typeface features you can use for such purposes.

Weight

Typefaces vary in *weight*—the width of the strokes that make up their letterforms. For example, the letterforms of Cooper Black in Figure 1.7 have thicker strokes than do the

FIGURE 1.7   Weight of Cooper Black and Aldus typefaces.

letterforms of Aldus. Thus, we can say that Cooper Black is a heavier typeface than Aldus, and that Aldus is lighter than Cooper Black.

Figure 1.7 illustrates the different weights of two typefaces. However, even within one typeface, *bold* type style, a weightier, or thicker style, can be used to differentiate elements. One common strategy is to use boldface type to highlight a word or phrase. For example, you could emphasize the word *unplug* in a warning to users of instructions:

Unplug the coffee grinder before cleaning the blades.

Similarly, bold type can be used to introduce a new term. Bold type will signal to your readers that you want to draw their attention to a particular word or phrase, as follows.

Typography is the craft of composing and arranging type.

In this case, the word being introduced, *typography*, is set off from the definition that follows it.

Besides using bold, you can also use a heavier typeface from the same *type family*; that is, you can use a typeface that has the same basic design, but differs in weight. For example, a common typeface, Palatino, has a variety of family members. The ones shown here differ in weight.

Palatino Black

Palatino Medium

Palatino Roman

Palatino Light

Within a type family, such as Palatino, the shape of typefaces remains largely constant.

If you used Palatino Roman (as opposed to Palatino Italic) throughout the body text of your document, you could use Palatino Black, a heavier typeface, to introduce new terminology. Our definition of the term *typography,* for example, might look like this:

Typography is the craft of composing and arranging type.

One advantage of using a heavier member of a type family rather than using the Bold feature of your word processing software is that typographers have designed the typeface family members carefully for letterform proportion and spacing between letterforms, enhancing legibility and readability. Note the difference between using a different typeface, Palatino Black, in our definition and using the bolded Palatino Roman:

Palatino Black:	**Typography** is the craft of composing and arranging type.
Bolded Palatino Roman:	**Typography** is the craft of composing and arranging type.

Palatino Black more clearly distinguishes the new term from the rest of the text, and it also maintains letterform proportions and spacing between letters that are more pleasing to the eye. Typographers and document designers, therefore, tend to prefer switching to a new, heavier typeface from the same family rather than simply bolding the type.

However, even the most steadfast of typographers would have to admit that simply bolding the typeface you are already using is typically easier since it requires just a few key strokes. To bold type in Word, you simply press the <B> key while holding down the <Control> key. In contrast, to change from one type to another, such as from Palatino Roman to Palatino Black, you have to select the Home tab at the top of the screen and then scroll through the selection of fonts until you find the one you are looking for.

Exercise D

1. For each set of sentences (a–c), pick out the following and explain your assessments:
    - A typeface in a weight for regular body text
    - That same typeface, but in bold
    - A different typeface of greater weight from that typeface's family

    a. The quick brown fox jumps over the lazy dog.

    The quick brown fox jumps over the lazy dog.

    The quick brown fox jumps over the lazy dog.

    b. The quick brown fox jumps over the lazy dog.

    The quick brown fox jumps over the lazy dog.

    The quick brown fox jumps over the lazy dog.

    c. THE QUICK BROWN FOX JUMPS OVER THE LAZY DOG.

    THE QUICK BROWN FOX JUMPS OVER THE LAZY DOG.

    THE QUICK BROWN FOX JUMPS OVER THE LAZY DOG.

2. How could you use type weight to differentiate text elements in the following passage?

    > A thermocouple is a tool (like a thermometer) that is used to measure temperature in a combustion turbine. Consisting of a temperature-sensing shaft, connecting threads, and a data-relay head, a thermocouple senses thermo-electric temperature.

Shape

Type can vary in shape as well as weight, and you can modify a typeface's shape to differentiate a word or phrase from the text around it. Perhaps the easiest and most common way to modify shape is to use *italics*, in which the letterforms slant to the right. Note the difference between Times New Roman and its italicized version:

Regular: Quit justifying your typefaces.

Italics: *Quit justifying your typefaces.*

If you look closely, though, you will see that the two versions contain different letterforms. The italicized uppercase *Q* has a longer tail, and the *f* descends below the baseline. The *a* in the word *typefaces* has a different shape from the regular version as well.

FIGURE 1.8   Double-story and single-story letterforms.

The regular type displays a *double-story a*, and the italic type displays a *single-story a*. The difference can be seen more clearly in Figure 1.8.

Because of these differences in shape, italics can be used to differentiate words from surrounding text. This property means that you can use italics to emphasize words or phrases. For example, if you are a manager who wants to stress that every employee of your organization needs to attend an important meeting, you could use italics to emphasize the words *all employees*:

All employees must attend the meeting at 2:00 p.m. tomorrow, April 9.

Some stylebooks suggest that writers use italics to mark foreign words. For example, you could mark a phrase that has been borrowed from French:

I revise and edit until I find the *mot juste*.

Of course, italics are also used to indicate book, magazine, journal, and newspaper titles as well, as in the following passage:

The *Washington Post* ran an article yesterday that cites Dr. David Allen, coauthor of the book *Politics for Idiots*. The *Post* article quotes Allen as saying that people should read academic periodicals like *Scientific American* in addition to magazines like *Time* to get information about advances in health care.

Yet another way to employ shape to differentiate textual elements is to use *small caps*, or small capital letters. SMALL CAPS, like bold and italics, are available in most word processing software. Small caps differ from regular type in that their letterforms are characterized by a rectangular shape. Note the difference between Times New Roman and the small caps version:

Regular: Quit justifying your typefaces.

Small Caps: QUIT JUSTIFYING YOUR TYPEFACES.

The rectangular shape of small caps makes them useful for differentiating headings and new terminology from the regular, body text of your document.

At the same time, many experts claim that when small caps are used in long stretches of text, the rectangular shape of the letterforms degrades the text's readability (e.g., Kostelnick & Roberts, 1998, p. 144; Williams, 2008, p. 36). Small caps lack distinction in shape; as a result, the word shape, or *bouma*, is rectangular and undifferentiated from that of other words in small caps. Note how the lack of distinctions among lowercase small caps creates a nearly rectangular bouma in the word *risky*, and compare this rectangular bouma to that of the word in regular type:

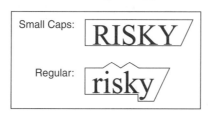

The small caps in *risky* are the same height, and the *y* does not descend below the baseline. In contrast, in the regular type, the dot on the *i* contributes to an irregular shape. So too does the *ascender* of the *k,* the part of the lowercase letter that extends above the height of the lowercase *s* in *risky.* The *descender* of the *y,* the part of the lowercase letter that drops below the baseline, also contributes to an irregular shape. Some experts think that an irregular bouma facilitates the identification and comprehension of words. They argue that a lack of differentiation in letterforms may only slightly decrease the legibility of a single word but may substantially reduce a text's readability when small caps are used over long stretches of text. Not all researchers agree on the role of bouma in word identification (Larson, 2004, provides a comprehensive discussion; see also Adams, 1979; Rayner, 1975). Nonetheless, a safe guideline is to reserve small caps for single words or short stretches of text.

Whether or not word shape substantially affects readability, small caps are definitely a better alternative than *all caps* (all capital letters) for differentiating one textual element from others. Type in ALL CAPS creates too much white space within and between letterforms to be comfortably read over long stretches of text. As can be seen in the following examples, the use of small caps creates less white space than does the use of all caps, resulting in more readable text. In addition, small caps allow a distinction between lowercase and uppercase letterforms, as can be seen by comparing the lowercase letterforms with the capitals *B, H,* and *W*:

Small caps: A BRIEF HISTORY OF THE WORLD

All caps: A BRIEF HISTORY OF THE WORLD

Before closing this section, it is important to discuss the extent to which you should use <u>underlining</u>, another standard feature of word processing software. To put it plainly, it's best to avoid underlining text. Underlining does not contrast words and phrases as well as **bold**, *italics*, or SMALL CAPS, and it interferes with legibility and readability.

Underlining especially interferes with readability over stretches of text by taking up what would otherwise be white space between lines, called *leading*. An adequate amount of leading is needed to distinguish between two lines of text. More egregiously, underlining slashes through letterform descenders. Thus, underlining may interfere with word identification. The following passage is set in large type so that you can clearly see how underlining slashes through the descenders of letterforms and fills up leading between lines of text:

<u>This study takes one step toward understanding how typeface personality is generated. Further research is still necessary.</u>

As Robin Williams writes, "never should you underline words in print. Never. That's a law" (Williams, 2008, p. 139). If you need more convincing, look at Figure 1.9, which shows the havoc that underlining, aided and abetted by all-caps type, wreaks on readability.

Figure 1.9 suggests that Williams's law is a good one to follow when designing print documents (as is the guideline about avoiding all caps for body text). That said, we will see later that Williams's law can be broken when designing Web sites.

FIGURE 1.9   Underlining and all caps text decrease readability in a flyer.

Exercise E

1. How could you use small caps to differentiate text elements in the following passage?

> Central to our claim is the notion of speech act, an action that is accomplished (or at least attempted) by an utterance, the language produced in a specific setting by a specific speaker. The illocutionary force of an utterance refers to the effect intended by its speaker. The perlocutionary force refers to the actual effect of an utterance.

2. How could you use italics to differentiate text elements in the following passage?

> N.B. is an abbreviation for nota bene, which means "note well." The abbreviation is usually written with majuscule (French for "uppercase") letters. The term is also frequently used as a column or newsletter title, as in the magazine Science. (http://en.wikipedia.org/wiki/List_of_Latin_abbreviations)

Size

Another way to differentiate textual elements is to modify the size of your typeface. Typeface size is measured in *points*, with one point equal to 1/72 inch. The practice of measuring the size of typefaces (as well as the leading between lines of type) in points comes from traditional typesetting, in which typesetters used one metal block for each character. These blocks were measured in points (Craig & Bevington, 1999, p. 17). Point size is illustrated here with examples in Times New Roman:

8-point: Times New Roman

10-point: Times New Roman

12-point: Times New Roman

14-point: Times New Roman

Text typefaces are designed to be read in 12- or 14-point (or smaller) type. Most professional print documents are set between 10 and 12 points. The default setting on most word processing software is 12-point type. The use of 12-point type for the body of documents stems from its easy readability. Also, research has shown that readers prefer type that is 10 points or larger (Bernard & Mills, 2000).

Modifying type size, however, is another way to distinguish among textual elements. For example, you could use a smaller typeface for captions on your visual elements, such as graphs. By consistently using a smaller typeface for that purpose, you help your readers identify content even before they read it. You can also modify type size to differentiate headings and subheadings from the body text of your document, using a different type size to show the level of generality of each section. For example, you could use 18-point type for section headings and 16-point type for subheadings. We say more in Chapter 3 about using type to organize your document. For now, we simply discuss how type size affects readability.

Type smaller than 10 points makes most people strain to read both print and online documents. The following paragraph, for example, is difficult to read because it is set in 8-point type.

Small type, like this 8-point Times New Roman, is less readable for most people because it makes them strain to identify words. It decreases the white space within letterforms and the white space between words. Also, it places more words on each line, making readers wait longer than usual for a line break.

On the other hand, type that is larger than 14 points, such as that in the next paragraph, is less readable than 10-to-12-point type because it generates too much white space within and between letters.

Large type, such as this 16-point type, is less readable for most people because it generates lines of text with just a few words, making readers scan more lines to get the same amount of information they would if the text were set in 12-point type. Also, because it generates more white space between and within letterforms, large type lessens readers' ability to scan lines of text efficiently.

Therefore, in most situations, you should stick to 10- to 12-point type for the body text of your documents.

There are, however, a few exceptions. Small type—if it is legible—can be useful when space is at a premium. For example, you can use small type to fit labels into visual elements such as drawings, diagrams, and maps. Figure 1.10 shows how small, yet legible, type labels streets and public transportation stops on a map. Figure 1.11 shows how small, yet legible, type labels an illustration in a set of instructions. The legibility of your labels is more important than their readability, given that labels generally consist of just a few words.

Similarly, you can use small type to present a large quantity of data in a table. This way, you can fit the data into their assigned columns or cells. Users of most tables will not be bothered by small type because they are interested in locating specific cells and line items, not in reading the entire table. Consider the list of prices in Figure 1.12, taken from a catalog for coaxial and fiber optic cables.

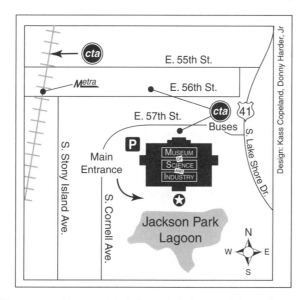

FIGURE 1.10   Legible type used in map labels (actual size). Copyright Redmoon Theater. Used by permission. (Visit www.pearsonhighered.com/riley to view this figure in more detail.)

Even though the type in Figure 1.12 is small, readers can still find the type of cable that they are looking for because the information is organized in a logical way—by dimensions and order amount. Therefore, small type is acceptable here because readers do not have to read every line or column of the table to find the information they are looking for.

Exceptions to the proscription against large type are situations in which your audience may have some visual impairment. People who have difficulty seeing 10- or 12-point type benefit from 14- or 16-point type. They get no benefit, however, from type that is larger than 20 points (Text Matters, n.d.).

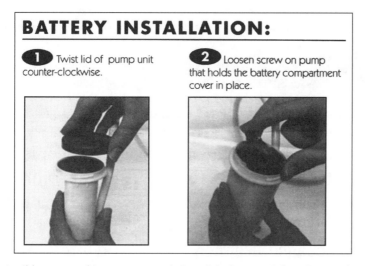

FIGURE 1.11   Legible type used in a user manual. Copyright Summer Infant Corporation. Used by permission. (Visit www.pearsonhighered.com/riley to view this figure in more detail.)

```
┌─────────────────────────────────────────────────────────────────┐
│          50 OHM, PE-SR402AL (.141" TINNED ALUMINUM)               │
│  Model No.      Length      1-24      25-49     50-99      100 +   │
│  PE34208-12      12"       $62.00    $57.66    $53.32    $49.60    │
│  PE34208-24      24"        67.15     62.45     57.75     53.72    │
│  PE34208-36      36"        72.30     67.24     62.18     57.84    │
│  PE34208-48      48"        77.45     72.03     66.61     61.96    │
│  PE34208-60      60"        82.55     76.77     70.99     66.04    │
│  PE34208-XX      Any     Same-Day Shipment / See Website for Pricing│
│                                                                   │
│          50 OHM, PE-SR402FL (.141" RE-SHAPEABLE)                  │
│  Model No.      Length      1-24      25-49     50-99      100 +   │
│  PE3417-12       12"       $54.80    $50.96    $47.13    $43.84    │
│  PE3417-24       24"        58.60     54.50     50.40     46.88    │
│  PE3417-36       36"        62.35     57.99     53.62     49.88    │
│  PE3417-48       48"        66.20     61.57     56.93     52.96    │
│  PE3417-60       60"        70.00     65.10     60.20     56.00    │
│  PE3417-XX       Any     Same-Day Shipment / See Website for Pricing│
│                                                                   │
│          50 OHM, PE-047SR (.047" BARE COPPER)                     │
│  Model No.      Length      1-24      25-49     50-99      100 +   │
│  PE3147-12       12"      $102.05    $94.91    $87.76    $81.64    │
│  PE3147-24       24"       108.35    100.77     93.18     86.68    │
│  PE3147-36       36"       114.65    106.62     98.60     91.72    │
│  PE3147-48       48"       120.95    112.48    104.02     96.76    │
│  PE3147-60       60"       127.30    118.39    109.48    101.84    │
│  PE3147-XX       Any     Same-Day Shipment / See Website for Pricing│
│                                                                   │
│          50 OHM, PE-SR047AL (.047" TINNED ALUMINUM)               │
│  Model No.      Length      1-24      25-49     50-99      100 +   │
│  PE3259-12       12"      $101.00    $93.93    $86.86    $80.80    │
│  PE3259-24       24"       106.25     98.81     91.38     85.00    │
│  PE3259-36       36"       111.50    103.70     95.89     89.20    │
│  PE3259-48       48"       116.75    108.58    100.41     93.40    │
│  PE3259-60       60"       122.00    113.46    104.92     97.60    │
│  PE3259-XX       Any     Same-Day Shipment / See Website for Pricing│
│                                                                   │
│          50 OHM, PE-SR047FL (.047" RE-SHAPEABLE)                  │
│  Model No.      Length      1-24      25-49     50-99      100 +   │
│  PE34209-12      12"       $93.75    $87.19    $80.63    $75.00    │
│  PE34209-24      24"        97.55     90.72     83.89     78.04    │
│  PE34209-36      36"       101.45     94.35     87.25     81.16    │
│  PE34209-48      48"       105.15     97.79     90.43     84.12    │
│  PE34209-60      60"       109.00    101.37     93.74     87.20    │
│  PE34209-XX      Any     Same-Day Shipment / See Website for Pricing│
└─────────────────────────────────────────────────────────────────┘
```

FIGURE 1.12   Small type in a catalog (actual size). Copyright Pasternack Enterprises. Used by permission.

Exercise F

1. Rank the following paragraphs (a–c) from most readable to least readable.

   a. Large type is less readable for most people because it generates lines of text with just a few words, making readers scan more lines to get the same amount of information they would if the text were set in 12-point type. Also, because it generates more white space between and within letterforms, large type lessens readers' ability to scan lines of text efficiently.

b. Large type is less readable for most people because it generates lines of text with just a few words, making readers scan more lines to get the same amount of information they would if the text were set in 12-point type. Also, because it generates more white space between and within letterforms, large type lessens readers' ability to scan lines of text efficiently.

c. Large type is less readable for most people because it generates lines of text with just a few words, making readers scan more lines to get the same amount of information they would if the text were set in 12-point type.

2. Explain your rankings. Specifically, analyze how line length affects readability.

Conclusion

When you modify a textual element by changing the weight, shape, or size of its typeface, you differentiate that textual element from others in your document. Consequently, you need to be consistent in how you modify typeface. If you use italics for emphasis, make sure that you *always* use it for emphasis. Similarly, if you use smaller type, such as 10-point type, to label and caption visual elements such as drawings, use that same size in the visual elements throughout your document.

Summary of Key Concepts and Terms

all caps	display typeface	legibility	single-story
ascender	double-story	pitch	small caps
baseline	fixed pitch	point	text typefaces
bold	italics	readability	type family
bouma	kerning	sans serif	variable pitch
descender	leading	serif	weight

Review Questions

1. What is a text typeface? Which of the following typefaces is a text typeface?
   a. Linotext: The quick brown fox jumps over the lazy dog.
   b. Rockwell: **The quick brown fox jumps over the lazy dog.**
   c. Smaragd: THE QUICK BROWN FOX JUMPS OVER THE LAZY DOG.
   d. Motter Corpus: **The quick brown fox jumps over the lazy dog.**

2. Which typeface weight is heavier: black or medium?

3. Which variety of typeface do readers seem to prefer in online documents: serif or sans serif?

4. Name three ways that you can use type to differentiate a textual element from the type that surrounds it.

Open-Ended Exercises

1. Find an advertisement for a prescription drug (e.g., Lipitor) in a magazine. Compare the use of large-size type to small-size type in the advertisement. Why do you think that drug manufacturers use small-size type in the disclaimers within their magazine advertisements? To what extent do you think this practice is ethical?

2. For what purposes has the author used bold, italics, and small caps in the following paragraph?

When a person COMPLIMENTS someone, that person not only indicates approval of the compliment-recipient's accomplishment or possession, but also demonstrates that he or she is **paying attention** to the recipient's experience. According to Brown and Levinson's *Politeness: Some Universals in Language Usage*, people thus build social relationships with compliments, an outcome that puts compliments into the category of POSITIVE POLITENESS STRATEGIES.

3. Beatrice Warde, an editor for the Monotype Corporation, said that typography should be invisible, like the glass of a window: "The book typographer has the job of erecting a window between the reader inside the room and that landscape which is the author's words. He may put up a stained-glass window of marvellous beauty, but a failure as a window; that is, he may use some rich superb type like text gothic that is good to be looked at, not *through*" (1995, p. 76).

  a. To what extent do you think that Warde is right?

  b. Warde's comment is about the typography in books. To what extent is her comment true in relation to instruction manuals or company Web pages?

4. How do you change the default font setting on your word processing software?

5. Many people consider using all caps in e-mails or online chat to be rude behavior. Based on what you have read in this chapter and what you know about online etiquette, why do you think that this is the case?

6. Some typefaces are closely associated with computers, but these typefaces may or may not be readable. To what extent are the following typefaces readable? Explain your assessments in terms of typeface weight and shape and specific features of letterforms.

OCR-A: The quick brown fox jumps over the lazy dog.

Russell Square: The quick brown fox jumps over the lazy dog.

7. Use your own word processing software to make the text from the flyer in Figure 1.9 more legible and readable.

Suggestions for Further Reading

Two of the books in the reference section at the end of the book are especially good resources for learning about typography: Craig and Bevington (1999) clearly explain basic technical issues, while Williams (2008) discusses typography from the point of view of a document designer.

Choosing Typography to Create a Persona

This chapter focuses on choosing typefaces that contribute a persona, or attitude, appropriate for the tone and purpose of your document. By the end of this chapter, you should be able to do the following:

- Identify typeface anatomical features that contribute to persona
- Identify typefaces with professional and friendly personas
- Identify typefaces with mixed-persona characteristics

OVERVIEW OF RELEVANT DESIGN CONCEPTS AND PRINCIPLES

As important as the usability of your document is, it is not the only consideration in visual composing. It is also important to use typography that contributes to the personality or attitude of the document. The typographer Will-Harris writes, "There are no good and bad typefaces; there are *appropriate* and *inappropriate* typefaces" (quoted in Burmark, 2002, p. 20). One of the most critical choices you make in visual composing is selecting typefaces that are appropriate—that contribute to the tone and personality you want your document to convey.

To achieve this goal, you'll want to be able to analyze the features that contribute to the tone and personality of a typeface—for example, that convey a professional or friendly impression. After all, you have access to thousands of typefaces: More than 167,333 fonts are for sale on one Web site alone (Fonts.com, 2010), and new typefaces are created every day. Each of these typefaces is appropriate for some document—but not necessarily for the document you are working on at any given time. Unless you are an experienced designer, you can easily derail your message if you rely solely on intuition or personal preference to select typefaces.

WHY THESE PRINCIPLES ARE IMPORTANT

Selecting appropriate typefaces for the body of your text is critical because your audience will encounter them throughout your document, which reinforces the persona conveyed by those typefaces. Whatever you write—a report for work, a newsletter for a community group, a flyer for an open house—typography can help convey your intended tone. Writing a letter to your extended family during the holiday season is different from writing a letter to the head of the Exxon Corporation to complain about pollution. Because these two documents are so different in their audiences and purposes, their typography can and should reflect those differences.

Rest assured, though, that you already know something about typeface persona. Here's a clear-cut example. We think of wedding invitations as formal documents because they (1) use standard language, (2) are planned, (3) have permanency, and (4) are often costly to produce (Walker, 2001, p. 43). Therefore, we associate the typefaces that tend to be used in wedding invitations, such as Snell Roundhand Std Script and Copperplate Gothic 32BC, shown here, with a formal persona.

Snell Roundhand Std Script: *A calligraphic script used in wedding invitations.*

Copperplate Gothic 32BC: ANOTHER TYPEFACE USED IN INVITATIONS.

In short, you can recognize a formal typeface when you see one.

In contrast to wedding invitations, many business memos are not thoroughly planned and are often not revised. They are often not saved, and they cost little to produce. We think of memos as less formal documents, and the typefaces that we use for them reflect that status. For memos, we tend to use common typefaces such as Times New Roman or Helvetica, set as the default typefaces on our word processing software.

Research shows that a typeface's *anatomical features* will contribute to its persona (e.g., Brumberger, 2003a, b; Walker, Smith, & Livingston, 1986). Such features include details such as how round the *o* and *e* are and how tall the *h* and *k* are compared to the *x* letterform. This chapter shows you how to analyze typefaces in a systematic way so that you can predict the extent to which they convey a professional or friendly persona.

CONVEYING A PROFESSIONAL PERSONA

When writing for an organization, you usually want your typeface to contribute to a professional tone. That is, you want your document to convey that you and your organization are competent and trustworthy.

Many people fall back on commonly used typefaces such as Times New Roman, which has gained popularity because it succeeds at conveying a professional tone. However, you can "push the envelope" a bit by experimenting with other typefaces. This section discusses some strategies for analyzing typefaces as you encounter them, based on research about typeface and tone (Mackiewicz, 2005). In particular, it shows you how to examine five basic letterforms—capital *J* and lowercase *a*, *g*, *e*, and *n*—for features that create a professional tone. It also looks at other features that contribute to tone, such as weight, thick-to-thin transition, and proportion.

Complexity and Perfection

One property of typefaces having a professional persona is complexity in their letterforms. In characters that have two possible structures, such as *a* and *g*, professional typefaces display the more complex option. Professional typefaces also display perfection in their letterforms: They are unbroken, with horizontal features that run parallel to the baseline. Figure 2.1 analyzes the five basic letterforms and shows how their features help create the professional personality conveyed by the typeface Meridien.

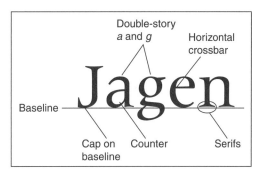

FIGURE 2.1 Five letterforms from Meridien.

Meridien's capital *J* sits on the baseline rather than dipping below it as typefaces rated low for professionalism often do. Also, the crossbar on the *e* letterform is horizontal rather than oblique. Both these features show perfection and reinforce the fact that Meridien is machine made rather than handwritten. It also has double-story *a* and *g* letterforms, a feature that shows complexity and is rated high for professionalism.

Exercise A

1. Which of the following *e* letterforms (a–f) have oblique crossbars?

2. Which of the following *a* and *g* letterforms (a–f) are single-story?

Moderate Weight

If a typeface is to be used for the body text of a document, it should display a moderate thickness in its strokes, that is, a moderate weight, rather than strokes that are excessively thin or thick. Thin strokes create light type, which is difficult to read and, therefore, does not suggest a professional persona (Williams, 2008, p. 34). The same is true for very heavy strokes, which create dark pages that are difficult to read (Craig & Bevington, 1999, p. 29).

The examples in Figure 2.2 show how different weights can create light and dark stretches of text. Note that the *counters*, the enclosed spaces within characters as in *o* and *d*, tend to close up in heavy typefaces such as Eras Ult BT, "reducing legibility and creating a sparkling quality in the type that inhibits comfortable reading" (Craig & Bevington, 1999, p. 29).

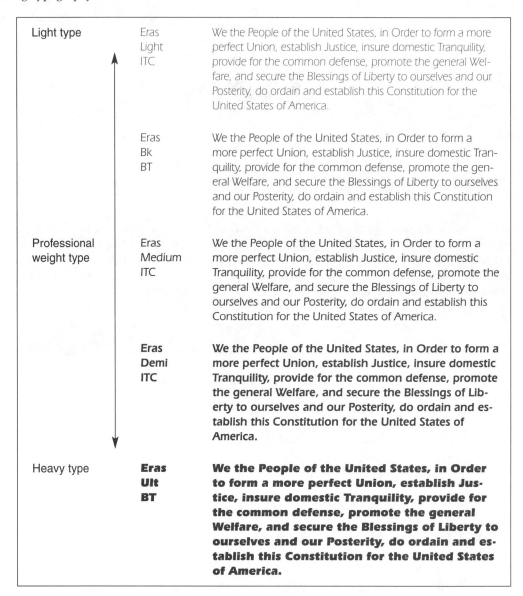

FIGURE 2.2   Spectrum of typeface weight and professionalism.

Typeface names may include helpful descriptive terms such as (listed from "lightest" to "heaviest"): *light, book, medium, demi, bold, heavy, black*, and *extra bold*. Normally, the most professional weight is "medium."

Minimal Thick-to-Thin Transition

To convey a professional tone, a typeface must display, at most, a moderate *thick-to-thin transition*, the variation in a letterform stroke's thickness from one end to the other. In other words, the strokes of a letterform should not shift suddenly from very thick to very thin. The moderate thick-to-thin transition of Times New Roman can be seen in Figure 2.3, for example, in the bowl of the *a* letterform. Figure 2.3 also contrasts the moderate transition of Times New Roman with the severe thick-to-thin transition of Bodini. Times New Roman's strokes transition from thick to thin more gradually than Bodini's do. In

FIGURE 2.3 Spectrum of thick-to-thin transition.

Bodini, the strokes of the *a* shift from thick to thin more dramatically. At the opposite end of the spectrum, Helvetica displays little or no thick-to-thin transition in its strokes; typefaces that have no thick-to-thin transition are called *monoweight* typefaces.

Sans serif typefaces such as Helvetica are often monoweight. However, designers are creating more and more sans serif typefaces that display thick-to-thin transition, such as Gill Sans in Figure 2.3. In fact, there seems to be a demand for sans serif typefaces that display thick-to-thin transition. Gill Sans and Optima, for example, are two of the best-selling fonts on the www.fonts.com Web site (Fonts.com, 2010).

Exercise B

1. Assess the thick-to-thin transition of the following typefaces (a–f). Label them as (1) severe transition, (2) moderate transition, or (3) monoweight.

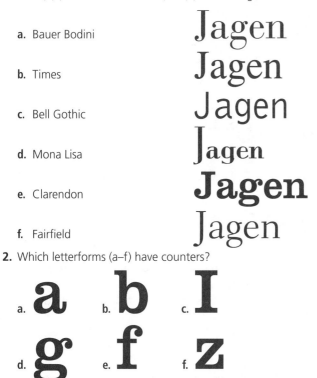

   a. Bauer Bodini   Jagen

   b. Times   Jagen

   c. Bell Gothic   Jagen

   d. Mona Lisa   Jagen

   e. Clarendon   **Jagen**

   f. Fairfield   Jagen

2. Which letterforms (a–f) have counters?

  a. **a**   b. **b**   c. **I**

  d. **g**   e. **f**   f. **z**

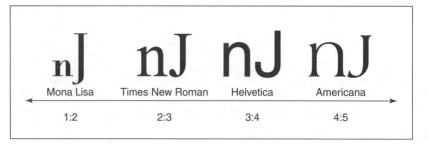

FIGURE 2.4   Spectrum of *x*-height to cap-height ratios.

Moderate Proportion

Another variable that contributes to a professional persona is the ratio of a typeface's *x-height* (the height of its *x* letterform) to *cap height* (the height of its uppercase letterforms), that is, its *proportion*. A moderate ratio is about 2:3 for serif typefaces and about 3:4 for sans serif typefaces. These ratios and others are illustrated in Figure 2.4 using the lowercase *n* (which has the same *x*-height as *x*) and the uppercase *J*.

Compare the moderate 2:3 ratio of Times New Roman and the 3:4 ratio of Helvetica with the 1:2 ratio of Mona Lisa and the 4:5 ratio of Americana. According to Schriver, typefaces with larger *x*-heights tend to look friendlier (Schriver, 1997, p. 259), and friendliness is a quality that tends to detract from a professional tone.

Exercise C

State whether or not the following typefaces (a–f) have *x*-height to cap-height ratios that would lend a professional personality to a typeface used in the body text of a document. Explain the reasons for your assessments.

a. nJ   b. nJ   c. nJ

d. N J   e. nJ   f. nJ

To summarize, it is challenging to describe a professional typeface in terms of anatomical features, but we can say that there are certain anatomical features that contribute to a professional personality. These features are listed in Table 2.1, with positive and negative examples of each feature.

CONVEYING A FRIENDLY PERSONA

Research suggests that anatomical features that mimic handwriting greatly contribute to the perception of friendliness. Specifically, letterforms that are imperfect and simple contribute to a friendly personality. What anatomical features, then, create the look of imperfection and simplicity? One again, we can return to the five basic letterforms for

TABLE 2.1 Examples of professional features of typefaces.

Professional feature	Yes	No
Moderate weight	Jagen	**Jagen**
Moderate or monoweight thick-to-thin transition	Jagen	Jagen
Moderate x-height to cap-height ratio (2:3 through 3:4)	Jagen	Jagen
Uppercase J that sits on the baseline	Jagen	Jagen
Horizontal crossbar on the e letterform	Jagen	Jagen
Double-story a and g letterforms	Jagen	*Jagen*

some answers to this question. Figure 2.5 shows the five basic letterforms of a typeface rated high for friendliness, Giddyup Web.

Broken construction is one anatomical feature that contributes to a friendly tone. For example, the counter of Giddyup Web's *g* letterform is broken on the right-hand side, and its single-story *a* is broken at the bottom. Broken construction evokes handwriting by displaying imperfection. In other words, we do not always create perfect letterforms when we write by hand; we do not always close the counters of letterforms such as lowercase *g* and *p* or uppercase *D* and *Q*.

Giddyup Web exemplifies friendly typefaces in other ways. Its *J* letterform descends below the baseline, beyond the typical boundary of uppercase letterforms. It displays an oblique, rather than perfectly horizontal, crossbar on its *e* letterform, another feature that conveys imperfection. These anatomical features mimic handwriting and thus humanize the typeface.

Handwritten single-story *a* and *g* letterforms are simpler than double-story ones and, thus, are easier to write with a pen or pencil. Giddyup Web has a single-story *a* letterform. Giddyup Web's *g* letterform is single-story, too. However, the tail of the *g* curls in, making the letterform approach double-story status but simultaneously highlighting the difficulty of creating a handwritten double-story *g*. These characteristics humanize the typeface and thus convey friendliness.

One other anatomical feature that appears to be closely associated with a friendly personality is rounded *terminals*, which are the ends of the strokes of a letterform. As shown in Figure 2.5, Giddyup Web has rounded terminals to evoke text written with a ballpoint pen.

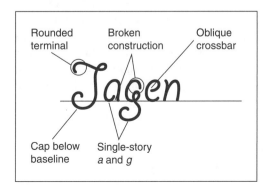

FIGURE 2.5 Five letterforms from Giddyup Web.

TABLE 2.2 Examples of friendly features of typefaces.		
Friendly feature	**Yes**	**No**
Broken construction	Jagen	**Jagen**
Rounded terminals	Jagen	Jagen
Uppercase *J* that dips below the baseline	Jagen	Jagen
Oblique crossbar on the *e* letterform	Jagen	Jagen
Single-story *a* and *g* letterforms	Jagen	Jagen

In summary, it is a bit easier to identify the anatomical features associated with a friendly typeface persona than those associated with a professional persona. Features of friendly typefaces are listed in Table 2.2, with positive and negative examples of each feature. These anatomical features humanize typefaces; thus people tend to perceive them as friendly.

Exercise D

List five anatomical features associated with a friendly personality that are displayed in the following letterforms.

MIXING TYPEFACE PERSONALITIES

You may encounter a situation in which you want to use a typeface that conveys professionalism but also seems a bit friendlier in personality than default typefaces such as Times New Roman or Helvetica. For example, if you are creating a newsletter for parents of kids who are enrolled in a neighborhood hockey program, you might want a typeface that contributes both professionalism (to convey a sense of responsibility) and friendliness (to convey a sense of fun). You can analyze the five basic letterforms to choose an appropriate typeface. For example, consider Souvenir, whose uppercase *J* and lowercase *a*, *g*, *e*, and *n* are displayed in Figure 2.6.

Souvenir is a serif typeface that displays moderate thick-to-thin transition within its strokes. It has a double-story *a*. It also has a cap *J* that sits on the baseline rather than dipping below it. These anatomical features are consistent with typefaces perceived to be professional.

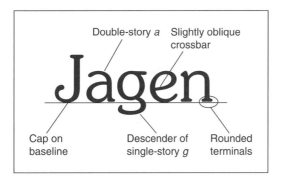

FIGURE 2.6   Five letterforms from Souvenir.

Souvenir also displays some of the characteristics that contribute to a friendly personality, although they are offset by some subtle features that link it to a professional persona. It has rounded terminals and an oblique crossbar on its *e*; however, that crossbar is close to horizontal. It also has a single-story *g*, as friendly typefaces often do. However, the descender of its *g* is more complex than most single-story *g* letterforms. Its descender projects out of the bowl to the right before curving back in toward the left. In contrast, most single-story *g* letterforms project downward, perpendicular to the baseline.

Look again at the typeface in the body text of the Ben & Jerry's brochure, shown in Figure 2.7. This typeface displays professional and friendly characteristics. It has double-story *a* and *g*, along with a horizontal crossbar on its *e*. These characteristics convey professionalism. In terms of friendliness, the typeface has rounded terminals and capital letters that dip below the baseline.

Exercise E

1. List three anatomical features associated with a professional personality that Caxton Lt (following) displays.

2. List three anatomical features associated with a friendly personality that Caxton Lt displays.

Year One of successful implementation. Our thanks to the St. Albans Cooperative Creamery of Vermont and the University of Vermont for their support in a commitment we believe can help improve the environmental and social impacts of dairy farming.

FIGURE 2.7   A typeface that mixes professional and friendly characteristics. Ben & Jerry's Thoughts on 2005 Social and Environmental Performance. Copyright Ben & Jerry's. Used by permission. (Visit www.pearsonhighered.com/riley to view this figure in color.)

Conclusion

We have seen that it is possible to analyze the anatomical features of a typeface for its tone or personality. Specifically, we have seen that it is possible to analyze five basic letterforms to help us determine if the typeface is essentially traditional, professional, or friendly.

Summary of Key Concepts and Terms

anatomical feature	counter	proportion	thick-to-thin transition
broken construction	monoweight	terminals	x-height
cap height			

Review Questions

1. What is the difference between typeface weight and thick-to-thin transition?
2. Which variety of typeface is more often monoweight: serif or sans serif?
3. Which variety of typefaces has taller x-heights: serif or sans serif?
4. Which is weightier: a book-weight typeface or a demi-weight typeface?
5. What is the difference between a single-story *a* and a double-story *a*?

Open-Ended Exercises

1. Examine the following typefaces (a–d) and rank them from most friendly to least friendly. What anatomical features do the most friendly typefaces have in common?

   a. Calvert   Jagen

   b. Bauhaus Medium   Jagen

   c. Kinesis   Jagen

   d. Benguiat   Jagen

2. Examine the fonts that are available to you in your word processing software. Find one serif font that conveys a professional personality. Find one that conveys a friendly personality. Describe the differences between the two.

3. The following word is set in Helvetica. Use a black marker to make it friendlier:

4. According to Walker (2001), formal documents have the following properties:

   (1) Use standard language
   (2) Are planned
   (3) Have permanency
   (4) Are often costly to produce (p. 43)

   Apply the characteristics of formal documents to the following:

   a. A tear-out recipe card from *Gourmet* magazine.
   b. An e-mail from a manager to a team of employees that lists agenda items for a meeting the next day.
   c. A newspaper.

5. Some typefaces are closely associated with computers and can be useful in procedural writing about computers or electronic devices when instructing the user to type or press some combination of keys or buttons. Technical or futuristic typeface personalities harmonize with technical tasks, such as installing software or programming a DVD player. As a result, if you use a legible one, such as OCR-A, you not only differentiate the words of your instructions from the words that the user should type, but you also reinforce the purpose of the document. For example, if you were writing instructions for copying the contents of a directory, you might write the following:

   At the C: prompt, type `copy dir b`

In this example, OCR-A is used for the words that the user should type (*copy dir b*), and Times New Roman is used for the instructions to the users (*At the C: prompt, type*). However, such typefaces may or may not be professional. To what extent are the following typefaces professional? Explain.

OCR-B:	The quick brown fox jumps over the lazy dog.
Eurostyle Medium:	The quick brown fox jumps over the lazy dog.
Briem Akademi Std:	The quick brown fox jumps over the lazy dog.

Suggestions for Further Reading

The following article discusses the importance of typography in technical communication:

Mackiewicz, J. (2004). What technical writing students should know about typeface personality. *Journal of Technical Writing and Communication, 34,* 113–131.

The following article reports empirical research on typeface personality:

Rowe, C. L. (1982). The connotative dimensions of selected display typefaces. *Information Design Journal, 3,* 30–37.

Establishing Visual Hierarchies

This chapter focuses on establishing visual hierarchies—on helping readers see the relationships among different parts of a text through the use of features such as headings, bullets, and numbered lists. By the end of this chapter, you should be able to do the following:

- Identify standard formats used for headings in professional publications
- Identify uses for bulleted and numbered lists
- Identify uses for headers and footers
- Identify uses for other visual elements such as drop caps and pull quotes
- Recognize and correct problems in faulty parallelism

OVERVIEW OF RELEVANT DESIGN CONCEPTS AND PRINCIPLES

Chapters 1 and 2 looked at ways to choose typography that is appropriate for the task at hand. We also looked at how to modify the look of a typeface by using effects such as boldface, italics, small caps, and other variations.

One principle established in Chapters 1 and 2 was that choosing and modifying a typeface should ultimately complement the verbal message. Likewise, we saw that modifications to typography should be handled in a way that unifies the text—for example, by using the same typographical effect (e.g., boldface) for the same purpose throughout the text.

In this chapter, we look at further ways to use typography to reinforce verbal messages, focusing on how headings and lists can help readers understand the organization of informative writing—the kind of writing often used in technical, scientific, business, and academic settings.

WHY THESE PRINCIPLES ARE IMPORTANT

When you think about how and why readers use informative texts and the environments in which they use them, the benefits of headings and lists become clearer. First, readers of informative texts are often trying to scan documents to get details needed to perform a task or make a decision. If you have ever tried to read instructions while you were assembling a piece of furniture, installing a printer, or even following a recipe, then you know the kind of situation in which these readers find themselves.

Second, headings and lists help readers locate and process information more easily than text without these features. For example, users can scan a *vertical list* (also known as a *stacked list*) in 80% of the time it takes them to read a *horizontal list* (also known as a *run-in list*, i.e., one set in the same format as a regular paragraph of text; USDHH, 2006, 12.2). *Headings*, words or short phrases that divide body text and signal its content, as well as signals such as numbers, also help readers remember information during tests of immediate and delayed recall (Hyönä & Lorch, 2004; Lorch & Chen, 1986; Lorch & Lorch, 1995, 1996; Williams & Spyridakis, 1992) and comprehension (Bartell, Schultz, & Spyridakis, 2006; Schultz & Spyridakis, 2004). Further, when asked about their preference for the same passage with or without headings, readers tend to prefer texts with headings. The following patterns emerge from studies of the effect of headings on reader comprehension:

> If a passage is quite simple—due to its shortness, high familiarity, or ease in terms of readability—then proficient adult readers may not need or benefit from headings. Conversely, if a passage is difficult—due to its length, its low familiarity, or its difficulty in terms of readability—then readers will need textual guidance and will benefit from headings. (Williams & Spyridakis, 1992, p. 65)

Third, readers of informative texts are often distracted and pressured for time. Cubicle workers, busy administrators, lab technicians, and parents assembling birthday presents are all working in environments that have frequent interruptions, noise (both literal and metaphorical), and other demands on their attention. These are not readers settling in for a leisurely soak in the tub with their favorite novel. Instead, these are readers who may repeatedly have to turn away from a text, come back to it, and find their place. Using headings and lists can help such readers keep track of where they are in the text. If they have to set the text aside and come back to it, headings and lists can help readers pick up where they left off.

Fourth, even for readers using a text in a less distracted environment, evidence from the study of *schema theory* reinforces the usefulness of organizational signals such as headings. A schema (plural: schemata) is a framework for organizing knowledge about the world. Schema theory proposes that readers understand text better when they are able to integrate the text into preexisting knowledge (represented in the schema). One type of schema is a *script,* a mental representation of the prototypical sequence of events in a familiar situation. For example, it has been hypothesized that a "restaurant script" would be organized according to scenes such as Entering, Ordering, Eating, and Exiting. Other schemata are conceptual rather than procedural (i.e., they represent nontemporal ways of organizing information). Scripts and other schemata provide us with a structured framework for processing the information encountered in a text. Research supports the use of structural clues that support the user's schema for the information in the text; for example, Resnick and Sanchez (2004) found that users were better at searching Web sites with labels that clearly mirrored a schema for the content being searched.

Exercise A

Scientific articles are often described as adhering to an "IMRAD" (or "IMRD") structure. Based on your examination of articles from scientific journals, what does IMRAD stand for?

By helping readers integrate a text into an existing schema, headings can greatly aid readers in their processing of a text. As evidence, in a famous experiment, research participants were asked to read the following passage, put it aside, and list as many points from the passage as they could remember.

Exercise B

Read the following passage, put it aside, and then, on a piece of paper, list as many points from the passage as you can remember. Set this list aside.

> The procedure is actually quite simple. First, you arrange things into different groups. Of course, one pile may be sufficient depending on how much there is to do. If you have to go somewhere else due to lack of facilities, that is the next step; otherwise you are pretty well set. It is important not to overdo things. That is, it is better to do too few things at once than too many. In the short run this may not seem important, but complications can arise. A mistake can be expensive as well. At first the whole procedure will seem complicated. Soon, however, it will become just another fact of life. . . . (Duin, 1989, p. 97)

Some research participants were given just the passage, while others were given the title of the passage before they started reading. (The title of the passage is revealed to you later in this chapter.) The latter participants were able to recall a significantly greater amount of information from the passage. This result indicates that readers rely on information in headings—such as titles—to help them process the information in a text.

In short, headings and similar visual signals help readers in several ways. First, they help readers construct a schema of the text, which in turn enhances readers' ability to recall and comprehend topics within the text. Second, they help readers group information within the text. Third, they help readers understand hierarchical relations among different parts of information in the text—for example, the fact that one section of a text is a subpart of a more general section.

STANDARD FORMATS FOR HEADINGS IN PROFESSIONAL PUBLICATIONS

Unnumbered Headings

Headings in print publications in professional writing tend to be unified either through the use of visual strategies or through the use of numbering. Most publications

TABLE 3.1 Examples of combinations tested by Williams and Spyridakis (1992).

Variable	Example
Size	Heading Heading
Size + position	Heading [centered]
Size + case	HEADING
Size + underline	<u>Heading</u>
Size + case + underline	<u>HEADING</u>
Position + case + underline	<u>HEADING</u> [centered]
Size + position + case + underline	<u>HEADING</u> [centered]

use unnumbered headings that are distinguished visually through size, typography, typographic effects, indentation and positioning, or some combination of these elements.

Research indicates that different types of headings create different perceptions on the part of readers about the relative importance of information. For example, Williams and Spyridakis (1992) asked research participants to judge 16 headings constructed using four variables:

- Size
- Case (upper or upper and lower)
- Position (centered, flush left, indented, embedded)
- Underlining (present or absent).

Participants were judging their perception of the heading's superordinate status with respect to the text. The combinations exemplified in Table 3.1 were tested. Williams and Spyridakis's main finding was that readers always perceive type size as the most important cue to the hierarchy of information, more so than position, case, or underlining.

In looking at the variable of position, the participants in Williams and Spyridakis's study consistently perceived centered headings as most important and embedded headings as least important. There was some inconsistency in how participants interpreted the difference between flush left and indented headings. Flush left headings were sometimes ranked as superordinate to indented headings (the intended interpretation), but other times ranked as subordinate to indented headings (the unexpected interpretation). For this reason, Williams and Spyridakis advise against using both flush left and indented headings in the same document.

Figures 3.1 and 3.2 show examples of unnumbered heading styles commonly used in professional writing. Within each figure, headings are listed at five different levels of scope. First-level headings are at the highest (i.e., most general) level within an article, book chapter, or report section. At the opposite end, fifth-level headings are at the lowest level, meaning that no other divisions with headings would occur within a section having a fifth-level heading.

Heading 1: 12-point Arial bold

Heading 2: 11-point Arial bold

Heading 3: 11-point Arial bold

Heading 4: 9-point Arial bold

Heading 5: 10-point Times Roman italics

Body text: 10-point Times Roman

FIGURE 3.1   Microsoft Office 2003 "Contemporary Report" headings.

HEADING 1: 9-POINT GARAMOND, BOLD, CAPS, CENTERED, 50% GRAY
0.75 RULES TOP AND BOTTOM

HEADING 2: 9-POINT GARAMOND, BOLD, CAPS, CENTERED

HEADING 3: 10-POINT GARAMOND, BOLD, CAPS, FLUSH LEFT

Heading 4: 12-point Garamond, italics, initial cap, indented 0.25 inches

Heading 5: 11-point Garamond, bold, initial cap, flush left

Body text: 11-point Garamond

FIGURE 3.2   Microsoft Office 2003 "Elegant Report" headings.

Exercise C

How well do the heading systems illustrated in Figures 3.1 and 3.2 adhere to the recommendations implied by the Williams and Spyridakis (1992) study? Identify particular points at which the heading systems do and do not reflect the study's findings.

Exercise D

Using Microsoft Word, create a new document using a report template. To access this template in Word 2003, go to File > New > Template on my computer > Reports > Professional Report. In Word 2007, go to File > New > Installed templates and select a report template such as Oriel. Identify the headings for levels 1–5, using enough detail about size, typography, and placement to allow you to reproduce them in a new document. (*Hint:* To find the details about a heading, turn on Styles and Formatting [Format > Styles and Formatting] in Word 2003 or Styles in Word 2007.) Hover your mouse over the name of the heading to reveal its specifications.

Exercise E

Examine the "Contemporary" and "Elegant" heading styles described previously. What generalizations can you draw about the visual cues that are assumed to make a header look stronger or weaker than the heading at the next level? An example of a generalization might be the following: If two headings both use the same typeface style and size, then making one bold will make it look stronger.

Exercise F

Williams (2003) claims that boldface type actually looks smaller than lightface type of the same size. This effect arises from the fact that boldface closes up the amount of white space in the interior of each letter and thus makes it look smaller. If Williams is accurate, what implications (if any) does this claim have for either of the heading systems outlined previously?

Numbered Headings

Numbered headings in general, and *decimal numbering* in particular, tend to be associated with technical reports or with documents such as user manuals in which it is desirable that the reader be able to cross-reference very specific parts of the document (e.g., "See Section 3.2 for instructions on how to use this feature").

The decimal numbering system for headings is quite easy to construct and has the advantage of giving the reader an instant answer to the question, Where am I in this document? Here's how the decimal numbering system works.

1.   First-level heading
1.2.   Second-level heading
1.2.1. Third-level heading
1.2.2. Another third-level heading
1.3.   Second-level heading
1.3.1. Third-level heading
1.3.2. Another third-level heading
1.4.   Second-level heading
2.   First-level heading

The following example shows this heading system in use.

1. Understanding your horse
     1.1. The herd instinct
     1.2. The "fight or flight" instinct
2. Types of horses
     2.1. Sport horses
     2.2. Work horses
3. Common medical conditions in horses
     3.1. Illnesses
          3.1.1. Digestive system
          3.1.2. Reproductive system
          3.1.3. Immune system
     3.2. Injuries
          3.2.1. Muscle and tendon injuries
          3.2.2. Wounds
          3.2.3. Splints and fractures
     3.3. Preventive medicine for your horse
          3.3.1. Daily and routine care
          3.3.2. Veterinary care
          3.3.3. Farrier and dentist care
4. Training your horse
     4.1.   Ground training and handling
               [etc.]

This heading system can also be used with visual cues (e.g., boldface) for different heading levels. However, those visual cues are somewhat less necessary because the numbers themselves let the reader know what the heading level is.

Frequency of Headings

Some research has been done on the relation between the frequency of headings and their effectiveness. Studies by Bartell, Schultz, and Spyridakis (2006) and Schultz and Spyridakis (2004) both found that medium-frequency headings were more effective than either high-frequency or no headings. High frequency was defined as one heading approximately every 100 words; medium frequency, approximately every 200 words; and low frequency, approximately every 300 words.

Running Headings and Footers

Headers (also known as running headings or running heads) and *footers* are items that "run" (i.e., that are repeated) from page to page throughout at least one section of a document. In keeping with the metaphor that the "head" of the page is at its top, an item that runs across the top of a page is known as a header, while one that runs across the bottom is known as a footer.

A header may contain one or more pieces of information, depending on the nature of the document and the header's place in the document. Typical pieces of information that you might find in a header include the following:

- Author's name
- Title of the document

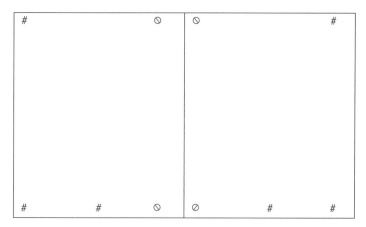

FIGURE 3.3   Placement guidelines for page numbers.

- Title of the chapter or section
- Page number

If a footer is also used, it generally contains only a page number.

Both headers and footers help to orient readers about what part of the document they are looking at. They can also be useful to the reader who is flipping through a document to find a particular page or section. Headers and footers are most useful to readers if you follow the guidelines discussed next.

Putting Page Numbers Where Readers Can Find Them

If you are setting up a header that will appear on facing left and right pages (as in an instruction manual that will be laid flat), place page numbers in the top outside corner of each page, the bottom outside corner of each page, or the bottom center of each page. These three positions are marked with a pound sign (#) in Figure 3.3. Avoid placing the page number in the *gutter*—that is, in the corner where the left and right pages come together. This position is marked with a prohibition symbol (⊘) in Figure 3.3.

Setting Up a Header and Footer

Setting up a header and footer is relatively easy in Word. In Word 2003, you can start from either File > Page Setup or by clicking the Page Setup icon (if it is showing on your toolbar). In Word 2007, Headers, Footers, and Page Number icons are found under the Insert tab.

Exercise G

Photocopy pages from at least three different complex, multipart documents with functional purposes (e.g., textbooks or long instruction manuals). Compare the decisions made about headers and footers in each document. Note in particular where they are placed and what type of information the document designer has included. Comment on any practices that you find especially effective or usable, especially from the perspective of a person trying to use the document.

Lorem ipsum dolor sit amet, consectetur adipisicing elit, sed do eiusmod tempor incididunt ut labore et dolore magna aliqua. Ut enim ad minim veniam, quis nostrud exercitation ullamco laboris nisi ut aliquip ex ea commodo consequat. Duis aute irure dolor in reprehenderit in voluptate velit esse cillum dolore eu fugiat nulla pariatur. Excepteur sint occaecat cupidatat non proident, sunt in culpa qui officia deserunt mollit anim id est laborum.

Lorem ipsum dolor sit amet, consectetur adipisicing elit, sed do eiusmod tempor incididunt ut labore et dolore magna aliqua. Ut enim ad minim veniam, quis nostrud exercitation ullamco laboris nisi ut aliquip ex ea commodo consequat. Duis aute irure dolor in reprehenderit in voluptate velit esse cillum dolore eu fugiat nulla pariatur. Excepteur sint occaecat cupidatat non proident, sunt in culpa qui fficia deserunt mollit anim id est laborum.

Lorem ipsum dolor sit amet, consectetur adipisicing elit, sed do eiusmod tempor incididunt ut labore et dolore magna aliqua. Ut enim ad minim veniam, quis nostrud exercitation ullamco laboris nisi ut aliquip ex ea commodo consequat. Duis aute irure dolor in reprehenderit in voluptate velit esse cillum dolore eu fugiat nulla pariatur. Excepteur sint occaecat cupidatat non proident, sunt in culpa qui officia deserunt mollit anim id est laborum.

Lorem ipsum dolor sit amet, consectetur adipisicing elit, sed do eiusmod tempor incididunt ut labore et dolore magna aliqua. Ut enim ad minim veniam, quis nostrud exercitation ullamco laboris nisi ut aliquip ex ea commodo consequat. Duis aute irure dolor in reprehenderit in voluptate velit esse cillum dolore eu fugiat nulla pariatur. Excepteur sint occaecat cupidatat non proident, sunt in culpa qui officia deserunt mollit anim id est laborum.

FIGURE 3.4 The same paragraph with four variations on drop caps.

OTHER VISUAL SIGNALS

In addition to some of the visual signals discussed so far, you may want to make use of some other visual signals that help draw readers' attention to specific content and that function there to highlight the importance of particular parts of the text.

Drop Caps

A *drop* (or *dropped*) *cap*, as the name implies, is a capital letter that is larger than the surrounding text and is "dropped," or lowered, into it. Figure 3.4 illustrates four variations on drop caps. The first three were created in Word using the Format > Drop Cap feature, using Bauer Bodoni and, in the third case, Linoscript Standard. The fourth is simply the result of selecting the first letter and enlarging it from 11 to 22 points.

Pull Quotes

A *pull quote* is a short excerpt from a text that is copied (i.e., "pulled out") in an enlarged format and inserted as a visual element into the page layout, as shown in the examples in Figures 3.5, 3.6, and 3.7. As Figure 3.7 shows, a pull quote may add further visual interest by "breaking the grid." (Chapter 5 discusses grids in more detail.)

Pull quotes are quite common in journalistic publications and in publicity materials, such as those shown in Figures 3.5 and 3.7. The use in Figure 3.6 of a pull quote in

Susan Feinberg Lectures at Beijing Institute of Technology

(cont'd from front cover)

As part of this trip, each faculty member in the group gave a presentation to his/her counterpart department at BIT. Feinberg presented an interactive lecture on "Technical Communication and Usability Studies" to BIT students. More than 75 students in the International Studies and Software Engineering programs at BIT attended and were introduced to the Technical Communication program at IIT. Key concepts in technical communication and usability studies were presented, followed by a demonstration of a usability test, a process for evaluating the design of a Website. Various audience members played the role of test subjects, while Feinberg facilitated the test. Attendees also had the opportunity to play the award-winning game "Scholars of the Lost Exhibit," which was developed by Feinberg's IPRO 329 and launched Fall 2006.

Feinberg remarked on "the warm hospitality and kind assistance of the international staff at BIT" as well as the "eagerness and excitement of the student response" to her presentation. Upon Feinberg's return, students have emailed her, thanking her for introducing technical communication and usability testing to them, and have expressed interest in attending IIT for further study.

> **Due to increasing globalization and expectations of students, prominent universities worldwide have been building partnerships with counterparts abroad.**

The partnership between IIT and BIT began after an initial recommendation by the Education Office of the Chinese Consulate General in Chicago. A group of IIT faculty and staff, including Wong, visited BIT in August 2003. Subsequently, the chancellor of BIT and a group of BIT faculty and administrators visited IIT in October 2003. These visits led to the current academic collaboration between IIT and BIT, which includes student exchanges and faculty visits.

During this visit to China, the group from IIT also attended the Chinese Opera of Beijing and the Great Wall of China, where they experienced the generosity and hospitality of Chinese families as many requested that their children pose for photographs with the group.

Wong's ongoing relationship with BIT made this visit possible. Feinberg's travel was supported by the Lewis Department of Humanities.

A friendly moment between Feinberg and a child at the Great Wall of China

The IIT group gathers in front of BIT's logo, which symbolizes an eagle transforming into a dove. From left: David Mao (BIT student), Thomas Wong, Gao Shan (Project Officer, International Office - BIT), Susan Feinberg, Judith Lederman, Norman Lederman, and Barry Feinberg

Feinberg speaks with two BIT students following her lecture on "Technical Communication and Usability Studies"

FIGURE 3.5 Newsletter page with pull quote. Copyright Illinois Institute of Technology. Used by permission. (Visit www.pearsonhighered.com/riley to view this figure in color.)

an academic journal, while somewhat less conventional, serves the dual purposes of highlighting a key finding from the article and of making what might otherwise be a "gray page" more inviting.

Note that in all three examples, the document designer has integrated the pull quote with the surrounding design by using both contrasting elements (especially size) and unifying elements. In Figure 3.5, the pull quote uses the same font as the photo captions and the same color as the background column for the photos. The red rules that set it apart echo another color used throughout the newsletter. In Figure 3.6, the pull quote uses the same font as that used for the page header. And in dimension. They had team leaders, who largely supervised and clarified questions. The team leaders, the first author was informed, held group meetings in the conference room once every month to evaluate the overall performances of different groups of employees and to set new goals for them. Meetings were accomplished in a manner that did not clearly demonstrate the power dimension. Team leaders held the meetings in the same conference room where the first author conducted her focus groups. With a white board lit up by lights from above, a television, and a computer, it was much like a university classroom in the United States. There was no fixed setup for the conference room, which was organized depending on the nature of the meetings. When the first author was there, wooden chairs with desks attached were organized in a semicircle in the center of the room. Unlike the main workplace with its colors and movement, this room seemed subdued with white walls, lack of wall décor, and windows overlooking the grounds.

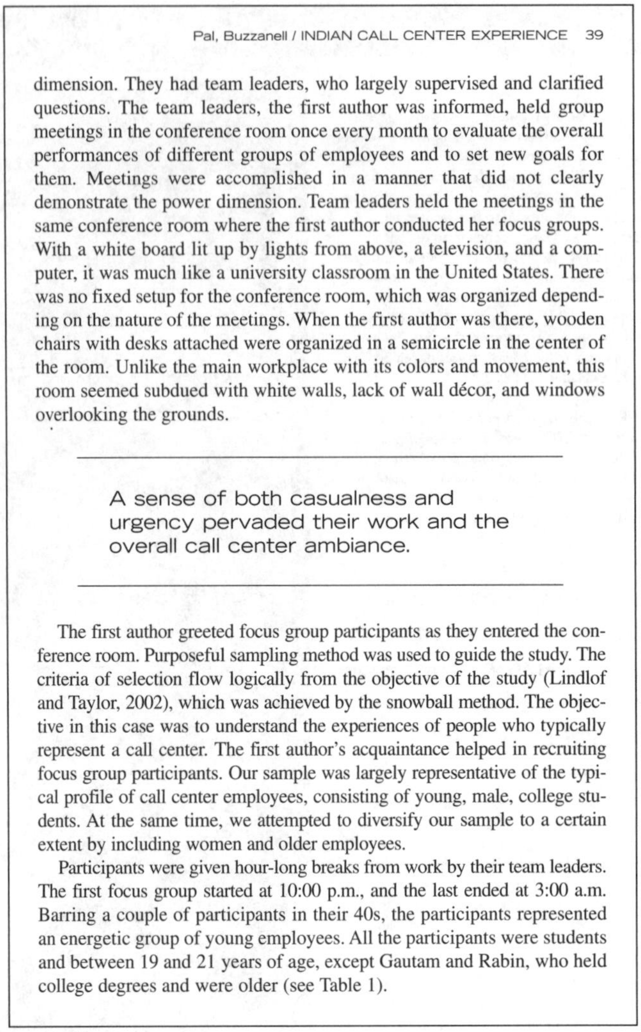

A sense of both casualness and urgency pervaded their work and the overall call center ambiance.

The first author greeted focus group participants as they entered the conference room. Purposeful sampling method was used to guide the study. The criteria of selection flow logically from the objective of the study (Lindlof and Taylor, 2002), which was achieved by the snowball method. The objective in this case was to understand the experiences of people who typically represent a call center. The first author's acquaintance helped in recruiting focus group participants. Our sample was largely representative of the typical profile of call center employees, consisting of young, male, college students. At the same time, we attempted to diversify our sample to a certain extent by including women and older employees.

Participants were given hour-long breaks from work by their team leaders. The first focus group started at 10:00 p.m., and the last ended at 3:00 a.m. Barring a couple of participants in their 40s, the participants represented an energetic group of young employees. All the participants were students and between 19 and 21 years of age, except Gautam and Rabin, who held college degrees and were older (see Table 1).

FIGURE 3.6   Page from *Journal of Business Communication* with pull quote. Copyright Association for Business Communication. Used by permission.

Figure 3.7, the pull quote uses the same color and font as that used for the story headline.

Exercise H

Examine some journalistic or publicity documents (magazines, newsletters, and annual reports are good prospects) for use of drop caps and pull quotes. Analyze the strategies and frequencies with which the document designers have integrated these elements into the visual design.

Toward a Vibrant Campus and Community Development

Building University Technology Park At IIT

By David Baker
Vice President for External Affairs

IIT's 1996 Main Campus Master Plan called for a "commercial zone" on the south end of campus. In 2000, as the City of Chicago decided to move its new police headquarters to near Main Campus and to take down public housing around IIT, President Lew Collens said, "Let's do a tech park." He turned to me and asked me to figure out how to do it. Needless to say it has had a big impact on me professionally.

By 2001, the key thinking behind the scenes became, "If we are going to build a tech park, who is going to pay for it?"

To begin financing, we turned first to the State of Illinois, which in 2001 committed $12 million to pay for the Incubator, an investment that inspired many others to get involved.

In 2002, after IIT sold the majority of its assets in IIT Research Institute (IITRI) to Alion Science and Technology, the south side of campus became available for the development of the park. IIT took control of two underutilized buildings and devised reinvestment strategies to renovate those buildings, which became the Incubator and Technology Business Center. None of this work required dollars from the Alion spin-off. Most important, we found a private developer-partner, Wexford Science and

Technology, who bought one of the old IITRI buildings from us and agreed to develop it.

There was still one big hurdle: we had to guarantee the developer that we would occupy the building. Somebody needed to lease a quarter of the building in order for the developer to proceed with the renovation financing.

Fortunately, the late Life Trustee Charlie Shaw worked with Lew and me to help the Board of Trustees understand that this was an appropriate risk.

Another critical step in the financing was obtaining Tax Increment Financing (TIF) status from the City of Chicago. It's a funny story.

We had completed and sent the city our TIF application. Someone from the Department of Planning and Development called us to meet.

> **One of the most distinctive aspects of the park is its integration with IIT's academic programs and vision.**

When we arrived, he said, "By the way, the mayor wants you to respect the green building standards, either by having a green roof or by meeting the Leadership in Energy and Environmental Design (LEED) standards."

I had been trying to convince the developer's lawyer to pay attention to whether we needed to meet these standards, but he told us the project was a renovation, so it did not apply.

That wasn't true. The man from Planning and Development insisted, "You've got to do this."

Everyone from our team exchanged a look.

But then our architect said, "That's no problem. I designed the building to meet the LEED standards; we just didn't want to pay to submit the paperwork."

2005

■ The City of Chicago's Commission on Chicago Landmarks awards official landmark status to Main Building and Machinery Hall.

■ The Mies van der Rohe Academic Campus of IIT's Main Campus is placed on the National Register of Historic Places.

■ Peter Lindsay Schaudt Landscape Architecture, Inc. receives the American Society of Landscape Architects General

34

FIGURE 3.7   Page from *IIT Magazine* with pull quote. Copyright Illinois Institute of Technology. Used by permission. (Visit www.pearsonhighered.com/riley to view this figure in color.)

FINE POINTS

Font Selection

For print texts where the body will be set in a serif font, it is usually better to set major headings in a sans serif font. For example, if the manuscript is Palatino, a sans serif font such as Humanist might be selected for headings. Choosing a sans serif font allows the heading to contrast with the body text on an important visual dimension. In turn, this contrast will allow the reader to associate each type of text clearly with one function (sans serif = heading, serif = body text).

In a style sheet or template that allows some lower level headings to be run into the text itself, those headings are sometimes set in the same serif font as the body. However, the headings should still be distinguished from the body text by a visual feature—for example, by using a bold or italicized version of the body typeface.

Numbers or Bullets?

The items in a vertical (stacked) list are usually set off by numbers or bullets. Numbered lists have two common uses. One is to show the chronological order of steps in a sequence. For example, the following list shows a set of instructions that must be followed in a certain order:

1. Remove the CD.
2. Remove the router.
3. Attach the feet to the router.
4. Insert the CD into your computer.
5. Click **Setup**.

The other common use for numbered lists is to show items the order of importance of the listed items. For example, the following list shows a set of goals from a strategic operating plan for an academic office related to undergraduate retention:

> Our goals for 2011 include the following:

1. Increase first-year student retention by 2%.
2. Reach 100% faculty compliance with reporting midterm grades.
3. Reduce by 5% the number of students on academic probation.

In short, when you use numbers to introduce the items in a list, your readers will assume that there is some sequence or priority order associated with the items.

Aside from these two uses, you should set off items in a *bullet list*. A bullet is a typographic symbol—often a dot (which resembles a bullet hole)—used to set some text apart. For example, the following list shows a set of tools needed to perform an oil change:

- Metric socket set
- Metric open-end wrench set
- Large grease gun with flex hose
- Small grease gun
- Molybdenum disulfide grease for both guns
- Oil filter wrench to fit your filter

You can use hyphens if bullets are not available. Some e-mail formats, for example, do not accommodate bulleted lists.

Formatting and Punctuating Items in a List

Various style guides differ in their advice on how to format and punctuate items in a list—for example on whether or not to capitalize each item and whether or not to follow each item with a period. If you are preparing a manuscript for an organization that uses a particular style guide, you should follow its guidelines. If you do not have a specific style guide, the following guidelines given by the *Chicago Manual of Style* are a good general-purpose choice.

- Do not use closing punctuation unless items consist of complete sentences.
- If items are numbered, follow the number with a period, and begin each item with a capital letter.

- Use hanging indentation for items running more than one line.
- For a long sentence with elements displayed in a vertical list, use a semicolon between each item and a period at the end of the final item. Begin each item with a lowercase letter.

Using Parallel Structure

Parallel structure, also called parallelism, refers to using similar types of grammatical patterns in similar types of document elements. For example, you may have noticed that the titles of the main chapters in this book all include a present participle ("-ing") verb, such as "Establishing." Although parallel structure is, strictly speaking, a writing issue rather than a document design issue, it is one to which you should be sensitive. Even if you are not the primary writer of a document, one of your tasks as a document designer may be to create headings for it, and when doing so you want to be aware of parallel structure.

When checking for parallel structure in a series of items distributed throughout a document, such as headings or chapter titles, start by isolating the series. For example, suppose you want to make sure that your report headings have parallel structure. As you go through the report, jot down the headings on a piece of paper or enter them into a separate table of contents file. You'll find that it's much easier to compare their structure if you can see them all at once.

Second, use a stacked list (i.e., a vertical format) to display the items being revised, especially when dealing with a complex series. For example, the following passage appears to contain a series of parallel verb phrases that might be converted to headings in an instruction manual for software.

> The software may be programmed to print checks with each employee's name and weekly salary, keep an up-to-date wage total, a summary of tax deductions, and file this information in employee accounts.

However, converting the series to a stacked list reveals its faulty parallelism:

- Print checks with each employee's name and weekly salary
- Keep an up-to-date wage total
- A summary of tax deductions
- File this information in employee accounts

The first, second, and fourth items are parallel verb phrases. The third item, though, is a noun phrase and is, therefore, not parallel. This problem can be corrected by converting the third item to a verb phrase.

- Summarize tax deductions

The series now has parallel structure, since each item consists of a verb phrase. These items, in turn, could form the basis for section headings in the instruction manual, as shown here:

Printing Checks for Employees

Keeping an Up-to-Date Wage Total

Summarizing Tax Deductions

Filing Information in Employee Accounts

Exercise I

Following is a list of tasks that might be used as the basis for headings within a document. Correct any problems in faulty parallelism; then formulate a series of headings from this list.

The software must do the following:

a. Handling of both incoming and outgoing books
b. Differentiate between textbooks and general books
c. Give credit for book returns
d. Printing customized forms
e. Generate operation reports

Conclusion

Headings and other visual signals—such as the title of the passage in Exercise B, "Washing Clothes"—help readers to recognize, recall, and comprehend text structure in several ways. By helping readers construct a schema of the text, such visual signals enable readers to forecast the topics that a text will cover and to recall and comprehend those topics. Reader comprehension is also enhanced by visual signals that help readers group and understand the relationships among different parts of the text. Finally, visual signals such as headers and footers help enhance the usability of a document by making it easy for readers to find information and keep track of their location with the document. Parallel structure helps to reinforce visual similarity for serial items such as headings by creating grammatical similarity.

Summary of Key Concepts and Terms

bullet list	gutter	parallel structure	script
decimal numbering	header	pull quote	stacked list
drop cap	heading	run-in list	vertical list
footer	horizontal list	schema theory	

Additional Exercises

1. Find another textbook, a user's manual, or another instructional document that has at least four levels of headings. Prepare a style sheet that shows the typographic specification for each heading. If you cannot identify the specific font by name, use terms such as those introduced in Chapters 1 and 2 to describe the font. For example, you may be able to identify a particular font as Humanist. However, you could also describe it as sans serif, monoweight, double-story.

   For each level of heading, also note additional cues used (e.g., boldface or italics) and describe its horizontal and vertical spacing (i.e., is it flush left? indented? centered? How many lines of space precede and follow it?).

2. Compare two academic journals that have the same trim size (e.g., 6 × 9 inches) and that use three or more levels of headings. Prepare a style sheet that shows the typographic specification for each heading. If you cannot identify the specific font by name, use terms such as those introduced in Chapters 1 and 2 to describe the font. For example, the headings in the three sample journal pages given in Figure 3.8 are in Franklin Gothic. However, you could also describe this font as sans serif, monoweight, double-story.

   For each level of heading, also note additional cues used (e.g., boldface or italics) and describe its horizontal and vertical spacing. (i.e., is it flush left? indented? centered? How many lines of space precede and follow it?). Also comment on the relation between any fonts used for headings versus the font used for body text.

   Finally, identify any similarities and differences between the visual strategies used by the journals to distinguish levels of headings. Which journal's system, in your opinion, is more successful, and why?

References

Bitzer, L. (1968). The rhetorical situation. *Philosophy and Rhetoric, 1,* 1-14.
Pare, A. (1993). Discourse regulations and the production of knowledge. In R. Spilka (Ed.), *Writing in the workplace: New research perspectives* (pp. 111-123). Carbondale: Southern Illinois University Press.
Stone, D. A. (1997). *Policy paradox: The art of political decision making.* New York: Norton.

WRITING GOVERNMENT POLICIES AND PROCEDURES IN PLAIN LANGUAGE

Don Byrne
Center for Plain Language
DOI: 10.1177/1080569907313376

ASK ORDINARY CITIZENS for an example of unreadable prose, and half of them will show you a government document; the other half will point to something written by a lawyer. As a government lawyer for more than 30 years, I wrote and reviewed safety regulations and technical policies and procedures for a major federal agency and eventually supervised other lawyers who did the same. Although I never met a technical document I didn't have the urge to rewrite, I always thought that what my fellow lawyers wrote was pretty clear. Then the plain-language movement came along, and I found I had a lot of room for improvement.

The Push for Plain Language in Government

The first major push to reform bureaucratic writing in the United States came in 1998 with President Clinton's memo declaring that "the Federal Government's writing must be in plain language." Other presidents had tried to improve government writing. Richard Nixon wanted the Federal Register, which publishes regulations and notices, to be written in "layman's terms." Jimmy Carter ordered that government regulations be "easy-to-understand by those who are required to comply with them." But the Clinton Administration went at plain language in a really big way.

Vice President Al Gore was assigned to monitor federal agencies and encourage them to communicate in plain language. He gave out monthly No Gobbledygook awards. His team held monthly meetings

of what was to become the Plain Language Action and Information Network (PLAIN). The network, composed of plain-language enthusiasts from federal agencies, developed a comprehensive Web site of resources for clear writing, www.plainlanguage.gov. Today, PLAIN volunteers teach plain-language principles to jam-packed classes of their fellow bureaucrats. So although there's still a lot of gobbledygook out there, I'll give you some examples of plain-language success stories.

But First, What Is Plain Language?

Plain language involves more than just a few simple techniques, such as using everyday words, short sentences, and active voice. Although there's no single definition, "plain language" basically stands for several dozen well-established principles of clear communication, including the following:

- planning, designing, and organizing documents with the readers in mind
- using sentences and paragraphs that lead readers through the document without taxing their memories
- providing informative headings, topic sentences, and frequent summaries that keep readers oriented and let them scan for what they need
- using vertical lists and tables that make information easy to absorb.

Plain-language manuals and guidelines can be accessed through www.plainlanguage.gov.

Plain language is reader oriented, not writer oriented. Acronyms, for example, may make the government writer's job easier, but a document full of them is distracting to the readers. That's why testing documents on typical readers (usability testing) is an essential plain-language principle. A simple test for plain language is whether readers can quickly and easily find what they need and understand it the first time they read it.

Why Do Many Writers Reject Plain Writing?

Writers who don't have a good grip on plain-language principles are often taken in by the myths about plain language. They think they'll have to dumb down their writing. They're afraid to write *use* because

utilize sounds more professional. Or they're afraid they will have to use a simple word at the expense of a more accurate one. But although some technical terms may be necessary, many turn out to be mere jargon. And when they can't be avoided, many can be explained for the reader.

But the most powerful myth is that plain language sacrifices precision. In fact, plain language improves both clarity and precision. Technical subjects are difficult enough without bogging down readers with ponderous prose. More than once I've offered a technical writer a plain-language translation of a long, complicated paragraph, only to have the writer recognize that the original was unclear, or even ambiguous.

Benefits of Plain Language

The benefits of expressing policies and procedures in plain language are many—not just for the government, but for any organization. If you look on www.plainlanguage.gov, you'll find 25 examples from government and business compiled by Joseph Kimble. I'll mention a few of the benefits here and give you some of Professor Kimble's examples.

Saves Government Time and Resources

The classic example of a plain-language success was the rewrite of the rules for ham radio operators by the U.S. Federal Communications Commission (FCC) in the early 1970s. The revised rules were easier for the operators to understand. For example, a heading that once read "Limitations on Antenna Structures" was rewritten as "How High May I Put My Antenna?" The result of the rewrite was fewer phone calls and letters from confused radio operators. In the end, the FCC was able to reassign five staff members to more productive work.

Increases Reader Understanding

In the early 1980s, the FCC reorganized and rewrote its regulations on pleasure boat radios. The agency decided to test reader comprehension of the new plain-language version. Out of 20 questions, readers using the old rules got an average of 10.66 questions right,

FIGURE 3.8 Sample pages from an academic journal (*Business Communication Quarterly*). Copyright Association for Business Communication. Used by permission.

Using Space to Enhance the Readability of Text

This chapter focuses on using *white space* (also known as *negative space*) to help readers locate and group information on a page. We look at how you can use variations in line spacing, margins, and justification to improve legibility and to help readers see the relationships among different parts of a text. While this chapter focuses on variations on the standard page size used in North America (8.5 × 11 inches), you will be able to apply these principles later to pages of different shapes and sizes. By the end of this chapter, you should be able to do the following:

- Understand the effects of white space on the legibility of text and on readers' preferences and perceptions about page content
- Select and vary the line height used in a block of text
- Select and vary the margins used in a document
- Select and vary the justification used in a block of text

OVERVIEW OF RELEVANT DESIGN CONCEPTS AND PRINCIPLES

In Chapter 3, we looked at how to use headings, bulleted lists, and numbered lists to reveal structure and to group related items in a text. In this chapter we look at additional ways to arrange text on a standard page in order to make the text more legible and to help readers see relationships among parts of a text. As in Chapter 3, our examples focus on informative writing, although the principles used in this chapter apply to other types of writing as well.

WHY THESE PRINCIPLES ARE IMPORTANT

When you use a word processing program, the default setting is typically for an 8.5 × 11 page with 12-point, Times New Roman typeface. Another default is 1.25-inch *margins*—the white space between the printed area of a page and the edge of the page—all around. However, numerous studies have demonstrated that these basic settings can be varied to enhance the greater legibility and readability of texts, two concepts introduced in Chapters 1 and 2. By way of review, legibility refers to how easy it is for readers to process the letterforms in a particular typeface. Readability refers to how easy it is for readers to process a body of text (for example, several lines, a paragraph, a page, or a longer document) in a particular typeface. So one design decision that affects readability is simply the choice of typeface. When designers talk about readability, they are often concerned with body text rather than display text (e.g., headlines).

The term *readability* is often used to refer to the concept of comprehensibility. For example, you may have used a *readability formula* such as the Flesch Index or the Fog Index that takes into account linguistic variables such as word structure and sentence length. Or you may be familiar with research on the relative comprehensibility of various syntactic structures (e.g., active voice vs. passive voice) or discourse patterns (e.g., the relative sequencing of familiar and unfamiliar information). Throughout this chapter, however, we focus on the visual elements of readability rather than on linguistic elements.

Additionally, a number of studies have tested not only readers' performance but also their subjective reactions to documents in which certain design elements have been varied. Testing readers' performance involves measuring activities such as the time it takes a reader to find a target word or the accuracy with which readers answer questions about their comprehension of a text they have just read. Testing subjective reactions, on the other hand, might involve presenting readers with three documents (with identical text but varied design) and asking them questions such as which one they prefer, which one they think would be most tiring to read, which one they find most credible, or which one they think was designed for an upper-class audience. Subjective reactions are often measured by having research participants choose a point on a *Likert scale*, a series of numbers (usually between 5 and 7) in which lower values are usually associated with lower agreement with a statement and higher values are associated with higher agreement. Figure 4.1 shows an example of a statement and the associated Likert scale that might be used to gauge a research participant's response.

The important distinction to note is that testing performance involves measuring readers' actual behaviors, while testing subjective reactions involves measuring readers' beliefs and attitudes. This distinction is especially important to keep in mind because the results of testing performance sometimes contradict the results of testing subjective reactions. It is not unusual for research participants to exhibit similar performance results on two documents (for example, to take the same amount of time to find target words in two documents) but then to have significantly different subjective reactions to the same two documents (for example, to strongly prefer one over the other, or to *think* that one took longer to read or would be harder to search). In short, readers' actual performance while using documents does not always coincide with their subjective reactions to the same documents.

Does this mean that the results of testing performance should "drive" design choices more than the results of testing subjective reactions? We might be tempted to answer yes, given that testing performance measures the way that participants actually behave when using a document. However, measurements of subjective reactions also

	Disagree	Strongly disagree	Somewhat disagree	Neither agree nor agree	Somewhat agree	Strongly agree
This advertisement looks like it was designed by a large company.	1	2	3	4	5	6

FIGURE 4.1   Example of Likert scale for gauging participant's subjective response.

give us important insights into participants' likes and dislikes as well as their impressions about the person or organization associated with the document. These are all part of what we might think of as the document's *rhetoric*—strategies that affect its appropriateness for its purpose and intended audience. Thus, when presented with findings in which design elements A and B correlate with no significant difference in performance and yet participants significantly prefer element B, we have an argument for choosing element B on the grounds that it appears to elicit a more positive reaction from users.

Visual factors that have been found to affect readability, especially of body text, are the following:

- Type size
- Use of *leading* (spaces between lines of type)
- Line length
- *Justification*
- The color, texture, or shading of the paper or printed background on which text appears
- The method used to (re)produce the document

This chapter focuses on the first four variables, especially as they affect text printed on 8.5 × 11 paper, but also considers these variables in digital documents such as Web pages. We address color and (re)production methods in later chapters.

TYPE SIZE

Choosing a type size for general-use reading is relatively easy: As a rule, typefaces used for body text are most readable between 10 and 14 points. However, more complex decisions arise when two variables are considered in more detail: the particular typeface being used and the audience for the document.

Text type in documents such as books, newspapers, and magazines tends to run between 10 and 12 points. However, when designing documents for readers at the younger and older ends of the age scale, larger type sizes may be appropriate. A standard recommendation for text intended for young children or beginning readers is to use approximately a 14-point size (Bernard, Mills, Frank, & McKown, 2001). At the opposite end of the age scale, several studies (e.g., Bernard, Liao, & Mills, 2001) have found that older adults prefer 14-point fonts over 10- or 12-point fonts for online reading.

Exercise A

Visit a public library and look at copies of the following items. If possible, photocopy a page from each one, since you will also need the items for Exercise B:

- A book designed for the 4- to 6-year-old age range (Many children's books list a recommended age range on their back covers, or a librarian can help you.)
- A book designed for adolescent readers
- A book or periodical (e.g., *Reader's Digest*) from the "Large-Print" section, if your library has one (A librarian should be able to direct you.)
- A copy of the same book or periodical from the section for general readers

Using a type gauge, measure the type size used in the body text of each of these items.

WHITE SPACE ON THE "LOCAL" LEVEL

Leading

Leading (rhymes with "wedding"), or *line spacing*, refers to the distance (in points) between the baseline of one line of type and the baseline of the line of type below it. Leading is also known as line height and line space, and the term *leading* is a carryover from earlier days of typesetting in which a strip of lead was used to separate lines of type.

It is commonplace in typography to identify type size and leading by using a pair of numbers, the first specifying the type size and the second specifying the amount of leading on which it should be set. For example, a specification such as "Times Roman 10/12" means to use 10-point type with 12 points of leading. A specification such as "Bodoni 12/14" means to use 12-point type with 14 points of leading.

The examples in Figure 4.2 show the same body of "Greeked" text (i.e., nonsense placeholder text) set in Aldus 10/11, 10/14, and 10/12 at identical line lengths.

You will probably find the leading in the first column a little "tight," or cramped; the leading in the middle column a little too "open," drawing your eye to the rows of white space separating the lines; and the leading in the rightmost column "just right."

Exercise B

Reexamine the items that you used in Exercise A. For each item, use a type gauge to determine the leading that is used. Then express the type size and leading using the format described previously (e.g., 10/12).

Aldus 10/11	Aldus 10/14	Aldus 10/12
Lorem ipsum dolor sit amet, consectetuer adipiscing elit, sed diam nonummy nibh euismod tincidunt ut laoreet dolore magna aliquam erat volutpat. Ut wisi enim ad minim veniam, quis nostrud exerci tation ullamcorper suscipit lobortis nisl ut aliquip ex ea commodo consequat. Duis autem vel eum iriure dolor in hendrerit in vulputate velit esse molestie consequat, vel illum dolore eu feugiat nulla facilisis at	Lorem ipsum dolor sit amet, consectetuer adipiscing elit, sed diam nonummy nibh euismod tincidunt ut laoreet dolore magna aliquam erat volutpat. Ut wisi enim ad minim veniam, quis nostrud exerci tation ullamcorper suscipit lobortis nisl ut aliquip ex ea commodo consequat. Duis autem vel eum iriure dolor in hendrerit in vulputate velit esse molestie consequat, vel illum dolore eu feugiat nulla facilisis at	Lorem ipsum dolor sit amet, consectetuer adipiscing elit, sed diam nonummy nibh euismod tincidunt ut laoreet dolore magna aliquam erat volutpat. Ut wisi enim ad minim veniam, quis nostrud exerci tation ullamcorper suscipit lobortis nisl ut aliquip ex ea commodo consequat. Duis autem vel eum iriure dolor in hendrerit in vulputate velit esse molestie consequat, vel illum dolore eu feugiat nulla facilisis at

FIGURE 4.2 Body text of 10 points, set in 11-point, 14-point, and 12-point leading.

Research studies show that the readability of a body of type can be impeded by either too little or too much leading. For example, Bernard, Chaparro, and Thomasson (2000) presented readers with identical Web site content presented in three different leading conditions and found that readers significantly preferred a medium amount of leading. It is interesting to note that different amounts of leading did not create a difference in performance among the three conditions; that is, readers were able to find information in all three conditions in about the same time and at about the same level of accuracy. What varied significantly was their level of satisfaction with, and preference for, the three conditions.

In a similar study, Weller (2004) compared readers' performance using texts of varying "local" and "overall" density as well as their subjective responses to these texts. Local density was measured by the proximity of characters to each other, while overall density was measured as a percentage of characters present in relation to overall space available. Weller found that higher local density had no significant effect on how long it took readers to search for target words. However, higher overall density did significantly decrease search time. In addition, there was a significant finding in terms of preference, in that 9 out of 10 participants least preferred the text with high overall density. In short, text with high overall density may deter both users' performance with online materials and their subjective judgment of how much they like them.

Adding to the complexity of decisions about leading is the fact that different fonts, even when set in the same point size, may have different *apparent* point sizes, depending largely on the font's *x*-height. (See Chapter 2 if you need to review this term.) For example, Figure 4.3 shows four different 10-point fonts set on 12-point leading: Times New Roman, Bodoni Book Light, Futura Light, and Helvetica. You will see that they convey subtle yet definite differences in apparent font size, with Bodoni Book Light looking quite a bit smaller than Helvetica. Correspondingly, the Bodoni leading will look more open to you, compared to the Helvetica leading.

Sometimes it is necessary to experiment to get a "feel" for the right leading for a particular typeface in a particular size. Line spacing is a fairly easy feature to change in Word. Here are three ways to access the feature in Word that allows you to change line spacing.

- In Word 2003, go to Format > Paragraph > Indents and Spacing > Line spacing. In Word 2007, from the Home tab, go to Paragraph > Indents and Spacing > Line spacing. The box labeled Line spacing gives you several options, one of which is to specify at exact point size for line spacing. To specify an exact point size, select Exactly and then type in the point size in the box labeled At.

or

- Find the Format Paragraph icon on your toolbar. Left-click and follow the instructions above to change the value in Line spacing.

Times New Roman	The quick brown fox jumped over the lazy dog. The quick brown fox jumped over the lazy dog.
Bodoni Book Light	The quick brown fox jumped over the lazy dog. The quick brown fox jumped over the lazy dog.
Futura Light	The quick brown fox jumped over the lazy dog. The quick brown fox jumped over the lazy dog.
Helvetica	The quick brown fox jumped over the lazy dog. The quick brown fox jumped over the lazy dog.

FIGURE 4.3   The same text set 10/12 in four different fonts.

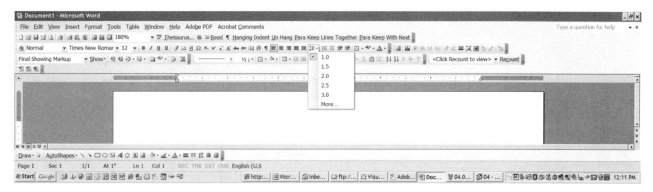

FIGURE 4.4   Presets in Word 2003's dropdown menu for line spacing. (Visit www.pearsonhighered.com/riley to view this figure in color.)

or

- Find the Line spacing icon on your toolbar. From the small drop-down arrow on the right of the icon, choose one of the preset line spacing options, or select More. Then follow the instructions above to change the value in Line spacing.

Figure 4.4 shows presets in the Word 2003 drop-down menu associated with the Line spacing icon.

Line Length

Line length is sometimes discussed in measurements using absolute terms (e.g., 5 inches, or 30 picas, or 13 centimeters), but it is also commonplace to discuss line length in terms of characters per line (*CPL*). This approach is useful because the readability of a particular line length is in many ways a function of the font and point size being used, which in turn affects the number of characters that can fit on each line. In other words, even at the same point size, different fonts will vary in the number of CPL that they can display in the same width. For example, Figure 4.5 illustrates a line of text in 12-point Times New Roman, Bodoni Book Light, Futura Light, and Helvetica. You can see variations in how many characters fit into the same width of space.

Shaikh (2005) tested participants reading a news article displayed at 35, 55, 75, and 95 CPL. Participants in that study read the 95 CPL text significantly faster than the other texts. The 95 CPL text was also found to yield significantly better comprehension than the 35 CPL text. Interestingly, reader preference tended to cluster at the extremes, with 60% of the participants choosing either 35 CPL (30%) or 95 CPL (30%) as their preferred line length. When asked to choose their least preferred line length, 45% of the participants chose 35 CPL, while 55% chose 95 CPL.

Rather more complicated results were obtained by Baker (2005). In that study, line length interacted with justification. Readers were presented with a story text set in one, two, or three columns (set, respectively, at column widths of 90, 45, or 30 CPL), with the

Times New Roman	The quick brown fox jumps over the lazy dog.
Bodoni Book Light	The quick brown fox jumps over the lazy dog.
Futura Light	The quick brown fox jumps over the lazy dog.
Helvetica	The quick brown fox jumps over the lazy dog.

FIGURE 4.5   The same line of text set in four different 12-point fonts.

text set either *fully justified* (i.e., text aligned on both the right and left sides) or *left-justified* (i.e., text aligned only on the left side). Thus a total of six conditions were tested (three column widths × two justifications). Results varied depending on whether the participants being tested were slow or fast readers. Slower readers read fastest and most efficiently using the one-column unjustified layout. In contrast, faster readers benefited most from the two-column fully justified layout.

WHITE SPACE ON THE GLOBAL LEVEL

When we talk about white space on the "global" level, we are talking about space on a larger scale, beyond the level of the line. As defined by Pracejus, Olsen, and O'Guinn (2006) with respect to its use in print advertisements, white space is "the conspicuously open space found between other design elements or objects within the borders of an ad" (p. 82). Technically, *negative space* is a more accurate term, since the open space in a color document is not necessarily white; but *white space* is a widely used and somewhat simpler term, and so we have adopted it in this discussion.

Margins and Gutters

As indicated, the default setting for margins in Word is 1.25 inches for the left and right margins.

VIEWING MARGINS AND PAGE LAYOUT   When laying out a text, it is often useful to be able to see the boundaries of margins (as well as of internal margins such as columns) and to be able to see multiple pages at one time. To see boundaries in Word 2003, go to Tools > Options > View and check the Text Boundaries box. Doing this will allow you to see the boundaries (although the boundaries themselves will not print as part of your text). Figure 4.6 shows a screenshot of a Word document with the View Text Boundaries feature activated. Note the faint lines around all four edges of the text area.

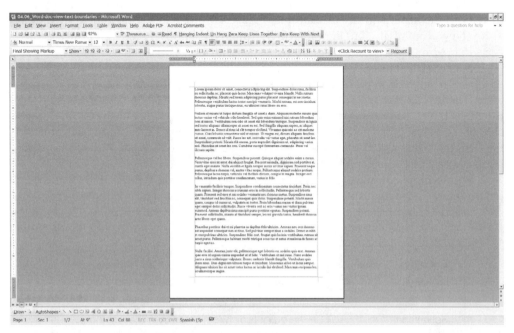

FIGURE 4.6   Word document with View Text Boundaries activated. (Visit www.pearsonhighered.com/riley to view this figure in color.)

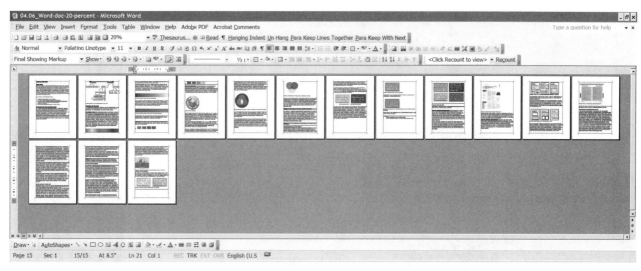

FIGURE 4.7 A 15-page Word document at 20% viewing size. (Visit www.pearsonhighered.com/riley to view this figure in color.)

To view page layout in Word 2003, look for a box on your toolbar that shows a percentage (e.g., 100%). From the drop-down arrow on the right of the box, choose Two Pages to see a two-page spread of your text. An alternative way to access the page layout view is to go to View > Zoom and then choose an option from that menu. Depending on what kind of mouse you use, you may also be able to zoom in and out by holding down the <Ctrl> button on your keyboard and rolling the scroll button on your mouse.

Figure 4.7 shows a screenshot of a 15-page Word document viewed at 20% size (Word can go down to a 10% view.) Although the text itself is too small to read, a low-percentage "thumbnail" view can be useful for getting a sense of the general text layout throughout a multipage document. For example, the thumbnails in Figure 4.7 allow us to see that there is a fairly even distribution of color graphics throughout this document but also that there are a few "text-heavy" pages (13 and 14 in particular).

CHANGING MARGIN SIZE   For many unbound documents intended for everyday use, the default margins, or even smaller (1-inch) margins, are fine. For documents that are to be bound or used for special purposes, however, it is often necessary to change margins from their default setting. For example, larger margins may be useful to readers who need to make notes on a document, such as a set of instructions.

There are several ways to change margin size in Word 2003:

- Go to File > Page Setup > Margins. You will have the option of accepting or changing the left, right, top, and bottom margins.

or

- Find the Page Setup icon on your toolbar. When you left-click on this icon, you will see the Margins tab just mentioned.

or

- Drag the margin markers on the ruler at the top of your document in Print Layout view (if you don't see a ruler, select View > Ruler).

Figure 4.8 shows a screenshot of the menu for changing margins in Word 2003.

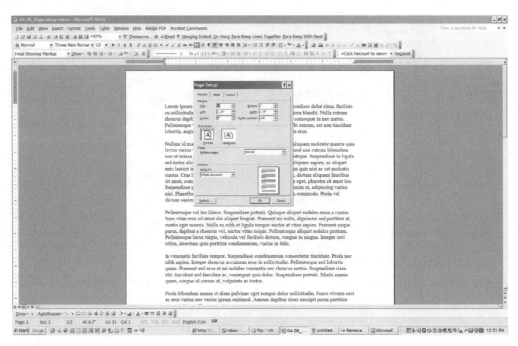

FIGURE 4.8 Page Setup menu in Word 2003, showing options for changing margins. (Visit www. pearsonhighered.com/riley to view this figure in color.)

PREPARING OFFSET MARGINS For documents that are to be printed double-sided and bound, consider preparing *offset* or *mirror margins*—that is, margins that automatically shift to allow for binding. In this type of setting, the inside (bound) margin, also known as the *gutter*, is automatically larger than the outside (unbound) margin, regardless of whether the page is an even-numbered (right-hand) page or an odd-numbered (left-hand) one. This larger inside margin takes into account that part of the margin will be used for binding.

A mockup of a two-page spread with offset margins is shown in Figure 4.9.

To prepare offset margins in Word 2003, use the following steps:

- Go to Page Setup > Margins.
- In the Multiple Pages box, select Mirror Margins. This setting will automatically redefine your left and right margins as inside and outside margins.
- In the top boxes containing margin measurements, redefine your margins to the desired size.

Exercise C

Select a Word document that has consistent margins throughout. Practice resetting them to mirror margins using the instructions just outlined. (In Word 2007, start with Page Layout.)

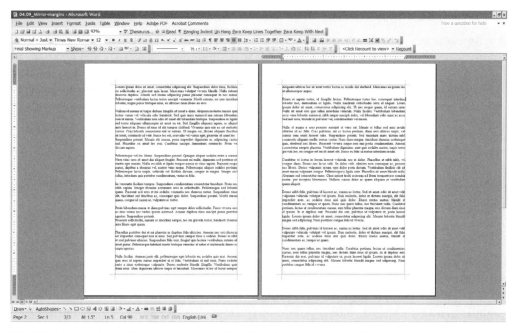

FIGURE 4.9   Mockup of two-page spread with offset (mirror) margins. (Visit www.pearsonhighered. com/riley to view this figure in color.)

Exercise D

Examine a document with offset binding, such as a spiral-bound report or textbook. What kind of difference do you find between the inside and outside margins?

Exercise E

Examine the margins in several books designed for functional use—for example, one in which the reader might want to make notes, such as a textbook or instruction manual. What strategies related to margin adjustment are used to enhance the document's functionality?

Adequate margins enhance readability and user attitudes toward documents. For example, Chaparro et al. (2004) compared texts with relatively large margins and open leading, relatively large margins and tight leading, relatively small margins and open leading, and relatively small margins and tight leading. Scores for both reading comprehension and for user preference and satisfaction were higher for the text with relatively larger margins—although participants read the text with smaller margins more quickly.

ALIGNMENT

Alignment refers to the placement of text relative to the left and right margins of a page, column, or other design unit. In discussing text, alignment is also known as justification. Most of the text that you will be dealing with will be *flush left* (also known as left aligned or left justified. Other categories are *flush right* (also known as *right aligned* or *right justified*) and *centered*. Fully justified (also shortened to *justified*) text aligns with the right and left margins. Columns in newspapers are usually fully justified. These different ways of aligning text are illustrated in Figure 4.10.

As you can see from Figure 4.10, left-aligned text falls at a consistent point with respect to the left margin, but the right-hand side of the text varies. For this reason, left-aligned text is also referred to as having a *ragged right* (sometimes shortened to a "rag right") margin; to set text ragged right means to set it left aligned.

The mirror image of left-aligned text is right-aligned text, in which each line ends at a consistent point with respect to the right margin, but the left-hand side of the text varies.

Right alignment is rarely used for body text, since readers (at least of Western languages) are used to having the left margin as a resting point when reading text. However, right-aligned text may be effective for short blocks such as a headline or a pull quote—a short piece of text that is "pulled out," enlarged, and set off from the surrounding text by a box or some other design element. (See Chapter 3 for examples.)

Every year, thousands of Lyric subscribers also purchase individual tickets—buying tickets for family and friends, or simply picking up operas that are not in their series. From July 24 through July 29—before we send out our massive mailing to former subscribers and the general public—we are offering a private sale just for subscribers.

For these six days only, our current subscribers can buy individual tickets via phone or internet, and they'll be getting the absolute best choice of the remaining seats before tickets are advertised to the general public. We are offering this opportunity only to current subscribers.

10a. Left-justified text

Every year, thousands of Lyric subscribers also purchase individual tickets—buying tickets for family and friends, or simply picking up operas that are not in their series. From July 24 through July 29—before we send out our massive mailing to former subscribers and the general public—we are offering a private sale just for subscribers.

For these six days only, our current subscribers can buy individual tickets via phone or internet, and they'll be getting the absolute best choice of the remaining seats before tickets are advertised to the general public. We are offering this opportunity only to current subscribers.

10b. Right-justified text

Every year, thousands of Lyric subscribers also purchase individual tickets—buying tickets for family and friends, or simply picking up operas that are not in their series. From July 24 through July 29—before we send out our massive mailing to former subscribers and the general public—we are offering a private sale just for subscribers.

For these six days only, our current subscribers can buy individual tickets via phone or internet, and they'll be getting the absolute best choice of the remaining seats before tickets are advertised to the general public. We are offering this opportunity only to current subscribers.

10c. Fully justified text

Every year, thousands of Lyric subscribers also purchase individual tickets—buying tickets for family and friends, or simply picking up operas that are not in their series. From July 24 through July 29—before we send out our massive mailing to former subscribers and the general public—we are offering a private sale just for subscribers.

For these six days only, our current subscribers can buy individual tickets via phone or internet, and they'll be getting the absolute best choice of the remaining seats before tickets are advertised to the general public. We are offering this opportunity only to current subscribers.

10d. Centered text

FIGURE 4.10 The same text aligned in four different ways.

Exercise F

Examine a recent print issue of a magazine such as *Newsweek*, *The New Yorker*, or *People*, and find four examples of right-aligned text in advertisements and in feature stories. To what purposes is right-aligned text put? Does there seem to be an upper limit on the amount of text set this way? What other types of alignment are used in the same advertisement or story?

As the name implies, *centered* text is aligned symmetrically around a point equidistant from the left and right margins. As a result, centered text has ragged margins on both the left and right. Like right-aligned text, centered text is usually reserved for display text such as headlines or for other short blocks of text and is rarely used for body text or other text intended for extended reading.

Special care must be taken with justified text to make sure that unsightly "rivers"—noticeable gaps of white space between words—do not appear in the text. Rivers are more likely to occur when justification is used on an unhyphenated text with a short line space, as in Figure 4.10c. In this situation, the amount of white space needed to fill out the line must be distributed among only four or five words, creating relatively large chunks of space between them. You can see this effect in the first paragraph of Figure 4.10c and throughout the first five lines of the second paragraph (where a noticeable column of white space appears near the left margin).

Figure 4.11 shows the effects of allowing hyphenation in the justified text from Figure 4.10c. You will notice that the rivers have largely (but not entirely) disappeared, since adding hyphenation allows more options in where the line can be broken. Hyphenation, though, can raise its own problems—for example, too many consecutive hyphenated lines can be distracting.

Special care should also be used with centered and right-aligned text to make sure that line breaks coincide with breaks at the linguistic level. Rather than simply letting

Every year, thousands of Lyric subscribers also purchase individual tickets—buying tickets for family and friends, or simply picking up operas that are not in their series. From July 24 through July 29—before we send out our massive mailing to former subscribers and the general public—we are offering a private sale just for subscribers.

For these six days only, our current subscribers can buy individual tickets via phone or internet, and they'll be getting the absolute best choice of the remaining seats before tickets are advertised to the general public. We are offering this opportunity only to current subscribers.

FIGURE 4.11   Text from Figure 4.10c, with hyphenation added.

> Every year, thousands of Lyric subscribers also purchase individual tickets—
> buying tickets for family and friends, or simply picking up operas that are not in
> their series. From July 24 through July 29—before we send out our massive
> mailing to former subscribers and the general public—we are offering a private
> sale just for subscribers.

FIGURE 4.12   Centered text with lines wrapped automatically.

> Every year, thousands of Lyric subscribers also purchase individual tickets—
> buying tickets for family and friends, or simply picking up operas
> that are not in their series. From July 24 through July 29—before we send out
> our massive mailing to former subscribers and the general public—
> we are offering a private sale just for subscribers.

FIGURE 4.13   Centered text with line breaks adjusted.

the lines wrap automatically, look for logical phrasal boundaries, and break the text at those points. For example, Figure 4.12 shows centered text in which lines have been allowed to wrap automatically, while Figure 4.13 shows the same text in which line breaks have been adjusted (using a hard return) to coincide with linguistic units.

Exercise G

Below is some additional centered text in which lines have been allowed to wrap automatically. How would you adjust the line breaks to make them coincide more closely with linguistic units (while still keeping fairly even line lengths)?

> For these six days only, our current subscribers can buy individual tickets via
> phone or internet, and they'll be getting the absolute best choice of the remaining
> seats before tickets are advertised to the general public. We are offering this
> opportunity only to current subscribers.

It is interesting to compare the different tones created by different types of alignment. We saw in the chapters on fonts that fonts in which characters display complexity and perfection tend to create more formal or professional personas. In the same way, lines that are of even length or symmetrically aligned, as found in justified or centered text, tend to create a more formal, conservative, or traditional feeling. Traditionally, for example, the text on an invitation to a wedding (or to a similarly serious event) is centered.

In contrast, lines that are of uneven length or that are unsymmetrically aligned create a more modern, less traditional feeling. Compared to centered text, for example, right-aligned text creates a more unpredictable effect. Likewise, setting the body text of a book flush left is a less conservative design decision than setting it justified. Traditionally, books and glossy, bound publications, such as annual reports, have represented a major investment of time and money, since they have had to be professionally designed, typeset, and produced—although the advent of desktop publishing and digital printing has dramatically changed those requirements—and justified text reflects the high-stakes nature of these publications. More and more, though, even bound publications are seen with left-aligned text.

Debate exists over the relative merits of justified and left-aligned body text. On the one hand, justified text creates a high-end appearance—if done properly. On the other hand, some researchers argue that left alignment aids readers by keeping the spacing between words consistent, and there is evidence that left-aligned text appears to be read more quickly than justified text (Baker, 2005). One study further complicates matters by suggesting that different types of readers prefer different alignments: Slower readers performed better on left-aligned text presented in one column of 90 CPL, while faster readers performed better when the same text was presented in two justified columns of 45 CPL (Baker).

Conclusion

Considerations about introducing horizontal and vertical space within the 8.5 × 11 page must take into account several design variables: type size and font; leading; line length; margins and gutters; and alignment. Research offers a number of guidelines for decisions about each of these individual components. However, as a document designer, you must keep in mind the fact that these variables interact with one another, which may lead to the inevitable need for trial and error in fine-tuning your decisions about a particular document.

Summary of Key Concepts and Terms

alignment	justification	line spacing	readability formula
centered	justified	margin	rhetoric
CPL	leading	mirror margin	right aligned
flush left	left aligned	negative space	right justified
flush right	left justified	offset margin	white space
fully justified	Likert scale	ragged right	
gutter			

Additional Exercises

1. Visit www.aarp.org to examine a site specifically aimed at older adults. What accommodations to this audience can you find, in terms of site design and viewing options?

2. Browse some sample wedding invitations online (entering "wedding invitation" into a search engine such as Google will turn up plenty of sites). Does centered text still seem to dominate the samples? What less conservative elements do you find being used as alternatives to centered text?

3. Examine at least four books that use left alignment (rather than full justification) for the body text. Are there any common denominators in their subject matter, authorship, or year of publication that might account for the use of this less traditional way of setting body text?

4. Following are five passages that appeared on a flyer whose purpose was to announce an upcoming philosophy conference and to invite submissions of papers for the conference. Line breaks are shown as they appeared on the flyer. Revise each passage to make the line break(s) at a point that better coincides with a linguistic unit. Keep the same font used in each original passage, and try to stay within approximately the same number of lines as the original passage. *Note:* In the last passage, the name of the speaker is James Parkison; the information in front of his name lists two honorary titles associated with his university appointment.

PASSAGE A:

Suggestions for commentators and session chairs, including self-nominations, are
welcome and encouraged.

PASSAGE B:

Papers should be suitable for blind reviewing and should not exceed 3000 words
in length. Abstract should not exceed 150 words.

PASSAGE C:

U.S. Postal Submissions: Send three copies of your paper to: Todd
Anderson, Secretary/Treasurer of the LPA, Department of Philosophy,
Campus Box 2309, Anywhere State University, Anywhere, LA
99999

PASSAGE D:

Papers in any area of philosophy are welcome.

PASSAGE E:

Keynote Speaker:
Regents Professor & Martha M. Meyers Research Professor James
Parkison (University of Somewhere)

5

Designing the 8.5 × 11 Page

This chapter focuses on strategies for laying out text and images on the familiar 8.5 × 11 page size. However, the concepts and strategies introduced are relevant to all types of page sizes and dimensions, both print and electronic. By the end of this chapter, you should be able to do the following:

- Describe the nature of a grid
- Identify the purpose of a grid
- Choose an appropriate grid for different page layout needs
- Balance elements on a page

OVERVIEW OF RELEVANT DESIGN CONCEPTS AND PRINCIPLES

Chapter 4 looked at preliminary issues in using space on the 8.5 × 11 page. In that chapter, we touched on concerns related to line length and white space. The principles and guidelines covered so far are adequate for dealing with text-heavy documents that conform to a one-column layout.

However, more robust strategies are needed for organizing the pages of more complex documents. Complexity can refer to combinations of text and images, multi-column layouts, or multipage documents that introduce variations in page layout. In this chapter, we examine the *grid*—regularly spaced horizontal and vertical lines used as a reference for locating text and images—as a tool for managing complexity and for achieving a unified design throughout a document.

WHY THESE PRINCIPLES ARE IMPORTANT

Design that works—design that is both aesthetically pleasing and responsive to the user's needs—reflects an understanding of *how* users respond to the relationship between the elements on a page. To some degree, developing an eye for good design is a talent. However, as with other talents, there are many strategies that can be consciously studied and learned—both rules of thumb that have been handed down by successful designers and more research-based principles developed in fields like psychology. Grid systems represent a principled way to visualize, design, and user-test the structure of single pages within a document, as well as a way to unify multiple pages within a document (so that, for example, page 2 of a newsletter looks like it "goes with" page 6 of the same newsletter).

In particular, good design, especially in functional documents, integrates text and images in a way that meets users' expectations and patterns of use (both of which are largely unconscious), yet also engages the user, as appropriate, with creative and original choices. Judicious use of elements such as the grid can help you, as a document designer, to lay out the page in a way that is consistent with what we know about how viewers use documents and is also aesthetically interesting and attractive to the user.

Numerous *eyetracking* studies, for example, have provided evidence for how readers view documents. Eyetracking is a method of measuring the length of a reader's gaze (*fixations*) as well as the paths of the reader's eye movements (*saccades)* through a document. Using a camera that tracks the direction and rate of eye movement, an eyetracking system can generate an image with *heat maps*, which are color representations of the values of a variable, such as the duration of fixations throughout a document. Figure 5.1 shows an example of such a heat map, showing the *F-shaped pattern* that is often attributed to readers of Web pages (Nielsen, 2006).

The various colors in Figure 5.1 indicate areas receiving different amounts of attention from the reader. In descending order of the amount of attention received, areas are coded red, yellow, or blue. (Gray areas received no attention.) Some recurring patterns described by Nielsen (2006) are as follows:

- Users first read in a horizontal movement, usually across the upper part of the content area. This initial element forms the F's top bar.
- Next, users move down the page a bit and then read across in a second horizontal movement that typically covers a shorter area than the previous movement. This additional element forms the F's lower bar.
- Finally, users scan the content's left side in a vertical movement. Sometimes this is a fairly slow and systematic scan that appears as a solid stripe on an eyetracking heat map. Other times users move faster, creating a spottier heatmap. This last element forms the F's stem.

Likewise, other studies have provided guidelines for structuring print and Web documents for ease of use. For example, Mayer, Dyck, and Cook (1984), Spyridakis (2000), and Williams (2000) argue that readers find documents easier to read if items are aligned vertically (i.e., on a common left-hand margin).

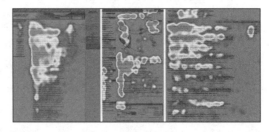

FIGURE 5.1   Images from eyetracking studies of three Web pages, showing a (roughly) F-shaped reading pattern in each case. Source: http://www.useit.com/alertbox/reading_pattern.html. Copyright Jakob Nielsen. Used by permission. (Visit www.pearsonhighered.com/riley to see this figure in color.)

Findings such as these can be incorporated into a grid structure with the goal of creating a page structure that places important information in appropriate places and that facilitates users' interactions with the document.

The use of a grid is also closely related to principles of *Gestalt theory*, in particular principles that have to do with alignment. Gestalt theory is a set of principles having to do with how humans perceive and organize information on an automatic, unconscious level. Originally developed within psychology, principles of Gestalt theory have since been extended to other fields as diverse as visual design, music theory, and graph drawing (Chang & Nesbitt, 2006; for historical perspectives on the grid, see Samara, 2005). Three central tenets of Gestalt theory related to the user of grids are, first, the principle of *similarity*, specifically that "Elements will tend to be grouped together if their attributes are perceived as related"; second, the principle of *continuation*, that "elements will be grouped together if a continuous pattern can be interpreted and this pattern will be assumed to continue even if some parts are hidden; and third, the principle of *balance* or *symmetry*, that humans "tend to feel more comfortable with a 'sense of equilibrium'" (Chang & Nesbitt, 2006, pp. 11–13; see also Riley & Parker, 1998). These important properties of similarity, continuation, and balance are reinforced by the use of visual alignment (among other design strategies). Alignment, in turn, is aided by the use of a grid.

Exercise A

Figure 5.2 shows an 8.5 × 11 inside page from a newsletter for an academic department. The designer, James Maciukenas, has used methods for aligning elements both vertically and horizontally. Examine the image carefully, using a rule or other straightedge as needed, and identify at least three instances of vertical alignment and at least three instances of horizontal alignment.

Exercise B

What function, other than alignment, is served by the dashed lines used in the page shown in Figure 5.2? Why might this strategy be needed on this page? Think in terms of readability.

Exercise C

In addition to alignment, what other design strategies are used in the page in Figure 5.2 to reinforce the principle of similarity? Identify at least two.

CSEP Celebrates 30th Anniversary

CSEP celebrated its 30th anniversary in February 2007 with an invited lecture by **John Rowe** (Chairman, President, and CEO of Exelon Corporation, and Chair of IIT's Board of Trustees). Speaking to a packed crowd in MTCC auditorium, Rowe focused on the complex ethical dimensions of his role at Exelon, one of America's largest utility companies. In his featured talk, "The Many Faces of Stewardship," Rowe described his efforts to address ethical issues such as environmentalism and workplace diversity.

For more on this story, visit www.iit.edu/departments/humanities/csep30th.html

Ethics Bowl Team Places Second in Upper Midwest Regional Competition

On December 2, IIT's Ethics Bowl Team placed second out of 12 schools in the Upper Midwest Regional Ethics Bowl. The team's performance qualified it to compete against top teams from across the U.S. at the National Championship of the Intercollegiate Ethics Bowl (IEB), held in February. Although IIT did not finish in the top eight nationally, team sponsor Professor **Robert Ladenson** reports that team members **Vaibhav Agrawal**, **Waseem Ahmed**, **Robert Brozyna**, and **Elena Davis** acquitted themselves well against keen competition.

The IEB also received the 2006 prize for Excellence and Innovation in Philosophy Programs, awarded by the American Philosophical Association and the Philosophy Documentation Center. This award recognizes philosophy programs of innovation, excellence, and inspiration. The IEB is an academic competition with rules and procedures designed to model the best approaches to reasoning about applied and practical ethics. It was created at the Center for the Study of Ethics in the Professions by Ladenson.

Spring 2007 Sawyier Philosophy Lecture

The spring 2007 Sawyier Philosophy Lecture in Science, Technology, and Society featured a talk on "Science, the Integrity of Nature and Human Welfare" by **Hugh Lacey**. Lacey is Senior Research Scholar/Scheuer Family Professor Emeritus of Philosophy at Swarthmore College, Swarthmore, PA, and Visiting Professor, Universidade de São Paulo, Brazil. Speaking on April 20 at the MTCC auditorium, Lacey discussed how to conduct scientific research to ensure that the integrity of nature is respected.

Lacey's lecture was made possible by a generous gift from the late **Fay Sawyier**, Professor Emerita of philosophy, who was an IIT faculty member from 1975-1988.

The planned speaker for the fall 2007 Sawyier Philosophy Lecture is Heather Douglas, a philosopher at the University of Tennessee. Douglas' talk, tentatively scheduled for Friday, October 26, is free and open to the public.

For updates, email Professor **Warren Schmaus** at schmaus@iit.edu or visit the Humanities Website: www.iit.edu/departments/humanities

Sawyier Predoctoral Fellows

Brandon Fogel and **Soazig Le Bihan** have joined us as Sawyier Predoctoral Fellows, teaching undergraduate courses in humanities and philosophy while finishing their dissertations.

Fogel is completing his Ph.D. from the University of Notre Dame; Le Bihan is completing her Ph.D. through a joint program between the University of Nancy 2 (France) and the University of Bielefeld (Germany). Both scholars specialize in the philosophy of physics.

The Sawyier Fellowships are made possible by a generous gift from the late **Fay Sawyier**, Professor Emerita of philosophy, who was an IIT faculty member from 1975-1988.

FIGURE 5.2 Inside page from 8.5 × 11 newsletter. Designer: James Maciukenas. Copyright Illinois Institute of Technology. Used by permission. (Visit www.pearsonhighered.com/riley to see this figure in color.)

THE GRID CONCEPT

In many ways, the concept of a grid is quite simple. A grid is a set of horizontal and vertical lines dividing the page into rectangles. The grid itself is not directly visible in the final document. Instead, during the design process, you can make the grid viewable on-screen in order to facilitate your work. A grid works analogously to the frame of a house—it cannot be seen once the house is built, but it reflects the basic design of the

Chapter 5 • Designing the 8.5 × 11 Page

house and guides the builder during construction. In the same way, a layout grid does not show in the final document, but it does show onscreen during the document design process to guide the designer.

When designing a document, you will use the grid during the layout process as an aid to placing, aligning, and sizing text and visuals and to maintaining a consistent proportion when working with elements such as photographs or blocks of text. This consistency is especially important when working with multipage documents such as reports, instruction manuals, newsletters, brochures, and the like. You might also want to create a grid for single-page items that will be companions in a set (for example, a series of single-page fact sheets about common medical conditions, displayed in the waiting area of a doctor's office). In addition to creating a unified look within or among documents, using a grid can also save you time, since it provides you with a starting point for laying out each page.

Figure 5.3 shows examples of four different grids for an 8.5 × 11 page:

- Figure 5.3a: 2 columns × 3 rows, with 6 grid units
- Figure 5.3b: 3 columns × 4 rows, with 12 grid units
- Figure 5.3c: 6 columns × 6 rows, with 36 grid units
- Figure 5.3d: 5 columns × 1 row, with 5 grid units

In these examples, each grid has equal margins all around (1 inch in full size), but keep in mind that margins may vary from inside to outside as well as from top to bottom.

Creating a Grid

Different types of publications and document purposes call for different types of grids. The type of grid that you create for a specific document depends largely on how many

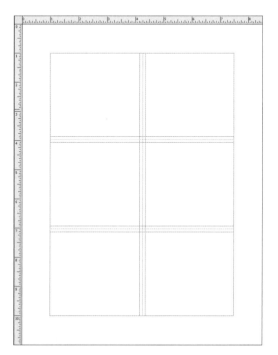

FIGURE 5.3 Four examples of grids for an 8.5 ×11 page. (Visit www.pearsonhighered.com/riley to see this figure in color.)
FIGURE 5.3a 2 × 3 grid.

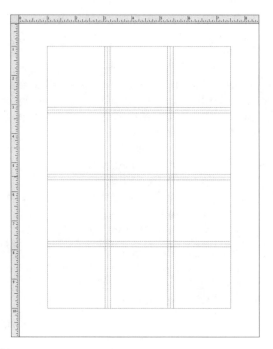

FIGURE 5.3b   3 × 4 grid.

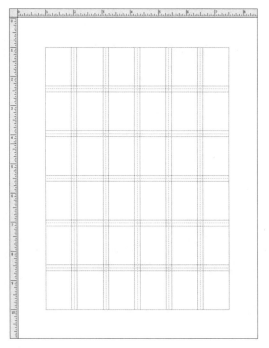

FIGURE 5.3c   6 × 6 grid.

types of textual or visual units you will be working with, as well as their size. As a general rule, the more complex the elements to be laid out, the more useful a smaller grid will be, since a grid with more divisions allows for more variations in its adaptation to specific text and images. Conversely, if the elements to be laid out are few and simple, a relatively simple grid will suffice.

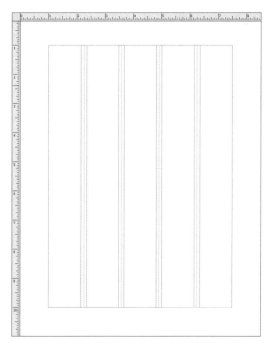

FIGURE 5.3d   5 × 1 grid.

For example, the 2 × 3 grid in Figure 5.3a would be suitable for a report that is primarily text with a few illustrations, tables, or graphs or for a journal that runs primarily single-column copy. Figure 5.3b would accommodate a journal or newsletter in which the copy will run in columns and in which more photographs of varying sizes will appear. Figure 5.3c, the most complex of the four grids, would allow for the greatest number of variations in layout of material and might be used for a more complex newsletter or annual report. Figure 5.3d would also accommodate a relatively complex layout. Since Figure 5.3d has grid units only for columns, rather than for both columns and rows, it would be more appropriate for a document that relies primarily on text (which tends to run in columns).

Therefore, choosing a grid requires knowing in advance—or at least predicting with some accuracy—certain facts about the material to be laid out, the preferred font size (since font size will interact with column width), the number and type of visual elements such as photographs, tables, and figures, and the amount of text and relative length of the individual text units (e.g., the mixture of long and short articles in a newsletter). As you can see, although constructing a grid is an early step in document design, it presupposes that much of the content of the document has already been created, or at least planned.

Exercise D

Examine the MSN homepage at http://www.msn.com/. Can you work backward to "reverse-engineer" the underlying grid of this page?

Exercise E

Examine a recent print issue of an academic journal published in 6 × 9 format (a common journal size). Work backward to construct the underlying page grid(s) used in the part of the journal that displays articles. If possible, try to examine pages that are entirely text as well as pages that display figures or tables. Based on your analysis, determine if the grid changes to accommodate these different content types.

Using a Grid

It is important to understand that grid units serve as guides for placing and sizing elements rather than as "holders" for elements. Just because a grid has five column units, this does not mean that each column of text must be one column unit wide. For example, Figure 5.3d has five column units, each 1.3 inches, or 7.8 picas, wide. However, this does not mean that each column of text must be 1.3 inches wide. Instead, it means that, as a rule of thumb, a given column of text should be some *multiple* of 1.3 inches wide. As an illustration, Figure 5.4 shows the identical text laid out in different ways using the five-column grid from Figure 5.3d.

As you can see, Figure 5.4a lays the text out in a one-column grid. Figure 5.4b uses two one-column units for the same text, and Figure 5.4c uses three one-column units. All three layouts would be possible within this same document, since all three follow the same grid.

Another point to note here is that just because text layout follows a grid, that does not insure its readability. For example, Figure 5.5 shows an enlarged excerpt from the

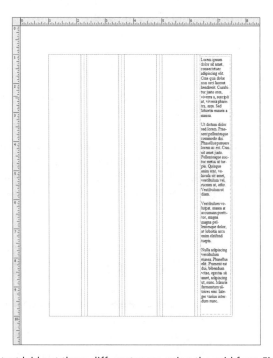

FIGURE 5.4 Identical text laid out three different ways, using the grid from Figure 5.3d. (Visit www.pearsonhighered.com/riley to see this figure in color.)
FIGURE 5.4a Text laid out in one column.

FIGURE 5.4b Text laid out in two columns.

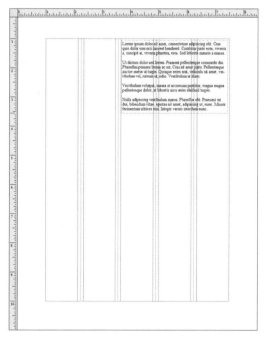

FIGURE 5.4c Text laid out in three columns.

one-column layout in Figure 5.4a. You can see from Figure 5.5 that the narrow column width accommodates only two to three words set in 10-point Times New Roman. This short line length might be acceptable for a caption or a very short paragraph but would be difficult to read for a longer passage, such as the full-column text shown in Figure 5.4a. Therefore, even though Figure 5.4a "obeys the grid," it does not illustrate an ideal design decision from the standpoint of readability.

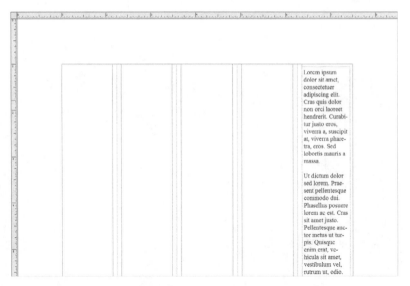

FIGURE 5.5   Enlarged excerpt from Figure 5.4a, showing effects of narrow column width on line length. (Visit www.pearsonhighered.com/riley to see this figure in color.)

Likewise, images such as photographs may need to be resized so that they span more than one grid unit in order to retain their interest and give readers an adequate amount of visual detail. As an example, examine the four page layouts in Figure 5.6. Here the same photo has been resized to span, respectively, one, two, three, and four grid units on an 8.5 × 11 page (shown here at about 30% of its actual size). However, not until we get to the three-unit span in Figure 5.6c does the photo have enough detail to become viewable and compelling.

Resizing photos "up" and giving them adequate space is an especially important consideration when laying out photographs of people, which often create a high degree of human interest for the document's stakeholders. For example, the page in

FIGURE 5.6a   Photo spanning one-column grid unit. Photograph copyright iStockphoto. Used by permission. (Visit www.pearsonhighered.com/riley to see this figure in color.)

FIGURE 5.6b   Photo spanning two one-column grid units. Photograph copyright iStockphoto. Used by permission. (Visit www.pearsonhighered.com/riley to see this figure in color.)

FIGURE 5.6c   Photo spanning three one-column grid units. Photograph copyright iStockphoto. Used by permission. (Visit www.pearsonhighered.com/riley to see this figure in color.)

Figure 5.6 could be from a newsletter going out from a university department to current students, alumni, and interested community members (including potential donors to the department). All these readers are likely to respond positively to seeing current students featured prominently. In Chapters 9 and 10, we will return in more detail to strategies for working with photographs; but for now the main point to keep in mind is that photos, like text, often need to span multiple smaller grid units to effectively engage the reader.

Mixing and Breaking Grids

Up to this point, we have looked at examples that adhere to a single grid. However, it is also common for multiple grids to be used in the same document and even on the same

FIGURE 5.6d   Photo spanning four one-column grid units. Photograph copyright iStockphoto. Used by permission. (Visit www.pearsonhighered.com/riley to see this figure in color.)

page. Mixing grids can be useful for avoiding a monotonous, predictable layout and for accommodating different types of material: for example, text versus images, or different types of text that require significantly different formatting from each other.

As an example, Figure 5.7a shows a two-column grid, while Figure 5.7b shows a five-column grid. Figure 5.7c shows a page laid out using the five-column grid on the

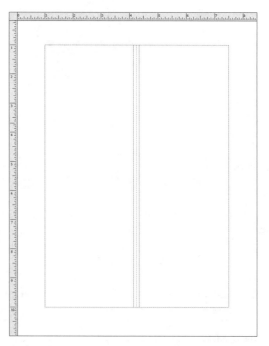

FIGURE 5.7   Separate grids combined on the same page. Photograph copyright iStockphoto. Used by permission. (Visit www.pearsonhighered.com/riley to see this figure in color.)
FIGURE 5.7a.   Two-column grid. (Visit www.pearsonhighered.com/riley to see this figure in color.)

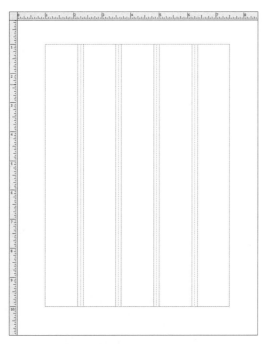

FIGURE 5.7b   Five-column grid. (Visit www.pearsonhighered.com/riley to see this figure in color.)

FIGURE 5.7c   Effects of stacking a five-column grid on top of a two-column grid. (Visit www. pearsonhighered.com/riley to see this figure in color.)

top half and the two-column grid on the bottom half. In Figure 5.7c, the use of the two-column grid on the bottom half introduces stability to the bottom of the page, since each column is wider than its counterpart on the top half of the page.

Using a Grid to Establish Balance and Symmetry

Earlier in this chapter, we mentioned the Gestalt principle of balance, which states that viewers are pleased by a sense of equilibrium among visual elements. In everyday language, it is commonplace to use *balance* interchangeably with *symmetry*. When considering document design, however, the two concepts, while related, must be distinguished. Symmetry refers to the repetition or equal distribution of identical (or nearly identical) visual elements on both sides of a central axis—either right and left or top and bottom. Figure 5.8 illustrates several instances of symmetrical design.

All three designs in Figure 5.8 illustrate left-right symmetry, that is, symmetry on both sides of a vertical axis. If you were to fold the image of each design in half lengthwise, you would find an even distribution of visual elements to the left and right of the

FIGURE 5.8   Three examples of symmetrical design. Photographs copyright iStockphoto. Used by permission. (Visit www.pearsonhighered.com/riley to see this figure in color.)
FIGURE 5.8a   The Parthenon. (Visit www.pearsonhighered.com/riley to see this figure in color.)

FIGURE 5.8b   Oriental rug. (Visit www.pearsonhighered.com/riley to see this figure in color.)

FIGURE 5.8c   Wedding invitation. (Visit www.pearsonhighered.com/riley to see this figure in color.)

fold. Figure 5.8b further illustrates top-bottom symmetry, that is, symmetry on both sides of a horizontal axis.

As illustrated in Figure 5.8, symmetry is characteristic of many classical designs and can impart a traditional, formal feeling and a feeling of stability. At the same time, symmetry can impart a feeling of predictability that may be somewhat less dynamic and visually interesting than we want. What we need, then, are strategies that allow the viewer to maintain a sense of visual equilibrium, yet that introduce elements of visual interest. The somewhat more complicated notion of balance can help you as a designer move beyond symmetry to achieve these goals.

The concept of balance has to do with the relative distribution on the page of elements with varying visual "weight," or "strength." Like symmetry, balance is usually discussed in terms of the opposition between left-right or top-bottom sections of a page. Unlike symmetry, however, balance may be achieved by strategies other than repetition or use of identical elements—strategies that allow the designer to introduce more variety into the page design. Arntson (2007, pp. 72–75) provides a useful summary of strategies through which balance can be achieved, even in the absence of symmetry:

- **Location:** Smaller shapes at the periphery of a page can balance larger shapes at the center.
- **Three-dimensionality:** Shapes with spatial depth are stronger than two-dimensional shapes.
- **Size:** Larger shapes are stronger than smaller shapes.
- **Texture:** Shapes with visual texture are stronger than those without visual texture.
- **Isolation:** An isolated shape is visually stronger than one surrounded by other shapes.
- **Subject matter:** An intrinsically interesting visual element is stronger than less interesting elements.
- **Contrast:** Elements with high visual contrast are stronger than those without. For example, elements with brighter and more intense colors are stronger than elements with toned-down colors. In black and white, comparatively darker or more solid graphic elements are stronger than lighter elements.
- **Shape:** Complex shapes are stronger than simpler shapes.

Exercise F

The specific strategies just outlined appear to fall into three general strategies: placement, size, and appearance. Identify which strategy or strategies belong in each category.

Exercise G

Referring to the bulleted list of strategies for creating balance, identify the strategies used in the designs in Figure 5.9. Consider balance across both the vertical axis (i.e., left to right) and the horizontal axis (i.e., top to bottom).

Exercise H

Return to the newsletter page shown in Figure 5.2. Identify at least three techniques used to establish balance on the page.

FIGURE 5.9 Postcard publicizing lecture. Designer: James Maciukenas. Copyright Illinois Institute of Technology. Used by permission. (Visit www.pearsonhighered.com/riley to see this figure in color.)

Exercise I

Visit a poster site such as www.allposters.com or an image library such as ARTstor (artstor.org) and examine some vintage travel posters. Referring to the bulleted list of strategies for creating balance, identify the strategies used in at least three poster designs. Consider balance across both the vertical axis (i.e., left to right) and the horizontal axis (i.e., top to bottom). Look for examples in which multiple strategies are used, and be prepared to discuss them with your instructor and classmates.

Conclusion

Grids offer designers a way to organize elements on a page and to unify pages in a multipage document. Constructing a grid for a particular document involves an analysis of the type, number, and complexity of text and image units that the document will contain. In some cases, multiple grids may be combined within the document or even on one page of the document to create variety and accommodate different types of material. Within the framework of the grid, principles from Gestalt psychology such as continuation, similarity, and balance can be further put to use to create a page layout that is both usable and engaging.

Summary of Key Concepts and Terms

alignment	eyetracking	Gestalt theory	saccade
balance	fixation	grid	similarity
continuation	F-shaped pattern	heat map	symmetry

Additional Exercises

1. Examine the report at http://www.aucc.ca/_pdf/english/publications/trends_2007_vol2_e.pdf What grid, or grids, are used in this document? How is the choice of grid determined by content type?
2. View the tutorial at http://v4.designintellection.com/using-ms-excel-to-brainstorm-grids/ and use this technique to set up a grid in Excel for an 8.5 × 11 page with 12 columns of equal width.
3. Massachusetts Institute of Technology maintains an archive of its daily "Spotlight" Web pages at http://www.mit.edu/site/gallery/index.html. (You can also view an archive of additional pages at http://www.mit.edu/site/past/index.html.) Select three of the pages and identify the grid strategies used to align and unify visual and textual elements on the page.
4. Examine the pages of a professionally designed annual report (e.g., http://www.wto.org/english/res_e/reser_e/annual_report_e.htm). Select several pages from the report and identify the grid strategies used to align and unify visual and textual elements on the page.

Varying the Size and Shape of the Page

Chapters 4 and 5 focused on principles and strategies for designing single- and multiple-page documents based on an 8.5 × 11-inch page size. This chapter focuses on strategies for working with common variants on the 8.5 × 11-inch page size, such as trifold brochures, pamphlets, booklets, and tent cards. By the end of this chapter, you should be able to do the following:

- Understand effective uses for commonly used variants on the 8.5 × 11-inch page
- Be able to choose an appropriate grid for these common variants
- Understand principles that underlie how readers use these variant forms
- Understand strategies for rescaling, placing, and balancing elements across various pages of these variant forms
- Understand strategies for constructing a unified set of related documents

OVERVIEW OF RELEVANT DESIGN CONCEPTS AND PRINCIPLES

Many of the concepts and principles discussed in Chapters 4 and 5 carry over to this chapter. Regardless of what size or shape your document is, you always need to consider fundamental questions about font selection, line length, and use of horizontal and vertical white space. However, when we move to some of the formats discussed in this chapter—in particular, to folded documents, or to smaller documents based on a larger "parent" document—we need to consider new questions about how the audience will read and use these varied types of documents. For example, in a folded document such as a trifold brochure, we need to take into account the order in which the audience will encounter each panel of the brochure. Likewise, you may find yourself designing companion documents—for example, both a poster for an event and a companion postcard announcing the event. This chapter offers some guidelines about how to coordinate a *document set*, a group of visually related documents.

WHY THESE PRINCIPLES ARE IMPORTANT

Advice on effective design of documents such as brochures, tent cards, and postcards tends to rise not so much from findings of empirical research but rather from received opinion, common sense, and advice of expert designers. For example, research on brochures tends to focus on the content of the information rather than on their design. Researchers have studied brochure readability, particularly of public health brochures (e.g., Perloff & Ray, 1991; Springston & Champion, 2004) and sales brochures (e.g., Burton, 1991). Sales brochure research is particularly rich in relation to the travel industry (e.g., Hodgson, 1991, 1993). Gregory (2002/2003) and Schellens and de Jong (2004) studied persuasive language, argumentation, and visual strategies in brochures aimed at persuading, such as public health, environmental, and charity brochures. There is some degree to which this research about content ties in with design decisions. For example, a finding that visual images are an effective addition to persuasive brochures would obviously affect a design decision to include photography in brochures.

Even in the absence of extensive empirical research on design principles related to these variant documents, we can still return to general principles of design such as the elements of Gestalt theory discussed in Chapter 5. These principles lead us back to considerations about alignment, similarity, continuation, balance, and the use of a grid to achieve some of these qualities. As mentioned, we will also return to principles related to font selection, line length, and use of horizontal and vertical white space.

DESIGNING TRIFOLD BROCHURES

Brochures are a common document type, used for both informative and persuasive purposes—for example, to publicize businesses and products, academic programs, social services, and health and medical information.

Brochures come in many shapes and sizes, but the most common one is the *trifold* (also known as *c-fold*, or *letterfold*) *brochure*. As the name implies, this type of brochure is based on a piece of paper (usually 8.5 × 11) folded twice (like a business letter) to create a brochure with a total of six panels: three on the outside and three on the inside. Figure 6.1 shows an overview of a trifold brochure, while Figure 6.2 shows layout screens for a trifold brochure with panels numbered 1–6 for ease of use as we refer to them in the text.

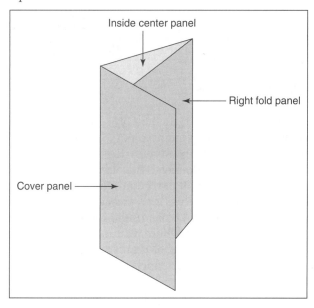

FIGURE 6.1 Overview of trifold brochure.

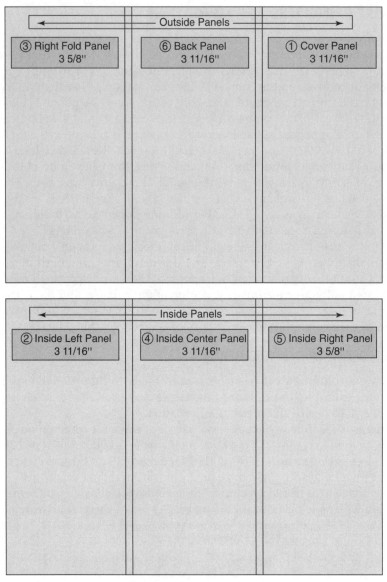

FIGURE 6.2   Layout screens for front and back of a trifold brochure, showing labeled panels. (Visit www.pearsonhighered.com/riley to see this figure in more detail.)

Working with folded documents such as brochures presents some special challenges for layout because the screen layout does not map directly onto the order in which the user will encounter the panels. For example, in the screen layout for a trifold brochure, you will see the cover panel (1) immediately to the right of the back panel (6). However, as the numbers indicate, these are not at all the order in which the user will encounter these panels. As a designer, you must keep this "disconnect" in mind as you proceed through the visualization and design process. Depending on your ability to mentally map the brochure layout onto the final folded brochure, you may want to prepare an actual piece of folded paper with the various panels labeled and numbered so that you can more easily visualize the relationships between the panels onscreen and in the actual folded piece.

Another detail to notice in Figure 6.2 relates to the grid system that was introduced in Chapter 5. The panels on a trifold brochure are not equal in size. This is because the right fold panel (numbers 3 outside and 5 inside) must be slightly narrower in order to fit under the cover panel once the brochure is folded.

Distributing Content Throughout a Brochure

Before moving to details in brochure layout, it is useful to begin with an overview of which content should go where in a brochure. Following are some general guidelines recommended by expert practitioners such as McWade (2003), Williams (2008), and others. These are illustrated with reference to the brochure proof pages in Figure 6.3.

- **Cover panel (1).** The cover panel has the most important job in the brochure: to make the reader open the brochure and keep reading. Typography, imagery, and content must come together in a way that delineates a clear but simple message, perhaps with a tagline that invites the reader to find out more. The sample brochure in Figure 6.3 is intended primarily for potential students interested in a doctoral program in technical communication (and perhaps for their advisors). Therefore, photographs of actual students from a variety of demographic groups were chosen for the cover panel.
- **Inside left panel (2) and right fold panel (3).** These are the first panels your reader will encounter upon opening the brochure. As such, they should contain copy and images that create interest or a strong selling point for your brochure's product or service. In the brochure in Figure 6.3, panel (2) contains key information about the degrees being publicized, while panel (3) features student photos and a list of courses.
- **Inside panels (4) and (5).** These panels should continue to draw readers in and sustain their interest. The panels in the sample brochure in Figure 6.3 do this by providing additional pictures and including details about program resources.
- **Back panel (6).** The back panel is where readers expect to find contact information. Often, the back panel repeats the organization's logo, a key image, or both. These strategies are used in the sample brochure in Figure 6.3. Depending on your content, you may also want to include a map on the back panel.

Strategies for Brochure Layout

Like other multipage documents, multipanel documents such as brochures are easier to design and execute if you establish a grid. You can see that the brochure in Figure 6.3 makes use of a one-column, three-row grid that breaks the panel horizontally into three roughly equal units. Solid lines and variations in color are used to further reinforce the structure of the grid and to both separate and unify visual and textual content.

For example, the contrasting blue and white backgrounds in panels (2) and (4), respectively, help to direct the reader's eye movement *down* each panel (rather than *across* the top of panel (2) to the top of panel (4), another possible—but in this case unintended—direction). Likewise, the thick red rule across the top of panels (2) and (4) establishes a distinct visual area for essential content about the program. The red rule also pulls together the brochure visually, since it echoes the red on the cover panel—which, in turn, uses one of the IIT school colors.

Brochure text generally needs to be clearly confined within each panel. That is, you ordinarily do not want text to run horizontally across a fold line, since you don't want the text creased during the fold process and rendered unreadable. For this reason, you want to make sure that you leave an adequate margin on both sides of the gutter of each fold line. Likewise, you want to avoid running your text too close to the outer margins, in case errors in alignment or trimming arise during the printing process. These precautions are doubly important if you are dealing with a printer whose work quality is relatively unknown to you. In terms of type size, Williams (2008) recommends using a font smaller than 12 points for body text in a brochure in order to accommodate the shorter line lengths found in this type of document.

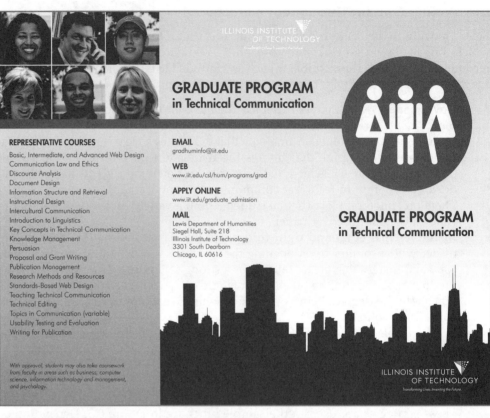

FIGURE 6.3 Sample brochure showing numbered panels. Designer: James Maciukenas. Copyright Illinois Institute of Technology. Used by permission. (Visit www.pearsonhighered.com/riley to see this figure in color.)

Pictures, rules, and color backgrounds, on the other hand, can run horizontally across panels in a brochure, since a fold line in these items will not affect readability. In the brochure in Figure 6.3, for example, images and rules extend across multiple panels at various points in the brochure. When extending graphic elements across a fold line, the main point is to make sure that the choice looks deliberate. For example, instead of extending a rule a quarter inch into the next panel (which might look like it resulted from a folding mistake), extend it several inches into, or all the way across, the next panel.

Exercise A

Collect some brochures and identify (if possible) the content distribution and grid structure used in each one. Does the distribution of content seem to follow the guidelines just given? If not, what are the differences? Likely places to find brochures include travel agencies, hospitals, and universities.

The paper you select for your brochure depends largely on its function, tone, and your production and budget constraints. If you have are designing a brochure for a luxury resort with full-color photographs, you will want choose paper that shows them to advantage. On the other hand, a brochure for a recycling center may call for recyled, matte paper in off-white tones. By working with a printer, you can select the best paper finish and weight for your project.

Exercise B

Analyze the paper choice in the brochures that you collected for Exercise A. Does the paper choice for each one seem deliberate and appropriate? Why or why not?

The trifold brochure design discussed in this section is the most common type and, depending on paper and color production options, can often be produced in-house using widely available stock paper (8.5 × 11 or 8.5 × 14). However, you should be aware that many other options exist for brochure sizes and fold patterns. A good source for ideas about other brochure variations is McWade (2003); this source illustrates several distinctive styles such as a square brochure, a miniature brochure with "peekaboo" panels, a pocket brochure, and a zigzag brochure. Most of these would require working with a professional printer to ensure quality production.

CREATING DOCUMENT SETS

Often you will need to construct different versions of a design in order to accommodate different media types, sizes, and stages of publicity. For example, the basic design of a company's letterhead may need to be adapted for use on envelopes, business cards, and mailing labels. Or a full-page ad may need to be adapted for a smaller space.

We will illustrate this process by looking at two related publicity documents for a university lecture: an 11 × 17-inch poster and a 4 × 6-inch postcard. Additionally, a version of the postcard image will be posted on the sponsoring department's Web site.

While these documents relate to the same event, they will be used at different times in the publicity schedule and will be targeted to different, although overlapping, audiences.

For the purposes of this discussion, the poster will be considered the "parent" document and the postcard the derivative, or "child," document. There are several reasons for envisioning the relationship in this way. First of all, the poster is a larger document and contains more verbal information as well as a larger image. Second, the poster will appear earlier in the publicity cycle than the postcards, since the posters will be posted around campus several weeks before the event, while the postcards will go out as a more targeted reminder to selected faculty, staff, and students about a week before the event.

Figure 6.4 shows a reduced version of the 11 × 17-inch poster that will form the basis for the postcard and Web versions. Our goal is to create a 4 × 6-inch postcard that can be printed on both sides but must have an address area suitable for mailing through the U.S. Postal Service (USPS). (It will also be distributed to some students in class and by campus mail.) As with the poster, the postcard can use color and imagery as well as text.

Our goal is not to create a miniature version of the poster. Instead, our goal is to create a postcard version that shares the "look and feel" of our poster but that is adapted appropriately to the postcard medium and its audiences. This means that the layout, font selection, imagery, and color palette of the postcard should echo the poster. A faculty member who sees the poster around campus and then later gets a copy of the postcard through campus mail should recognize the two documents as publicizing the same event.

Some strategies and constraints to consider when "versioning" a 4 × 6-inch postcard from an 11 × 17-inch poster include the following:

- Because of the size difference, you will need to make choices about what to cut or resize from your poster. For example, the poster in Figure 6.4 contains a large image and quite a long abstract (summary) of the talk (provided by the speaker). Clearly, the entire abstract from the poster is not going to fit on a postcard, unless it is reduced to such a small size that readers will have difficulty reading it.

FIGURE 6.4 Poster (actual size 11 × 17 inches) advertising university lecture. Designer: James Maciukenas. Copyright Illinois Institute of Technology. Used by permission. (Visit www.pearsonhighered.com/riley to see this figure in color.)

- On the other hand, *some* text must carry over to the postcard so that the reader will receive the essential information about the event. We cannot assume that the reader will have seen the poster or will remember all the information on it. Figure 6.5 shows a companion postcard for the event publicized in Figure 6.4. Note that the front of the postcard carries over the same visual image and displays essential details about the event, while the back of the postcard contains a highly abbreviated version of the abstract.

FIGURE 6.5   Front and back of postcard publicizing lecture. Designer: James Maciukenas. Copyright Illinois Institute of Technology. Used by permission. (Visit www.pearsonhighered.com/riley to see this figure in color.)

FIGURE 6.6   Postcard using cropped images. (Visit www.pearsonhighered.com/riley to see this figure in color.)

- Rather than miniaturizing the entire poster image for use on the postcard, it may be effective to carry over a section of the poster image. An interesting full-scale excerpt cropped from a large image might be more compelling and intriguing than a complete but miniaturized image. (See Chapter 10, "Editing Photography," for strategies about cropping.) Figure 6.6 shows this strategy used on a postcard publicizing a lunchtime colloquium: instead of showing a image of an entire typewriter, the card shows just segments of typewriters.
- Color and font choices for both versions should be compatible with each other.
- When designing for a smaller scale, a common mistake is trying to fit too much into the design. Continue to aim for basic qualities such as a focal point, clean design, and use of proximity, alignment, repetition, and contrast (as discussed in Williams, 2008; see also Chapter 9).
- Keep in mind how recipients will use each version. For example, a postcard about an event might end up on a refrigerator door. That should tell you something about what should be on the front of it.
- Sometimes you have to follow rules and regulations that are outside of your control, such as the USPS regulations about postcards. For example, space for an address must be planned for the back of the postcard.

Exercise C

Compare the poster and postcard versions in Figures 6.4 and 6.5 with respect to the designer's decisions about the following: (a) visual elements repeated from the poster; (b) verbal elements repeated from the poster; and (c) layout decisions repeated from the poster (e.g., choices about the ordering of text). Also consider in what ways the two document differ. Speculate on the rationale behind the differences.

Exercise D

Figure 6.7 illustrates an 11 × 17-inch poster for a university lecture. Sketch a layout for a 4 × 6-inch postcard version. If you are interested in proceeding further than the sketch stage, the fonts used in the poster are Lithograph Light, Papyrus, and Kaufmann BT.

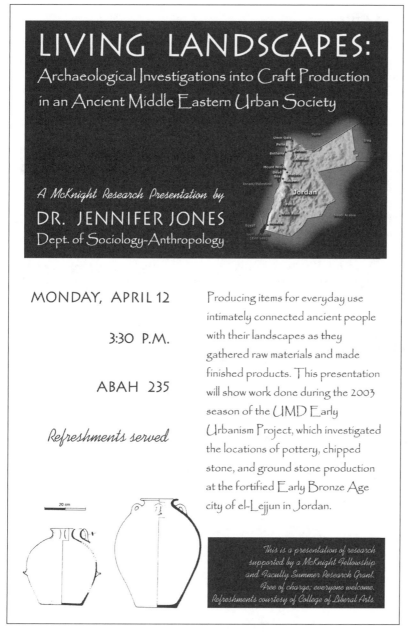

FIGURE 6.7 Black and white poster (actual size 11 × 17 inches) advertising a university lecture. (Visit www.pearsonhighered.com/riley to see this figure in more detail.)

Exercise E

Because of budget constraints, the 11 × 17-inch poster in Figure 6.7 had to be produced in-house and in black and white. Suggest a strategy for paper selection that might introduce some visual interest while remaining in keeping with the tone and subject matter of the talk. Keep in mind that any color selected will show through the reverse type as well as through the map image.

BUSINESS CARDS

Business cards are part of the standard suite of stationery for any individual or organization with a service or product to promote. Yet business cards present a special challenge because of the amount of information that must be contained in a very small space (2 × 3.5 inches). And, as Williams (2008) points out, "The amount of information you put on a business card has been growing—in addition to the standard address and phone, now you probably need your cell number, fax number, email address, and if you have a web site (which you should) your web address" (p. 114).

As a starting point for designing a business card, McWade (2003) suggests envisioning the 2 × 3.5-inch space as shown in Figure 6.8, creating a 2 × 2-inch square on the left that will contain a dominant image for the card. The 2 × 1.5-inch space on the right creates an area for text (i.e., the business name and contact information), allowing for left alignment of this material.

Figure 6.9 shows three sample cards based on this template and shown at approximately full size. You will see that the template is quite versatile and allows for both an image-based card (such as the two on the top) and one that is more text-based (such as the one on the bottom). In the top two examples, the dominant visual image (the photograph in the top card, the logo in the middle card, and the logotype in the bottom card) occupies the left space, while the contact information is neatly contained in the right space.

Exercise F

You may notice that the contact information area on the Keyboarders business card in Figure 6.9 deviates slightly from the 2 × 1.5-inch size suggested earlier. Based on a close examination of the card, why do you think this decision was made?

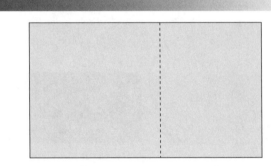

FIGURE 6.8   Business card template suggested by McWade (2003). (Visit www.pearsonhighered.com/riley to see this figure in more detail.)

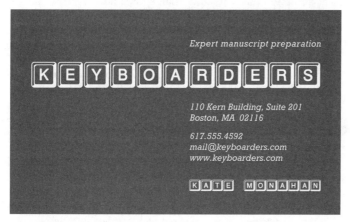

FIGURE 6.9   Three sample business cards designed using McWade's (2003) template. (Visit www.pearsonhighered.com/riley to see this figure in color.)

Conclusion

Commonly used variations on the size and shape of the 8.5 × 11-inch page include trifold brochures, postcards, and business cards. We have looked at strategies for selecting and placing elements within each of these types of documents. Given that these variants are often part of a document set, we have also considered strategies for creating visual coherence among related documents. While each of these variants on the 8.5 × 11-inch page calls for specialized design strategies, the basic principles discussed in Chapter 5—using a grid and establishing alignment, balance, and symmetry—continue to apply.

Summary of Key Concepts and Terms

c-fold brochure   document set   letterfold brochure   trifold brochure

Additional Exercises

At the end of this chapter and on the Companion Web site, you will find background information, copy, and photos for your use in designing three documents for a small business called Trail's End Farm: (1) an 8.5 × 11 trifold brochure, (2) an insert sheet for the brochure, and (3) a business card. Design as many of these items as your instructor assigns. If designing more than one of them, keep in mind strategies for creating a unified document set.

You are free to use full color on the brochure and business card and up to one color on the insert. The brochure should be suitable for printing on 8.5 × 11-inch paper as a double-sided trifold brochure. The insert requested is a one-panel (i.e., 8.5 × approx. 3.6 inches) insert containing rate information. The owners would like the insert delivered as a Word file that they can easily update themselves without having to reprint the entire brochure.

You are not expected to use all the photographs but may select from them as you wish. Assume that all were supplied by the business owners—the couple pictured in one of the photos—and represent scenes from their facility. You will also need to make decisions about which text to include and how to format it. For example, you may wish to convert some of the sentences to a bulleted list, and you may also add headings. However, you should not add or create facts or images other than those provided.

With your deliverables, also submit a separate document (up to two double-spaced pages) in which you explain and justify the design choices that you made. For the brochure, also include some discussion of the type and color of paper you would recommend to the clients, considering the intended use, subject matter, and readership of the documents.

Background Information about Trail's End Farm

Trail's End Farm was opened in 2000 by Annette and George Haygood. Annette works part-time as a nurse, and George is a construction supervisor who took early retirement shortly after he and Paulette opened Trail's End. Both have been riding and caring for horses all their lives, and in 2000 they finally decided to take the plunge and open a boarding facility. There was not enough of a market in the area to support a fancy facility aimed at people who show and compete their horses. However, their research showed that there was a market for a facility aimed primarily at owners who needed to board retired horses or horses in layup (i.e., horses needing recovery or rehabilitation after illness or injury).

Horses in layup or retirement need daily, or sometimes even more frequent, care. Often, however, the owner of the horse is unable to tend to the horse on a daily basis or even to visit it very frequently. Owners of horses in retirement or layup want to rest assured that their horses will be cared for by responsible, knowledgeable, and compassionate caretakers. Trail's End is not a lesson facility or a fancy,

ultramodern "show barn" for riders who want to compete in equestrian sports; however, the Haygoods take pride in the fact that the Trail's End facilities are safe, clean, and "horse-friendly." Being a former construction supervisor, George personally takes care of or oversees much of the upkeep of the facilities (such as fencing).

Although not aimed at riders who want to compete or take lessons, Trail's End does have an indoor arena that can be used for riding, handwalking, or lunging a horse. A network of riding trails circles the hay fields and the woods adjacent to the pastures.

Annette and George have provided you with the copy and photographs available on the Companion Web site. They need a brochure and business card that they can distribute to visitors, place with local veterinarians (who, in turn, might pass it on to clients when making barn calls), and place in tack shops and at horse shows. They want to appeal to owners from all riding disciplines (i.e., not just English or Western).

Using Tables to Display Information

This chapter examines the use of tables to display numerical and nonnumerical information. It looks at issues to consider in deciding when to use a table; conventions for table structure and layout; ways to make tables readable and usable; ways to integrate tables into the surrounding text; and strategies for writing explanatory material for tables, such as labels and titles.

After working through this chapter, you should be able to do the following:

- Apply criteria for deciding whether to use a table
- Construct effective tables using standard format features
- Use Word to create and modify the appearance of a table
- Integrate tables clearly into surrounding text by using clear callouts and previewing or reviewing table material in surrounding text

OVERVIEW OF RELEVANT DESIGN CONCEPTS AND PRINCIPLES

It may be helpful to start with some basic terminology and definitions. The essence of a table is that it allows the reader to relate information in *columns* (vertically arranged) and *rows* (horizontally arranged). The intersection of a row and a column is called a *cell*. For example, consider the table—which is not especially well formatted—shown in Figure 7.1. This table has two columns (Admitted and Enrolled), three rows (U.S. students, International students, and Citizenship unknown), and six cells (each containing a number).

Information displayed this way still comprises a table even if we remove the borders around and within it, as shown in Figure 7.2.

Table 1. Enrollment figures for spring 2010

	Admitted	Enrolled
U.S. students	203	107
International students	50	37
Citizenship unknown	6	6

FIGURE 7.1   Example of numerical table with borders.

Table 2. Enrollment figures for spring 2010

	Admitted	Enrolled
U.S. students	203	107
International students	50	37
Citizenship unknown	6	6

FIGURE 7.2   Example of numerical table without borders.

Table 3. Common Indo-European and non-Indo-European languages

Indo-European languages	Non-Indo-European languages
English	Arabic
French	Chinese
German	Japanese
Spanish	Swahili

FIGURE 7.3   Example of nonnumerical table with borders.

While we often think of numbers when we think of tables, tables also have important uses for displaying nonnumerical information as well. For example, Figure 7.3 (where, for the time being, we have again ignored formatting) lists common Indo-European and non-Indo-European languages.

Likewise, Figure 7.4 lists academic requirements and specifies whether they apply to undergraduate and graduate students.

Table 4. Final requirements for technical communication majors

	Required of undergraduates?	Required of graduate students?
Internship	Yes	Yes
Capstone course	Yes	No
Thesis project	No	Yes
Exit interview	No	Yes

FIGURE 7.4   Example of nonnumerical table without borders.

WHY THESE PRINCIPLES ARE IMPORTANT

We can see that Tables 1 through 4 use various formatting techniques, ranging from a full set of gridlines and borders (in Tables 1 and 3) to no gridlines or borders (in Tables 2 and 4), as well as various sorts of alignment and spacing to group material together. In choosing among these and other formatting options, as well as ways to implement those options, one of main principles of table construction has to do with what Tufte (2001) describes as maximizing the data-to-ink ratio. Doing so usually means reducing the amount of nondata ink (the amount of extraneous material, such as unnecessary gridlines), thereby focusing the reader's attention on ink that represents data (in the case of a table, items in a cell or information in related headings).

For example, instead of using gridlines, we can use spacing to group data into rows or columns, giving them visual *proximity*, or closeness. To illustrate the potential of spacing as a strategy for visually grouping data, compare Tables 5a, 5b, and 5c in Figure 7.5. Table 5a uses gridlines (lines separating columns and rows) to delineate data cells and other table components.

Table 5b in Figure 7.5, on the other hand, uses no gridlines whatsoever. We can see that the spacing between columns is much greater than the spacing between rows; therefore, it is fairly easy to distinguish columns of data but somewhat less easy to follow a row of data across the table.

Table 5c in Figure 7.5 uses a somewhat different strategy, introducing more white space between rows and therefore allowing readers to scan each row across more easily, since the space between rows is starting to approximate the space between columns.

Table 5d in Figure 7.5 takes another approach to grouping information, relying instead on *contrast*—the design principle of making two items that are not the same very different—rather than on spacing to keep the reader's eye moving across the row. The very faint (10%) gray fill color on alternate rows helps to group the data and might be a good alternative to spacing between rows if space is at a premium.

Table 5a. Heads and credit hours for fall 2009 for three departments.

		Full-Time		Part-Time		Total	
		Heads	Hours	Heads	Hours	Heads	Hours
English	**Deg**	15	143	13	60	28	203
	Cert	5	16	2	8	7	24
	Non	1	3	2	6	3	9
		21	**162**	**17**	**74**	**38**	**236**
History	**Deg**	77	728	78	269	155	997
	Cert	7	20	8	30	15	50
	Non	2	6	6	21	8	27
		86	**754**	**92**	**320**	**178**	**1,074**
Political Science	**Deg**	59	584	100	458	159	1,042
	Cert	0	0	5	16	5	16
	Non	0	0	20	74	20	74
		59	**584**	**125**	**548**	**184**	**1,132**

FIGURE 7.5 Strategies for grouping information within a table.
FIGURE 7.5a Use of gridlines to delineate cells within a table.

Table 5b. Heads and credit hours for fall 2009 for three departments.

		Full-Time		Part-Time		Total	
		Heads	Hours	Heads	Hours	Heads	Hours
English	**Deg**	15	143	13	60	28	203
	Cert	5	16	2	8	7	24
	Non	1	3	2	6	3	9
		21	**162**	**17**	**74**	**38**	**236**
History	**Deg**	77	728	78	269	155	997
	Cert	7	20	8	30	15	50
	Non	2	6	6	21	8	27
		86	**754**	**92**	**320**	**178**	**1,074**
Political Science	**Deg**	59	584	100	458	159	1,042
	Cert	0	0	5	16	5	16
	Non	0	0	20	74	20	74
		59	**584**	**125**	**548**	**184**	**1,132**

FIGURE 7.5b Table with gridlines deleted.

Table 5c. Heads and credit hours for fall 2009 for three departments.

		Full-Time		Part-Time		Total	
		Heads	Hours	Heads	Hours	Heads	Hours
English	**Deg**	15	143	13	60	28	203
	Cert	5	16	2	8	7	24
	Non	1	3	2	6	3	9
		21	**162**	**17**	**74**	**38**	**236**
History	**Deg**	77	728	78	269	155	997
	Cert	7	20	8	30	15	50
	Non	2	6	6	21	8	27
		86	**754**	**92**	**320**	**178**	**1,074**
Political Science	**Deg**	59	584	100	458	159	1,042
	Cert	0	0	5	16	5	16
	Non	0	0	20	74	20	74
		59	**584**	**125**	**548**	**184**	**1,132**

FIGURE 7.5c Use of white space to delineate columns and rows.

In short, decisions about whether to use a table to display information and about strategies for displaying information within a table can contribute greatly to the clarity and usability of detailed information that a reader might need.

Table 5d. Heads and credit hours for fall 2009 for three departments.

		Full-Time		Part-Time		Total	
		Heads	Hours	Heads	Hours	Heads	Hours
English	**Deg**	15	143	13	60	28	203
	Cert	5	16	2	8	7	24
	Non	1	3	2	6	3	9
		21	162	17	74	38	236
History	**Deg**	77	728	78	269	155	997
	Cert	7	20	8	30	15	50
	Non	2	6	6	21	8	27
		86	754	92	320	178	1,074
Political Science	**Deg**	59	584	100	458	159	1,042
	Cert	0	0	5	16	5	16
	Non	0	0	20	74	20	74
		59	584	125	548	184	1,132

FIGURE 7.5d   Use of shading to delineate rows.

DECIDING WHETHER TO USE A TABLE

In considering the issues outlined previously, the most fundamental question is whether or not to use a table. As with many design decisions, this one can best be made by looking at the document from the reader's viewpoint: Will a table make the document more usable and understandable to the reader? As you plan or review the draft of your document, you will want to keep several questions in mind.

Will the Reader Have to Process Complex Data or Large Amounts of Data?

It is hard for readers to track and compare a large series of numbers or other details if the information is presented in prose format (i.e., sentences and paragraphs). While "large" is a relative term—one that requires you to use your own judgment—a good rule of thumb is that items that would need more than four table cells present an opportunity for a table. Put another way, if a table requires only four cells, the data are "more efficiently presented in text" (American Psychological Association, 2001, p. 147).

For example, at one extreme, consider the text in passage (1). This passage compares only two items (in-state and out-of-state daycare operations) across two conditions (whether or not they have a state license). This comparison is hardly complex enough to need the table in Figure 7.6a to supplement or replace it:

1. While only 75% of in-home daycare operations are licensed by the state, 98% of out-of-home daycare operations have state licenses.

	State license	No state license
In-home daycare	75%	25%
Out-of-home daycare	98%	2%

FIGURE 7.6a   Example of unnecessary table.

	West Coast	Rockies	Midwest	Southeast	Northeast
Lightning	31%	64%			
Smoking	20%	10%	21%		26%
Debris burning			28%	19%	21%
Incendiary burning				39%	

FIGURE 7.6b   Example of table that clarifies complex text.

In contrast, passage (2) attempts to discuss two features (the two most common causes of forest fires) of five entities (regions of the United States):

2. On the West Coast, the most common causes of forest fire are lightning (31%) and smoking (20%). In the Rocky Mountain states, the most common causes are lightning (64%) and smoking (10%). In the Midwest, the most common causes are debris burning (28%) and smoking (21%). In the Southeast, the most common causes are incendiary burning (39%) and debris burning (19%). And in the Northeast, the most common causes are smoking (26%) and debris burning (21%).

The prose format of passage (2) makes it hard to compare the regions and causes and to see relationships within the information. The patterns in these data are much more apparent in the table in Figure 7.6b, where the reader can see all five regions simultaneously. For example, it does not take long to see that smoking is a major factor in four of the five regions. In contrast, incendiary burning is a major factor in only one region. (Whether a table is the *best* way to present this data is a question that we take up in Chapter 8.)

Will the Reader Want to Find or Refer Back to Data Quickly?

Tables make it easy for the reader to cross-reference data within a document. For example, if you were asked right now to find four examples of Indo-European languages, it would be easy for you to return to Table 3 (in Figure 7.3) and locate this information quite quickly. For this reason, tables and graphics can be especially useful for informative or instructional material, such as user manuals—documents that a reader may be trying to learn from or to use while performing a related task.

Will the Reader Want to Examine and Compare Precise Numerical Values?

A table is useful for displaying exact values or terms—for example, if the reader needs to be able to quickly locate exact dollar amounts or percentages. On the other hand, if all the reader needs to be able to do is estimate values and if you want instead to emphasize the overall "shape" of numerical data, a graph or chart (discussed in Chapter 8) is probably a better choice. As Robbins (2005) puts it, "Graphs are for the forest and tables are for the trees" (p. 344).

Will the Reader be Overwhelmed or Bored by a Number of Gray Pages?

One benefit of tables and graphics is that they break up gray pages, that is, pages that contain only prose text. This feature is especially important if you are trying explain complex or technical material to nonspecialists (although readers who are subject-matter experts will also welcome a break from uninterrupted blocks of text) or if you're constructing a lengthy document. In either case, tables and graphics can help to make a document more reader-friendly and interesting, compared to paragraph after paragraph of prose.

PARTS OF A TABLE

Fully constructed tables can have a number of parts. The most commonly used ones are listed here for your reference:

Column head	Table body
Column spanner	Label
Table spanner	Title
Stub head (row label)	Notes
Stub	

Most of these items are illustrated in Figure 7.7 and discussed in the sections that follow.

Column Head

A *column head* (also known as a column header or heading) is a label that identifies the content of one individual column. For example, in Figure 7.7, *Female* and *Male* are column heads.

Column Spanner

A *column spanner* is a heading that associates a set of two or more columns, usually by using a rule (i.e., a solid line) under the spanner. (Since the rule straddles several columns, a column spanner may also be called a *straddle rule*.) Column spanners are useful for helping the reader see categories within the columns that are being compared. For example, in Figure 7.7, the column spanners *Domestic* and *International* help the reader to see that the data for domestic and international students form subcategories within the data.

Exercise A

What is another way that the categories in Figure 7.7 could be grouped? How would the use of column spanners have to be adjusted? Would you change anything else if you regrouped the categories? Sketch out your answer.

Item tested	Domestic		International	
	Female	Male	Female	Male
Vocabulary	79.6	73.4	53.7	42.5
Spelling	73.5	70.9	68.3	59.7
Syntax	72.4	68.7	47.2	41.8

Source: Office of Institutional Research.

FIGURE 7.7 Examples of various components of a table.

Row Head

A *row head* (or row headers or headings) is a label that identifies the content of one individual row. For example, in Figure 7.7, *Vocabulary* is a row head.

Stub

The *stub* is the leftmost column, which typically identifies the information found in each row. In other words, the stub consists of a series of row heads. In Figure 7.7, the stub comprises three row heads: *Vocabulary*, *Spelling*, and *Syntax*.

Stub Head

The *stub head* identifies the category that the items in the stub have in common. For example, in Figure 7.7, *Item tested* is the stub head.

Table Body

The *table body* consists of all the cells that form the intersection of a column heading and a row heading. For example, in Figure 7.7, all cells in which numbers appear comprise the table body.

Horizontal Rule

A *horizontal rule* (line) is used under the table title, the column heads, and at the bottom of the table to separate it from the text that follows it. A horizontal rule is also used under any column spanners. It can also be used as a *table spanner*, a rule that divides the table's data horizontally so that two sets of data can share column headings.

Label

Formal tables (generally those with more than two columns) require a label that includes a sequential number—e.g., Table 4. (Tables are numbered as a different series from figures such as graphs, charts, and illustrations. For example, one document may have both a Table 4 and a Figure 4.) Within a larger document that has formal subparts such as chapters, it is often more convenient to use *double numeration*, such as Table 2.4. This type of numeration incorporates the number of the chapter (or other subdivision) into the label. For example, Table 2.4 indicates that the item being labeled is the fourth table in Chapter 2 of the document. If Chapter 3 also had four tables, they would be labeled as Table 3.1, Table 3.2, Table 3.3., and Table 3.4.

The benefit of double numeration is that it makes life easier when a table (or figure) is added or removed from a chapter. Without double numeration, for example, if Chapter 6 of a 10-chapter manual starts out with five tables and one is added, the new table would have a ripple effect that would necessitate renumbering the subsequent tables in Chapters 7–10 (as well as their references in the surrounding text). With double numeration, on the other hand, only the subsequent numbers within an individual chapter are affected if a table is added or subtracted from the initial number.

Title

The *table title* conventionally takes the form of a noun phrase (i.e., a noun plus any needed adjectives or other phrases that modify the noun). Generally speaking, the title should mention the units of measurement, the variable being measured, and the entities of interest. The most difficult challenge in constructing a table title is striking the right balance between general and specific information.

For example, as a title for the table in Figure 7.7, *Language scores of students* is far too general, even though technically it tells us the variable being measured (language scores) and the entities of interest (students). In contrast, a title such as *Test scores for first-year students in three areas of written English language* or *Written English language scores of domestic and international students entering fall 2009* approaches a better level of detail, since it narrows the class of "students" into domestic and international students who were new as of fall 2009. The more specific title also orients the reader to the points of comparison. Thus, the more detailed title provides readers with a kind of *schema*, a mental model, for interpreting the content of the table: that is, it prepares readers for what appears in the table and alerts them to the mental framework they will need to interpret the table.

Notes

Optional *notes* at the bottom of a table may serve one of several purposes. Two common ones are to identify the source of data and to identify the level of significance if the table reports statistical information.

Exercise B

Prepare a table title for the table in Figure 7.6b.

Exercise C

Identify the various parts of the table in Figure 7.6b.

FORMATTING TABLES IN MICROSOFT WORD

As discussed at the beginning of this chapter, effective table formatting is a matter of balancing enough detail to separate parts of the table without overwhelming the user with extraneous (i.e., nondata) ink. This section explains how to set up a table using the default settings in Microsoft Word and then how to change those settings to reflect the formatting guidelines given in this chapter. Knowing how to change the default settings is important because tables prepared according to the default settings in Word will have gridlines throughout, and usually we want to eliminate most of those gridlines to highlight the data itself.

Sketching Your Table

Before setting up your table in Word (or any other software), it is useful to start with a paper-and-pencil sketch so that you can visualize the table's basic format: the number of columns and rows needed (including a column for the stub head and a row for column heads), whether the table should have a landscape or a portrait orientation,

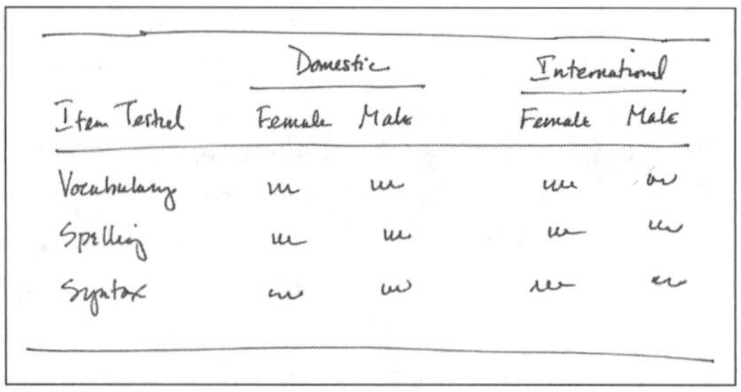

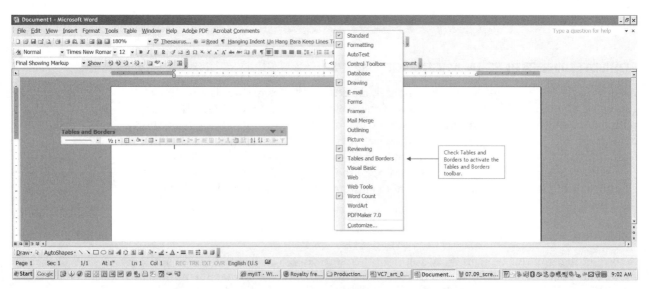

FIGURE 7.8   Sketch of table, showing basic layout of rows and columns.

whether any table spanners are needed within the table, and so on. While these elements can be modified later on, it's easier to start out with the basic shape of the table in place.

Figure 7.8 shows a sketch of how we want our final table to be set up. We can see that we need five rows and five columns. However, because we want to be able to add a column of space between the Domestic and International groups, we will set the table up for six columns.

Activating the Tables and Borders Toolbar

Word 2003 contains a Tables and Borders toolbar that provides a number of shortcuts you can use while constructing and formatting a table. Generally, the toolbar shortcuts are faster to use than the dropdown menu (although all the following tasks can also be done using the dropdown menu). To activate the toolbar, right-click into the blank toolbar area at the top of your Word screen. A vertical menu of various available toolbars should appear as a result. (See Figure 7.9.) Click on the Tables and Borders option so that a checkmark shows. You should now see a toolbar on your screen area, which you can move up and lock into your toolbar area if you wish.

FIGURE 7.9   Screenshot showing menu for Tables and Borders toolbar and resultant toolbar. (Visit www.pearsonhighered.com/riley to view this figure in color.)

FIGURE 7.10   Grid generated by Word for a table with six columns and five rows.

Creating a Grid for Your Table

There are several ways to create a table in Word. On a PC, one way that is both quick and that gives you control over the format of the table is to start by choosing Table from the standard toolbar. From Table, select Insert > Table. A popup window will ask how many columns and rows you want (you can easily change add and subtract rows later on). This is where your sketch comes in handy. Based on the sketch, we can see that we will need six columns and five rows. Selecting these options will create the grid shown in Figure 7.10.

We can now fill in the values for the various cells; the preliminary result is shown in Figure 7.11. Note that as you fill in the value for each cell, you can just hit the Tab key to move to the next cell to the right.

Modifying the Grid

Our grid is not yet set up exactly as it needs to be. Generally, we want to use alignment and spacing, rather than an abundance of horizontal and vertical rules, to show the relationships among parts of the table (Miller, 2004; Tufte, 2001). The table in Figure 7.11 has three problems with respect to this goal:

- The column headers *Domestic* and *International* are not spanning the columns *Female* and *Male* as they should be.
- The table contains too many horizontal rules.
- The table contains vertical rules.

We will fix these problems one by one.

First, the column headers *Domestic* and *International* need to be centered so that they span the cells *Female* and *Male*. In order to make this happen, we need to merge *Domestic* with the empty cell to its right and then center *Domestic*, as follows:

1. Left-click into the *Domestic* cell.
2. Drag the mouse across into the empty cell to the right.
3. Select Table > Merge Cells, or click the Merge icon on the Tables and Borders toolbar. (In Word 2007, select Merge from the Layout tab group.)
4. Do the same for the *International* cell.

	Domestic			International	
Item tested	Female	Male		Female	Male
Vocabulary	79.6	73.4		53.7	42.5
Spelling	73.5	70.9		68.3	59.7
Syntax	72.4	68.7		47.2	41.8

FIGURE 7.11   Grid with headers and values added.

Item tested	Domestic			International	
	Female	Male		Female	Male
Vocabulary	79.6	73.4		53.7	42.5
Spelling	73.5	70.9		68.3	59.7
Syntax	72.4	68.7		47.2	41.8

FIGURE 7.12   Grid with merged cells in top row.

Your grid should now look like the one in Figure 7.12.

Next, we want to center *Domestic* and *International*. As usual in Word, there are several ways to accomplish this. One is to right-click in the *Domestic* cell. Hover over Cell Alignment, and you will see nine different options for aligning the cell text. Choose one of the three centering options shown in the middle column. (The Cell Alignment icon is also available on the Tables and Borders toolbar.) Alternatively, left-click in the Domestic cell and then click on the centered text icon if it is displayed on your toolbar. (In Word 2007, the icon appears in the Home tab group.) Follow either of these procedures to center *International*. Your table should now look like the one in Figure 7.13.

Next, we need to eliminate the unneeded horizontal and vertical rules. We can do this by taking out all the rules and then reinserting just the horizontal rules that we want.

- To take out all the rules, right-click in the table; then select Borders and Shading. In the Borders window, select None and then OK. (The grid lines in the table will still be faintly visible in the screen view but will not appear when you print the page.)
- To insert a horizontal rule above *Female* and *Male*, select those cells (one pair at a time) and right-click. Then select Borders and Shading. In the Borders window, select Box; then unclick the left, right, and bottom borders from the Preview. Apply to Cell; then click OK. Follow the same procedure with the second pair of *Female* and *Male* cells. (In Word 2007, borders are part of the Design tab group.)

As an alternative method that is a bit faster, use the Tables and Border toolbar. Select a *Female* and *Male* pair of cells and then click the dropdown arrow in the borders preview. Choose the preview that shows just the top border, and that border will appear at the top of the cell.

Your table should now look like the one in Figure 7.14.

The last thing we need to do is adjust spacing and alignment.

- For the purposes of this exercise, we will set the rows at 1.5 spacing rather than at 1.0 (single) spacing: Select both rows, then select Format > Paragraph, and then select 1.5 in the Line spacing option. Alternatively, after selecting the rows, you can choose 1.5 spacing from the line spacing icon if it appears on your toolbar. (In Word 2007, paragraph spacing is part of the Page Layout tab group.)

Item tested	Domestic			International	
	Female	Male		Female	Male
Vocabulary	79.6	73.4		53.7	42.5
Spelling	73.5	70.9		68.3	59.7
Syntax	72.4	68.7		47.2	41.8

FIGURE 7.13   Grid with merged and centered cells in top row.

| Item tested | Domestic | | | International | |
	Female	Male		Female	Male
Vocabulary	79.6	73.4		53.7	42.5
Spelling	73.5	70.9		68.3	59.7
Syntax	72.4	68.7		47.2	41.8

FIGURE 7.14 Table with column spanners added.

- Next, decrease the size of the spacer column that separates *Domestic* and *International*. Do this by right-clicking within the column; then select Table Properties > Column and set the Preferred Width to 0.25 inch.
- Next, center the headings Female and Male: Select those cells; then select the centering icon from your toolbar.
- Next, align all of the numerical values flush right: Select those cells; then select the flush-right icon from your toolbar.
- At this point, the numerical values will be sitting too far to the right; we would prefer to have the *Female* and *Male* headers centered on top of each column of numbers. Rather than centering the numbers—which can misalign the decimal point—we will instead keep the numbers flush right but change the spacing on the right: Select the cells containing numerical values and then Table Properties > Cell > Options; then set the right margin value to 0.37 inch.

As practice, add lines across the entire table in three places: top, bottom, and under the headings row. Also add a line spanning the top of the Female and Male headings.

Your table should now look like the one in Figure 7.15.

As a final task, you will even up the vertical spacing by adding a little leading at the top of each row. Select the entire table; then choose Format > Paragraph and insert 6 points of space before. Your table should now look like the one in Figure 7.16.

| Item tested | Domestic | | | International | |
	Female	Male		Female	Male
Vocabulary	79.6	73.4		53.7	42.5
Spelling	73.5	70.9		68.3	59.7
Syntax	72.4	68.7		47.2	41.8

FIGURE 7.15 Table with spacing and alignment adjusted.

| Item tested | Domestic | | | International | |
	Female	Male		Female	Male
Vocabulary	79.6	73.4		53.7	42.5
Spelling	73.5	70.9		68.3	59.7
Syntax	72.4	68.7		47.2	41.8

FIGURE 7.16 Table with vertical spacing adjusted.

INTEGRATING TABLES INTO THE SURROUNDING TEXT

Integrating a table into the surrounding text is easy if you remember three "I" words:

- Introduce
- Identify
- Interpret

Introducing the Table

Prepare the reader by referring to the table *before* it appears. Introductory references can be handled in various ways; you will need to use your judgment about what works best for the document and the discourse context. In the text leading up to the visual, introduce the visual by mentioning its label and referring to it in an informative way. Rather than simply telling the reader to *See Table 3*, you can use the introductory sentence to help the reader to interpret the visual, as in the following examples.

- Nearly 35% of all cases are curable, as shown in Table 2.
- Only one subject identified all of the stimuli correctly (Table 4).
- Table 7 summarizes our sales figures for the past 2 years.

As an aside, by suggesting that you introduce the table before it appears in the text, we are implying that you have control over where the table itself will appear. In reality, however, the exact placement of a table in a finished document is not always under the author's control. This is especially likely if your document will be edited and produced by someone other than yourself.

For example, if you have a paper accepted for a conference proceedings or a trade magazine, you will probably be asked to submit the manuscript using an online submission process or as a file produced by a standard word processing program such as Microsoft Word. At this point, an editor and publisher will take over the production process to ensure that all submissions are uniformly formatted and produced. For this reason, editors often ask writers to put tables and figures at the end of a submitted manuscript and to insert a placeholder at the point where the table or figure should occur when the manuscript is typeset. Figure 7.17 shows an example from a manuscript page that uses this convention. While editors will try to get your table as close as possible to where you would like it in the final published product, be prepared for the fact that the table may not end up in the exact spot that you envision (unless you are asked to submit camera-ready copy).

Identifying the Table

Provide each table with a label that uniquely distinguishes it from any other tables or figures discussed in the surrounding text. While the details of numbering vary somewhat from one style guide to another, it is usually the case that, as mentioned, tables are numbered as a different series from figures (other graphical elements). This means that a document may have both a Table 1 and a Figure 1, both a Table 2 and a Figure 2, and so on.

For this reason, your text should always refer to an exact table number (e.g., *Table 7 summarizes our sales figures . . .*), not to a location relative to the text (e.g., *the previous table* or *the table below*). This is a good guideline to follow even in documents in which you control the layout, since it means that the reader will never have any doubt about exactly which table you are referring to.

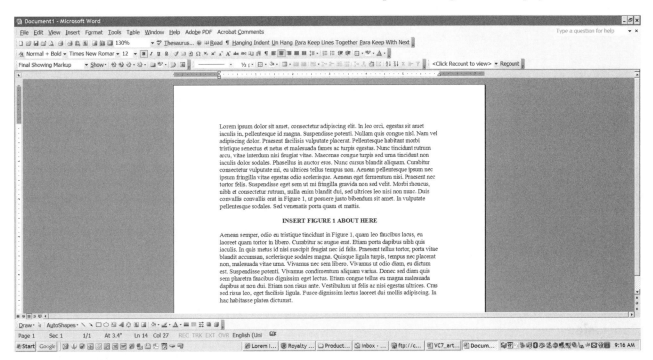

FIGURE 7.17   Manuscript page showing a placeholder callout for a figure. (Visit www. pearsonhighered.com/riley to view this figure in color.)

The table itself requires both a label and a title. The title should be a noun phrase (rather than a complete sentence) that captures an intermediate level of detail about the data in the table:

Table 3. Percentage of population below poverty level, 2004 and 2005

Table 6. Factors accounting for more than 50% of fires in five U.S. regions

Table 8. Fastest growing jobs in the computer sector

However, only the table's label (e.g., *Table 3*) need be mentioned in the surrounding text.

Interpreting the Table

Follow up with commentary in the text after the point at which the table itself is placed. The commentary should focus on the main trend that the reader should take away from the table. It may also point the reader toward any unusual deviations from that trend or details whose explanation may not be self-evident: for example, *As shown in Table 1, our sales typically drop during the first quarter. A recent exception was in 2009, when record-breaking sales of Mango Madness continued well past the holiday season and into Super Bowl Sunday.*

If you are preparing an academic paper for a class or journal, or a document for a large organization, you will probably be expected to adhere to a particular *style guide*. A style guide is a manual (either online or print) that specifies standards about how a document is to be prepared, especially with respect to details that come up during the writing and editing process—for example, format, punctuation, and usage. Examples of commonly used style guides used in academia are *Scientific Style and Format: The CSE Manual for Authors, Editors, and Publishers,* the *Publication Manual of the American Psychological Association*, and the *Chicago Manual of Style*. Examples of style guides produced by private or government entities are the *Microsoft Manual of Style for Technical Publications* and the *European Union Interinstitutional Style Guide.* Your department or organization may have its own style guide, especially if it produces documents such as manuals or technical reports on a regular basis.

Style guides differ on details related to format and document design. For example, you may wonder whether the text should use capitalize the word *table*, i.e., whether to say *as shown in Table 1* or *as shown in table 1*. The APA *Publication Manual* specifies *Table 1*, while the *Chicago Manual of Style* specifies *table 1*. Likewise, some style guides specify *headline style* for titles of tables and figures, whereas others specify *sentence style*. In headline style, the first letter of each main word is capitalized: for example, *Number of Uninsured Illinois Motorists by Age Group*. In sentence style, only the first letter of the first word (plus that of any proper nouns) is capitalized: for example, *Number of uninsured Illinois motorists by age group*.

If you are not told to follow a particular style guide, the important thing is to choose a format and use it consistently. In this case, for example, our personal prefer-ence is to use initial caps on terms such as *Table 1*, which makes them somewhat easier to find within the text.

Conclusion

Although tables are less useful than charts and graphs for showing readers the shape of data, they are useful when you want your reader to have access to large amounts of data and to be able to examine and compare precise numer-ical values. In laying out a table, the goal is to allow align-ment and spacing to signal relationships among headings and data points rather than to clutter the table with an overabundance of vertical and horizontal rules. Tables are integrated into the surrounding text by introducing, identi-fying, and interpreting the table.

Summary of Key Concepts and Terms

cell	headline style	row head	stub head
column	horizontal rule	schema	style guide
column head	notes	sentence style	table body
column spanner	proximity	straddle rule	table spanner
contrast	row	stub	table title
double numeration			

Additional Exercise

1. Using the process outlined in this chapter for format-ting tables in Microsoft Word, reformat one or more of the tables in Figure 7.3, 7.4, or 7.6. For additional help with formatting tables in Word 2003 and Word 2007, refer to the tutorials listed in the Web Resources for this book.

8

Displaying Information in Graphs and Charts

This chapter describes how you can use the visual language of graphs and charts to convey information that you cannot readily convey in prose. It also explains how you can decide which type of visual will best suit your readers' needs. In addition, it explains how to integrate graphs and charts into the text of your document. By the end of this chapter, you should be able to do the following:

- Understand the appropriate uses of graphs and charts, as opposed to tables
- Choose the appropriate type of graph or chart for the information you are trying to convey
- Understand conventions for visual and verbal information in graphs and charts
- Understand strategies for conveying information ethically in a graph or chart
- Use color effectively in a graph or chart
- Integrate graphs and charts effectively into the text that surrounds them

OVERVIEW OF RELEVANT DESIGN CONCEPTS AND PRINCIPLES

Some information is conveyed more clearly and efficiently in visual form, such as a graph or chart. For example, suppose you are revising management procedures for your company, and you need to explain the process by which a new employee is added to your company's payroll. You want to include the offices that must approve and process the addition. Rather than offering a long textual description, you might instead sketch a diagram containing a series of boxes connected by arrows (Figure 8.1).

Then, using your word processing software, you might replace your hand-drawn sketch with Word's shapes and text boxes (Figure 8.2). By designing a visual representation, you make the procedure more readily understandable.

Graphs and charts use lines, shapes, and colors to give your readers a different way to understand your meaning. You can use graphs, especially common types such

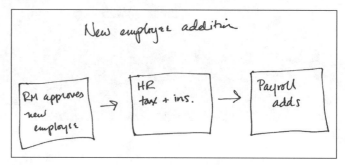

FIGURE 8.1 Hand-drawn sketch of a visual element.

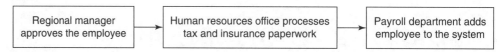

FIGURE 8.2 Shapes and text boxes in a visual element.

as the bar graph and line graph in Figures 8.3 and 8.4, to show patterns in your *quantitative data,* which are data that can be counted or expressed numerically.

You can also employ various types of charts to convey relationships, such as the relationship among the parts that compose a whole, as the pie chart in Figure 8.5 conveys. That is, the pie chart in Figure 8.5 shows the contribution of each country (i.e., the parts) to the world's total banana exports in 2006 (i.e., the whole).

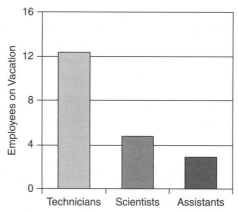

FIGURE 8.3 A bar graph. (Visit www.pearsonhighered.com/riley to view this figure in color.)

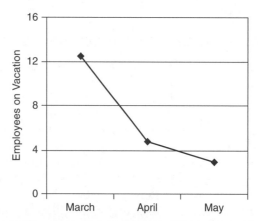

FIGURE 8.4 A line graph. (Visit www.pearsonhighered.com/riley to view this figure in color.)

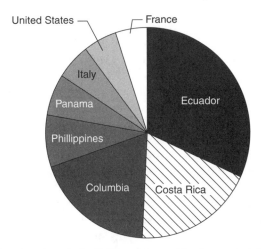

FIGURE 8.5 Pie chart showing the relationship among parts (each country's banana exports) to the whole (the world's total banana exports). (Visit www.pearsonhighered.com/riley to view this figure in more detail.)

WHY THESE PRINCIPLES ARE IMPORTANT

The value of graphs and charts is based on the *dual coding theory*, articulated by Paivio (1986). This theory proposes that people process words and images differently, through two different cognitive subsystems: "one specialized for the representation and processing of information concerning nonverbal objects and events, the other specialized for dealing with language" (p. 53). Thus, when you integrate visual elements with verbal elements, you give your readers two ways to process your message, which, in turn, fosters comprehension and recall. By doing so, you enhance the clarity and usability of your document.

DIFFERENTIATING GRAPHS AND CHARTS FROM TABLES

Indeed, a quick note is in order about why you might select a graph or chart rather than a table. You saw in Chapter 7 that tables are useful if readers need to be able to locate specific points in data. But when you want to help readers understand general patterns in data, consider using a graph or chart instead. Guthrie, Weber, and Kimmerly (1993) point out that graphs allow readers to get the "gist" of information (p. 188). As Meyer, Shamo, and Gopher (1999) write, "the transformation of regularities in the data into consistent visual patterns" is the "major advantage" of graphs (p. 572), a statement that applies to charts as well. In contrast to graphs and charts, tables do not show the gist of or regularities within data nearly as well.

Exercise A

If you wanted to display horsepower, miles per gallon, and price for five tractor models, would you use a table, or a graph or chart? Why? Try to state at least two reasons.

CHOOSING A GRAPH TYPE

So far we have discussed graphs and charts together, but what is the difference between the two? For many technical communicators, *graph* refers to a visual element that plots quantitative data on two axes (a horizontal *x-axis*, and a vertical *y-axis*. Technically, then, bar graphs and line graphs are truly graphs because they plot data on two axes. For example, changes in the amount of interior space in American-made cars over the past 20 years could be quantified and plotted on a bar or line graph.

However, other visual elements, such as pie charts and Gantt charts, also use space on the page to display data—they just don't use *x*- and *y*-axes. So, even though pie charts are often called pie graphs, we call them charts in this book. Pie and Gantt charts might be called "semiquantitative" in that both allow you to represent parts of a whole. Finally, some charts, such as flowcharts and organizational charts, are very different from graphs in that they do not show quantitative data at all. Flowcharts illustrate the steps or decisions involved in carrying out some process, while organizational charts display hierarchies, such as a military chain of command.

Figure 8.6 displays the spectrum of graphs and charts according to their suitability for displaying quantitative data. We focus for now on graphs and then move to charts later in the chapter..

Both bar and line graphs are quite common in professional writing, and both are good for showing comparisons, such as differences among the gross domestic products (GDPs) of the United States, Japan, and Germany or how much the average American's weight has changed over the past 50 years. However, the visual differences between bar and line graphs correspond to differences in the kind of quantitative data each is best at displaying. To see this, we need to distinguish between two major types of quantitative data.

One type, called *nominal*, or *categorical*, *data*, compares some property of discrete, nonoverlapping categories, such as countries. For example, the comparison of the GDPs of the United States, Japan, and Germany involves categories. Bar graphs, such as that in Figure 8.7, are especially useful for displaying categorical data (Carswell & Wickens, 1987; Shah, Mayer, & Hegarty, 1999; Zacks & Tversky, 1999). As Figure 8.7 shows, the categories are typically displayed on the *x*-axis in a bar graph; the value associated with each category is plotted on the *y*-axis.

Another type of quantitative data, called *interval data*, compares some property at points along a continuum, such as a timeline. For example, showing changes in the average American's weight involves comparing weight at different points in time. This example clearly illustrates the relation between a *dependent variable* and an *independent variable*. The value of the dependent variable changes when the value of the independent variable changes. Put another way, we can say that in this example, knowing the average American's weight depends on knowing the point of time at which we are looking. Thus, time is the independent variable in this example and would be shown on the *x*-axis of the line graph, while the dependent variable of weight would be shown on the *y*-axis.

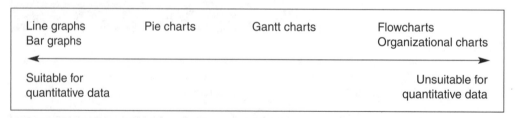

FIGURE 8.6 Suitability of various graph and chart types for displaying quantitative data.

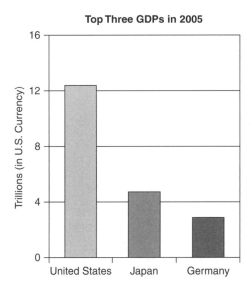

FIGURE 8.7 Effective bar graph. (Visit www.pearsonhighered.com/riley to view this figure in color.)

Line graphs, such as the one in Figure 8.8, are especially useful for displaying interval data and for showing trends. In fact, viewers of line graphs are more likely to describe trends than are viewers of bar graphs (Carswell, Emery, & Lonon, 1993; Meyer et al., 1999; Shah, Mayer, & Hegarty, 1999; Zacks & Tversky, 1999) and to be accurate in describing those trends (Carswell & Wickens, 1987; Meyer et al., 1999).

Because line graphs suggest trends so strongly, you should avoid using them for nominal data, such as gender (male or female) or city (Chicago, New Delhi, Tokyo, Amsterdam). For example, the line graph in Figure 8.9 incorrectly suggests a trend where one does not exist. Amsterdam, Chicago, New Delhi, and Tokyo are not points on a continuum. Instead, cities are nominal categories, such as species (mammal or reptile) or occupation (manager, writer, technician, or engineer). These categories cannot be measured in the same way as temperature or test scores, which fall along a continuum. That

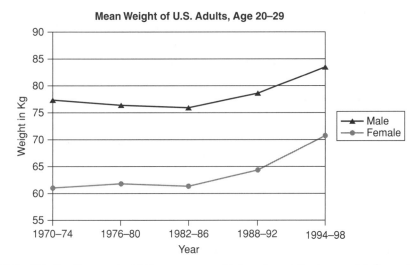

FIGURE 8.8 Effective line graph. (Visit www.pearsonhighered.com/riley to view this figure in color.)

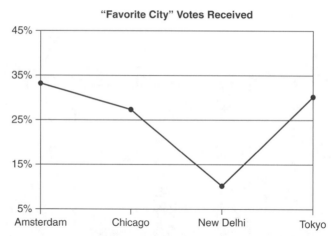

FIGURE 8.9   Misleading line graph. (Visit www.pearsonhighered.com/riley to view this figure in more detail.)

is, one mammal is not *more mammal* than another mammal—a particular animal either is or is not a mammal. Suggesting a trend among nominal categories by using a line graph, then, constitutes poor graphic design. You may end up leading your reader to an invalid conclusion similar to the one offered by a participant in Zacks and Tversky's study of graphs: "The more male a person is, the taller he/she is" (1999, p. 1076).

Exercise B

Would you use a bar graph or a line graph to display each of the following data sets? State at least one reason for each answer. Are there any cases where you could use either?

1. SAT scores of high school seniors in Illinois, Minnesota, and Wisconsin
2. Average hours of sleep per night for people in three different age groups
3. Average monthly rainfall in Chicago in 2010
4. Frequencies with which 175 third-grade girls and boys chose blue, green, pink, red, and purple as their "favorite color"
5. Average 15-, 20-, and 30-year mortgage rates for first-time home buyers in 2000, 2005, and 2010

CONVENTIONS OF EFFECTIVE GRAPHS

Effective graphs adhere to the conventions that viewers have come to associate with each graph type. They also emphasize any pattern that emerges in the data, conforming to viewers' perceptual expectations (e.g., "up is more" and "length is duration"), but they do so honestly. And they are easy to read and interpret.

In this section, we describe some conventional graphic components, referring to the names that Microsoft Excel and Word assign to them. These components have become conventional; therefore, viewers expect to see seem. This means that you should include them in your graph designs unless there is an overriding reason not to. The most common graph components are illustrated and labeled in Figure 8.10 and discussed shortly. (In the exercises at the end of this chapter, we show how you can

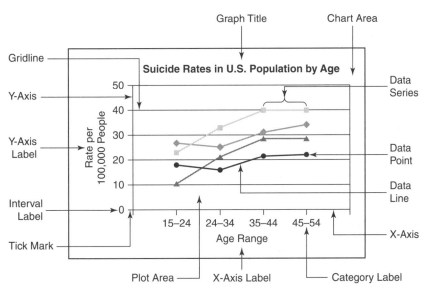

FIGURE 8.10   Verbal and visual components typically found in graphs. (Visit www.pearsonhighered .com/riley to view this figure in color.)

change the default settings in Excel and Word to enhance the usability and appearance of your graphs.)

Axes and Related Components

As mentioned earlier, graphs contain a horizontal axis, called the *x*-axis, and a vertical axis, called the *y*-axis. Data are plotted on bars or lines within the area defined by these two axes. Categories or intervals on each axis are indicated by *tick marks* so that reading the graph (and trying to determine accurate measures) is easy. Even though tick marks help readers to retrieve measurements, too many tick marks will clutter your graph.

Plot and Chart Areas

The *plot area* is the area defined by the axes. As a default setting, Word stretches *gridlines* across the plot area along the intervals that are set on the *y*-axis. As with tick marks, you will need to decide whether readers need gridlines to interpret the graphs accurately or whether they would benefit from less visual clutter. As with other lines in the plot area, gridlines should be kept thin, to limit nonessential ink (Tufte, 1983).

In contrast to the plot area, the *chart area* refers to the larger area that contains all the verbal and visual elements related to the graph. Thus, the chart area includes the plot area as well as other components such as the title and labels.

Data Display

The visual components of a graph, such as lines and bars, display measurements in the plot area. Figure 8.10 shows four *data lines*. Each line contains four *data points*, and each of these data points is a visual representation of one unit of data. Each line and its data points comprise a *data series*.

Verbal Components

Figure 8.10 also shows typical verbal components found in line and bar graphs, such as a *graph title, x-axis label, y-axis label,* and *category labels* and *interval labels.* Labels for categories and intervals name the tick marks on the *x*- and *y*-axes, respectively. We discuss techniques for constructing these verbal components later in this chapter.

CREATING ETHICAL GRAPHS

Before leaving this section on graph design, we must point out the need to convey information ethically. When graph designers discuss ethical graphs, they usually mean "honest" graphs—graphs that do not misrepresent the data that they contain. (However, some technical communication researchers also stress the need to humanize technical subjects when attempting to design ethical graphs; see Dragga & Voss, 2001.) To increase your chances of generating honest graphs, follow the three design principles discussed next.

Start the *y*-Axis at Zero

One convention of honest graphs is that their *y*-axis begins at zero. If you fail to start with zero, you distort the bars, diminishing their differences (Robbins, 2005, p. 239). Moreover, viewers will likely misinterpret the trend being shown because the starting point of the *y*-axis will affect the slope of the lines. Figure 8.11 shows how starting the *y*-axis with a number other than zero can be misleading, especially on a graph intended for comparison with one that does start at zero.

Because the graph on the left does not start at zero (but the graph on the right does), it appears at first that more Canadian geese nested in Chicago from 2005 to 2008 than from 2001 to 2004. Actually, however, the trends during the two time periods are similar.

Exercise C

Keeping in mind the qualities of ethical graphs, answer the following questions:

1. Are there any situations in which you might start the *y*-axis of a graph at a number other than zero?
2. How would you justify your design choice in this situation?
3. How could you alert the viewer to the fact that the *y*-axis does not start at zero?

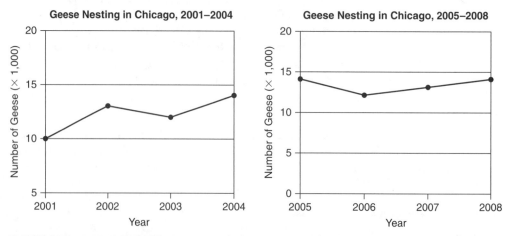

FIGURE 8.11 Example (left) of a graph that fails to start the *y*-axis at zero, creating a misleading comparison, and (right) of a graph that corrects this problem.

Use a 2:3 Aspect Ratio

A graph is honest when its *aspect ratio*, the ratio of its y- to its x-axis, generates a plot area designed to display the data objectively. Researchers have recommended using an aspect ratio of about 2:3 to achieve this goal, meaning that the x-axis should be about one third longer than the y-axis. Besides the 2:3 guideline, researchers have also recommended ratios of 1: $\sqrt{2}$ and 3:4. As Figure 8.12 shows, the difference between these three aspect ratios is negligible. Thus, any one of them is an effective starting point for graph design.

These ratios are commonly recommended because they bank the slope of lines, bars, and other graphical elements to 45° (called banking to 45°), which has been found to maximize accurate perceptions of data (Cleveland, McGill, & McGill, 1988). If the average slope of all of the lines in the graph (called the *orientation midangle*) is 45°, you optimize viewers' ability to make accurate readings and comparisons. Figure 8.12 shows a 45° angle superimposed over line graphs with various aspect ratios. In Figure 8.13, the graph lines (the lines with the dot points) together average a slope of 45°.

By comparison, in Figure 8.14, perception is distorted because the aspect ratio is about 2:1, giving the graph lines an average slope of about 75°. In Figure 8.15,

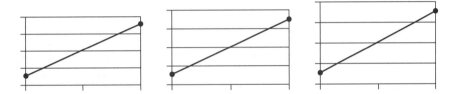

FIGURE 8.12   Graphs with aspect ratios of 2:3, 1: $\sqrt{2}$, and 3:4, respectively.

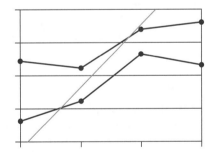

FIGURE 8.13   A 2:3 aspect ratio with an average line slope of 45°. (Visit www.pearsonhighered.com/ riley to view this figure in more detail.)

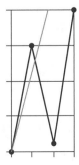

FIGURE 8.14   A 2:1 aspect ratio with an average line slope of 75°. (Visit www.pearsonhighered.com/ riley to view this figure in more detail.)

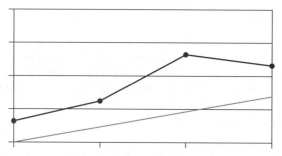

FIGURE 8.15 A 1:2 aspect ratio with an average line slope of 10°. (Visit www.pearsonhighered.com/riley to view this figure in more detail.)

perception is impaired because the aspect ratio is 1:2, giving the lines an average slope of just 10°. Figure 8.13 represents the data accurately and ethically. The slope of the graph lines averages 45°. In contrast, Figure 8.14 exaggerates the variable represented by the graph lines, while Figure 8.15 minimizes the variable represented by the lines.

Avoid Empty Dimensions

One final tip for creating honest graphs is to avoid "empty" dimensions, especially third dimensions in bar and line graphs and in pie charts that do not represent some variable. An *empty third dimension* conveys volume, and its size can be varied independently of the actual data. Thus, designers are free to adjust the size of the empty dimension in any way they wish, enhancing it or minimizing it, depending on their intent. For example, in Figure 8.16, the third dimension makes the bar representing Nevada appear much larger than it actually is in relation to the bar representing Arizona.

To summarize, bar and line graphs each have different functions. Bar graphs are best for displaying categorical data (e.g., the average height of different breeds of horses). In contrast, line graphs are better for displaying interval data (e.g., changes in the height of one breed over time). Whichever graph type you choose, you should design it honestly—which means, in general, starting the *y*-axis at zero, using a 2:3 aspect ratio, and avoiding empty dimensions.

CHOOSING A CHART TYPE

Charts, like graphs, use space to display information. However, charts and graphs differ in the type of information they display. This section discusses four types of charts that are common in professional documents. Pie and Gantt charts are semiquantitative

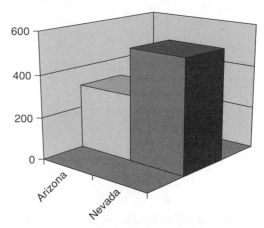

FIGURE 8.16 Bar graph with an empty, and misleading, third dimension. (Visit www.pearsonhighered.com/riley to view this figure in color.)

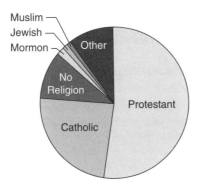

FIGURE 8.17   Pie chart showing relative proportions. (Visit www.pearsonhighered.com/riley to view this figure in color.)

in that they display part-to-whole measurements. In contrast, flowcharts and organizational charts display nonquantitative information.

Pie Charts

Pie charts are an excellent way to show relative proportions, that is, *how much* of the whole is comprised by each part (Kosslyn, 1994; Shah & Hoeffner, 2002, p. 53; Wilkinson, 1999). For example, Figure 8.17 displays the proportion of the U.S. population aligning itself with each of several religious beliefs.

On the other hand, it is difficult to compare exact values across different pie charts with precision because the wedge that corresponds to a given variable may change location and shape in each chart.

Exercise D

Consider the following pie charts, designed to show compare the top medal-winning countries in the 2000 and 2004 Summer Olympics.

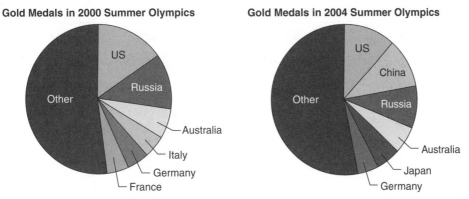

(Source: www.nationmaster.com. Visit www.pearsonhighered.com/riley to view this figure in color.)

How effective are side-by-side charts for this purpose? Is there another chart type that would display the information more effectively? If so, how would you design it?

Exercise E

Decide whether the following data would be suitable for display in a pie chart.

1. Percentage of freshman, sophomores, juniors, and seniors comprising a university hockey team
2. Number of Boeing employees who work in each of the following departments: human resources, engineering, information technology, communications
3. Number of books read by first, second, third, fourth, fifth, and sixth graders from a local elementary school during a summer reading program
4. Percentage of middle school, high school, and college students with summer jobs in 1980 and 2010

Gantt Charts

Gantt charts—named after Henry Laurence Gantt (1861–1919), the American engineer and management consultant who developed them ("History of Gantts")—are commonly used to show the duration of tasks in a project. In effect, then, they convey "parts-to-whole" information because they show the duration of different stages in a process—when a particular task will be done and how long it should take. For this reason, they are common in proposals and progress reports. For example, Figure 8.18 shows the duration of tasks involved in a research project.

A Gantt chart is organized so that the timetable of the project runs along the top and the tasks are listed on the left. This arrangement allows the viewer to see three variables at once: the sequence of tasks (by scanning the leftmost column from top to bottom), the duration of each task (by scanning from left to right), and the overlap

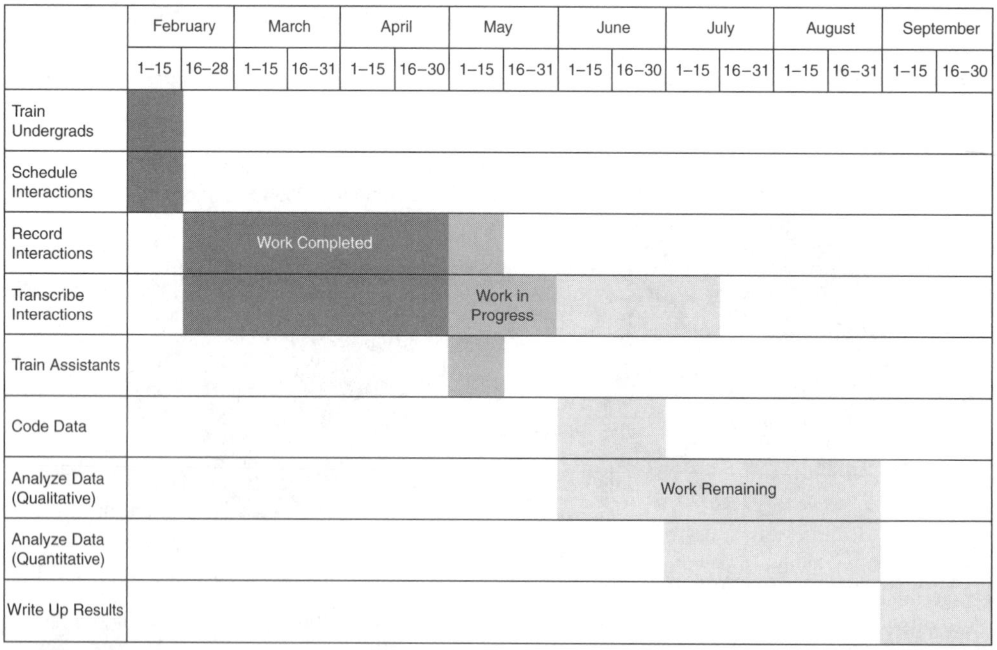

FIGURE 8.18   Gantt chart displaying tasks in a research project. (Visit www.pearsonhighered.com/riley to view this figure in more detail.)

between various activities, such as transcribing interactions and training assistants during the period from May 1 to May 15 (by scanning from top to bottom within the charted area).

Note that the Gantt chart in Figure 8.18 uses verbs at each step to reflect the fact that this chart illustrates steps in a procedure.

Flowcharts and Organizational Charts

Flowcharts and organizational charts use space on the page to display a process or structure, such as a decision-making process. For example, Figure 8.19 shows a flowchart from a set of instructions.

Well-designed flowcharts use shapes such as rectangles and diamonds consistently to illustrate parts of a process. For example, in Figure 8.19, questions are presented in trapezoids, and commands are displayed in rectangles. In Word, you can use the Drawing tools to choose and modify shapes and arrows and to layer text boxes containing the flowchart's questions and commands over their respective shapes. You can also modify a process type of Word's SmartArt. (You can find SmartArt at Insert > Illustrations.)

Exercise F

List three ways that the flowchart in Figure 8.19 could be changed to improve its effectiveness. Draw on design concepts from previous chapters, particularly chapters about typography. Supply reasons for your three-item list.

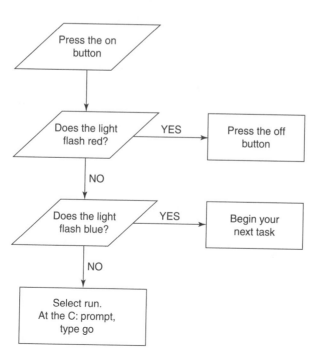

FIGURE 8.19 Flowchart of procedure for starting a computer.

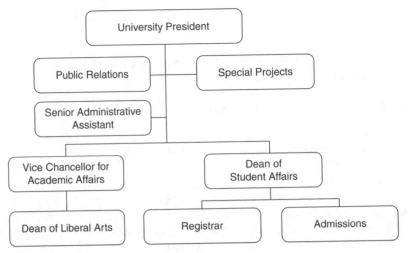

FIGURE 8.20 Organizational chart created in Word.

Organizational charts display structures and relationships within a group. Such charts are often used to display hierarchies of individuals or departments in an institution. For example, Figure 8.20 shows who reports to whom within a university administration.

Organizational charts use relative position to convey meaning; in particular, positions at the top are the most powerful. Similarly, such charts can be used to show the development of relationships over time, in which case readers usually assume that "top is earlier, bottom is more recent." A common type that relies on this pattern is the genealogy chart (or "family tree"). For example, Figure 8.21 shows how Indo-European languages developed over time as well as how existing languages are related to each other at the present.

In summary, flowcharts and organizational charts do not convey quantitative data. Instead, they use position to display relationships among entities in some larger process or group.

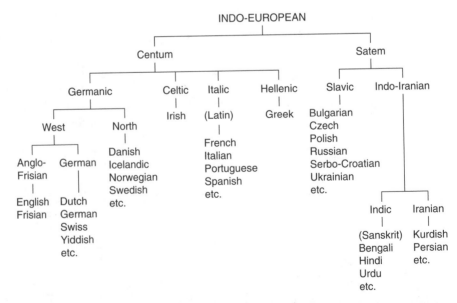

FIGURE 8.21 Chart showing the family tree of Indo-European languages.

USING COLOR IN GRAPHS AND CHARTS

Using color effectively, according to White (1990), requires thinking about color "from the very inception of an idea, when the information is being planned for presentation" (p. 48). He adds, "Color can never be used successfully if it is merely an afterthought" (p. 48). In addition, using color effectively does not mean simply assigning each variable a color, such as representing United States, Japan, and Germany with blue, maroon, and gold, respectively, in a bar graph. While representing variables with color does help viewers keep track of referents (Carpenter & Shah, 1998), you can do much more with color to aid readers' comprehension.

First, you can facilitate comprehension and decrease demands on graph viewers' working memory by capitalizing on conventional color associations (Carpenter & Shah, 1998). For example, a line graph comparing boys' and girls' average birth weights over time might use blue lines for boys and pink lines for girls. A bar chart showing an airline's earnings from 2000 to 2010 might use black bars for years of profit and red bars for years of loss. A pie chart displaying annual holiday spending in the United States might use red for Christmas, blue for Hanukkah, orange for Halloween, and pink for Valentine's Day.

Exercise G

How could color be used to group elements in the Gantt chart in Figure 8.18 and the Indo-European language chart in Figure 8.21?

Color is also useful for comparing variables across different graphs and charts (Lewandowsky & Spence, 1989). If you used blue to signal Baltimore, purple to signal Annapolis, and gray to signal Silver Spring, readers could easily locate information about each city across different graphs and charts showing average incomes, property tax, and population. The key is being consistent in your use of color throughout a document.

While color is a powerful tool, keep in mind that your readers may have to reproduce a color graph or chart in black and white. For example, your report may be photocopied on a black-and-white copier or printed out on a black-and-white printer. Therefore, be sure that distinctions do not rely solely on color. For example, the line graph in Figure 8.22 uses black to emphasize the data series related to Chicago. If the line graph in Figure 8.22 were going to be published online or if it were going to be printed in a color document, the line representing Chicago could be red, a color that would make it stand out even more.

Color and shading can also reinforce a trend in the graph or chart, as Figure 8.23 shows. If the graph in Figure 8.23 were to appear online or in a color printed document, you could use darker to lighter shades of blue to signal greatest to least square kilometers of water.

In short, as White writes, "If you know what your purpose is, you can use graphics and color to catapult it [the element for emphasis] into the viewer's mind" (1990, p. 57).

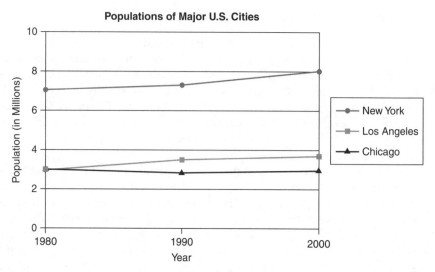

FIGURE 8.22 Line graph emphasizing one data series out of three. (Visit www.pearsonhighered.com/riley to view this figure in more detail.)

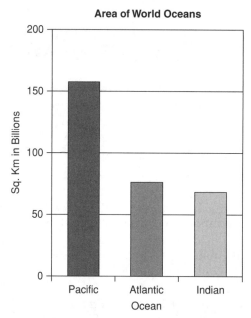

FIGURE 8.23 Bar graph using shading to reinforce a data trend. (Visit www.pearsonhighered.com/riley to view this figure in more detail.)

HOW PEOPLE PROCESS GRAPHS AND CHARTS

To select and design graphs and charts effectively, you need some understanding of the cognitive processes that readers go through when they encounter these visual elements. If you understand these processes, you can improve the reader's experience.

Essentially, readers go through three cognitive processes when they encounter a graph or chart. They first encode its visual array by scanning its arrangement and determining its important visual features. So, for example, a viewer of Figure 8.24 would first perceive the visual features—the line and its curve.

In the second process, viewers relate visual features of an array (such as the line and its curve) to the concepts that they represent (Bertin, 1983; Kosslyn, 1989; Pinker,

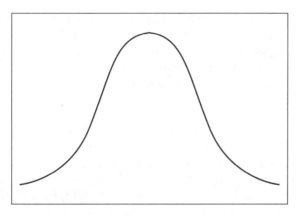

FIGURE 8.24   Elements perceived during the first two steps of graph comprehension.

1990). For example, someone viewing a line graph like that in Figure 8.24 would move from perceiving a curved line to, perhaps, perceiving a "bell curve." This viewer would be connecting the visual features, such as the curved line, with an abstract concept, such as a bell curve. The more clearly the visual features display a concept, such as a bell curve, or increase, or inverse relationship, the easier comprehension becomes.

This second process stems from how humans perceive, at a very basic level, the world around them. People seem to find it easier to interpret visuals that are *icons*, or visuals that look like what they represent. For example, Shah and Hoeffner (2002) propose that vertical rather than horizontal bars may be better in bar graphs that depict quantities of physical material (such as reams of paper, cords of wood, tons of taconite) because "a greater quantity of items usually corresponds to a taller pile" (p. 51). Keeping this connection in mind may help you to better represent certain types of information.

This second process is also influenced by the viewer's experience with graphs (and charts as well), what Pinker (1990) calls *graph schema*. Thus, a viewer with some background in statistics is more likely to relate the curved line in Figure 8.24 to the concept bell curve or normal distribution than someone without such a background.

The third and last step in the comprehension process is one in which the viewer maps the concept to specific referents. For example, a viewer of Figure 8.25 would map the concept *bell curve* to the labels of its axes ("percent of students" and "exam score").

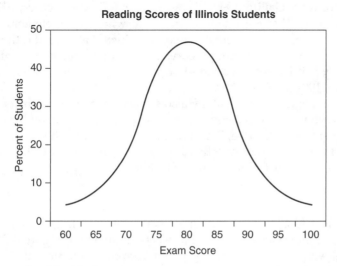

FIGURE 8.25   Example of the labeling process.

This third process, called the labeling process, involves recognizing the relationship between a visual element and verbal or numerical elements within the graph or chart. This process involves reading labels, including the *legend* (a verbal component, usually in a box next to a graph or chart, that explains the use of colors, shapes, patterns, or symbols) and quantitative values, and relating these to corresponding data points, lines, or shapes.

In most visual elements, *direct labeling* minimizes the cognitive work that a viewer must do to link a visual element, such as a wedge in a pie chart, to words or numbers. Direct labeling means that verbal and numerical elements are placed on, or very close to, the associated visual element. Direct labeling saves readers the trouble of locating a visual element's referent in a legend (also called a *key*), which can impede comprehension (especially if the legend is placed too far from the graph area).

Exercise H

Referring to the line graph in Figure 8.8, list three pieces of information that the viewer would know after the third step of graph comprehension.

LABELS, TITLES, AND CAPTIONS

Labels, titles, and captions are the verbal components that identify and explain visual components of a graph or chart. This section looks more closely at these verbal components and explains how they can be put to most effective use. We limit our discussion to graphs and charts in this chapter. However, keep in mind that the same principles apply to using labels, titles, and captions with other visual elements, such as tables, drawings, and photographs.

Very little research has investigated people's perceptions of verbal elements in graphs and charts. Most comes from cognitive studies in education that have examined how students learn and retain scientific explanations of phenomena such as lightning (Mayer, 1989; Mayer & Gallini, 1990; Mayer, Steinhoff, Bower, & Mars, 1995). Such studies indicate that cognitive processing is enhanced when visual elements (illustrations) are paired with verbal components (concise captions that describe the illustrations). These findings support dual coding theory, the idea that information can be processed more effectively if it is presented simultaneously via two modes—visual and verbal (Clark & Paivio, 1991; Paivio, 1986).

Research in cognitive psychology also shows that readers transfer and retain information best when the verbal component is concise, coherent, and coordinated with the visual element (Mayer, Bove, Bryman, Mars, & Tapangco, 1996). In addition, Kaufman and Tebelak suggest that effective captions can attract nontechnical readers who are skimming documents for information (1993, p. 337).

Labels

Labels guide the reader's interpretation of visual elements. In graphs, it is critical to label categories and intervals on the *x*- and *y*-axes, as shown in Figure 8.7. In charts, it is critical to label what the shapes, colors, patterns, and lines represent, as in Figure 8.26, which shows effective direct labeling of a pie chart.

Sectors of State Employment Opportunities

FIGURE 8.26   Pie chart with direct labels. (Visit www.pearsonhighered.com/riley to view this figure in color.)

In both graphs and charts, direct labeling is better than using a legend or key. Direct labeling entails either drawing a line between a label and the visual component that it represents or labeling the visual component itself. Either method helps the viewer to map visual components to their referents.

Sometimes, given enough space, it is possible to place labels directly on the visual components that they refer to. For example, in Figure 8.26, all labels have been placed directly on the corresponding pie wedges because each wedge has enough area to accommodate the label. Although it is not necessary to place labels on visual components, doing so is both conventional and effective.

Exercise I

How would the colors you use in a pie chart affect your decision about whether you could place labels directly on the wedges?

When space or the size of graphical elements does not permit direct labeling, indirect labeling is necessary. Indirect labeling requires the use of a legend. An example of a bar graph with a legend is shown in Figure 8.27.

Legends can be useful when graphs and charts get too complex for direct labels to integrate neatly, but they should be used only when direct labels would impede comprehension and, when used, should be placed near the visual elements to which they refer. In short, whenever possible, facilitate your reader's cognitive processing by designing your graphs so that you can use direct labeling.

Exercise J

How could you modify the graph in Figure 8.27 to avoid the need for a legend?

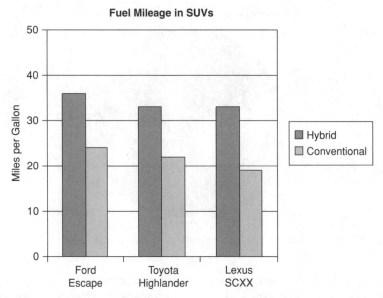

FIGURE 8.27 Bar graph with indirect labels in a legend. (Visit www.pearsonhighered.com/riley to view this figure in color.)

E. R. Tufte, a pioneer in graphic design, says that "friendly" labels contain words that are spelled out and are void of "mysterious" abbreviations (1983, p. 183). He also advises that if you are writing in a language read from left to right, such as English, your labels should run from left to right so that they can be read easily. The leftmost graph in Figure 8.28 displays this kind of label.

If your labels are longer than one or two short words, you will not be able to create horizontal labels that can be read left to right (or right to left in languages such as Arabic). Instead, you can use a label that can be read from left to right if readers turn their heads or turn the page. The middle graph in Figure 8.28 displays such a label.

Avoid stacking letters and numbers on top of each other in an effort to save space. People rarely see letters in English words stacked vertically, so stacked letters may impede their understanding of your graph. The rightmost graph in Figure 8.28 shows this kind of label—the kind you should avoid.

In addition, you can facilitate your reader's comprehension of both direct and indirect labels by using *parallel structure*, that is, identical lexical or syntactic form. For example, in the Gantt chart in Figure 8.18, the labels that describe tasks follow a pattern: They are all uninflected verbs (i.e., forms such as *train* and *analyze*, which have no verb ending). You can choose other verb forms for tasks in Gantt charts, such as present participles (i.e., with an -*ing* ending):

- Setting foundation
- Framing walls
- Shingling roof

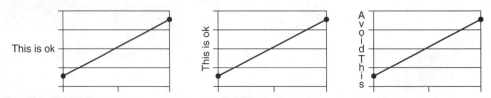

FIGURE 8.28 Two effective ways and one ineffective way to label visual elements.

- Insulating walls
- Installing wiring
- Taping sheetrock

When writing about actions (as in Gantt charts), look for verbs that are buried in nouns, such as *rehearsal* (*rehearse*), *content specification* (*specify content*), or *displacement* (*displace*).

In other types of graphs and charts, though, your labels will often consist of short noun phrases (e.g., *April, amplitude, charitable donations, cases of Ebola virus*). The same guideline applies: Pick one lexical or syntactic form and do your best to use it throughout your graph or chart.

Exercise K

Using parallel structure and uninflected verbs, list five steps in the process of registering for classes at your school.

Titles

A title should concisely and coherently describe the content of the graph or chart. That is, it should coordinate with the visual element to create a verbal-visual package. Titles are typically phrases rather than full sentences. Some graph and chart titles are listed here:

- Daily Availability of Electricity in Baghdad
- Distribution of Injuries in Mining Occupations
- U.S. Petroleum Sources after September 11, 2001
- Industry Spending on IT Equipment from 1995 to 2010

When composing a title for a graph or chart, start by asking yourself this basic question: What point does the graph or chart make? Your answer might be something like the following example: This line graph shows the effect that increased speed has on a car's consumption of gas. Your title might be "Effect of Speed on Gas Consumption." This title identifies the two variables displayed in the graph (i.e., speed and gas consumption) and indicates a relationship between them. You might be tempted to add the unit of measure (such as gallons) within a graph title, but such specificity within a title is often redundant. Units of measure can instead appear in the axis labels. In this case, the unit of measure, gallons, would appear in the label of the *y*-axis.

Exercise L

Edit these graph titles for conciseness:

1. The price of watermelon, honeydew, and cantaloupe in relation to customer demand (weekly bushels)
2. Effect of help-desk-employee enrollment in semiannual politeness training on length of customer calls
3. Altitude in Earth's atmosphere and aerosols in parts per billion

Captions

Captions are descriptions that elaborate (beyond the title) on the content of a visual element or how it should be interpreted. Captions typically take the form of one of more sentences. For example, following a title such as "Organizational Chart for Caliber University," the writer might continue with a caption such as "Note that lines of report divide broadly between academic and operational units." Captions can also run much longer than one sentence. Lengthy captions are fairly common in scientific and technical publications; as one author notes, they can "play a crucial role in shoring up or undermining an author's claims" because they can potentially provide a good deal of added information (Richards, 2003, p. 197).

However, even in very technical publications, there are differing opinions about how much verbal information should accompany a visual element. Dr. Nels Lersten, former editor-in-chief of *American Journal of Botany*, explained in an interview that one school of thought sees captions as document components that, when accompanying visual elements, tell a complete story in themselves (Richards, 2003, p. 198). The other school of thought favors "bare-bones" captions that leave explanation to the body of the document.

Tufte (1983, p. 182) recommends that captions distinguish between "exploratory" data and "settled" findings. A caption commenting on exploratory data should explain how to read the graph, especially if the graph is complex: for example, "Note that college students made the most calls to their parents in January and September." In contrast, the caption commenting on a settled finding should focus on the conclusion that can be drawn from the graph: for example, "College students miss their parents less as a semester progresses, evidenced by the decrease in calls home after January and September, the first months of the spring and fall semesters."

Integrating Graphs and Charts into Surrounding Text

As discussed in Chapter 7, integrating a visual element such as a graph or chart into the surrounding texts means introducing, identifying, and interpreting it. You may want to review the discussion in Chapter 7 about integrating tables, since it applies to graphs and charts as well.

Conclusion

This chapter has discussed strategies for choosing and preparing common types of graphs and charts to convey information that you cannot readily convey in prose. We have noted that, as opposed to tables, which are best suited to organizing and displaying particular, identifiable data points, graphs and charts are more suitable for showing the gist of your message, the "big picture," in other words. Because they show relationships, graphs and charts can tell a story in a way that tables cannot. In particular, graphs effectively convey quantitative information (bar graphs are for categorical data, and line graphs are for interval data). Charts visually support and enhance verbal information as well. Pie and Gantt charts are best suited for semiquantitative information, while flowcharts are for processes and organizational charts are for hierarchies. In addition, this chapter explained how people process graphs and charts and how you can design these visual elements effectively and ethically. It also discussed ways to enhance these visual elements with effective labels, titles, and captions.

Summary of Key Concepts and Terms

aspect ratio	chart area	dependent variable	graph schema
caption	data line	direct labeling	graph title
categorical data	data point	dual coding theory	icons
category label	data series	empty third dimension	independent variable

interval data	orientation midangle	tick mark	y-axis
interval label	parallel structure	title	y-axis label
label	plot area	x-axis	
nominal data	quantitative data	x-axis label	

Review Questions

1. Why are line graphs more effective for displaying trends?
2. What does dual coding theory predict about comprehension of visual and verbal information (e.g., viewing a flowchart and reading its labels, title, and caption)?
3. What are three characteristics of an ethical graph?
4. What kind of information do pie charts display most effectively?
5. What is the main purpose of a Gantt chart, and what content do Gantt charts typically contain?
6. How do flowcharts differ from organizational charts?
7. What are two ways that you can use color to convey information in graphs and charts more effectively?
8. What are three characteristics of effective labels?

Additional Exercises

1. Collect a sample of five graphs from newspapers, magazines, and Web sites. What kinds of data do they display? What design conventions are followed? What conventions are broken?
2. Collect a sample of five line graphs from newspapers, magazines, and Web sites. What are the aspect ratios of the graphs? Do the lines in the graphs display an orientation midangle of about 45°?
3. Collect a sample of five charts from newspapers, magazines, and Web sites. What kinds of information do the charts display? Do the authors refer to the charts in the text? Do the authors explain the charts?
4. If your intent is to persuade your readers with your document, to what extent is it ethical to modify the aspect ratio of a line graph so that the orientation midangle of its lines deviates from 45°, creating a graph that better supports your arguments? If your answer is "It depends," answer this: depends on what?
5. Collect a sample of five graphs or charts from newspapers, magazines, and Web sites. Analyze how color is used in each. To what extent does color convey information? To what extent is it decorative?
6. Collect a sample of five graphs from science- and health-related journals such as *Science* and *Journal of the*

American Medical Association. How many of the graphs have captions? Do the captions state the main points of the graphs, or do the captions state how to interpret the graphs?

7. Using the instructions on the Companion Website, change the following default graph, illustrating quarterly sales figures, so that it is more usable and sophisticated, like Figure 8.8.

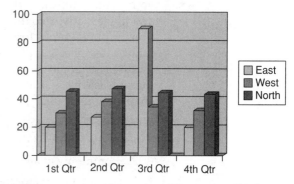

(Visit www.pearsonhighered.com/riley to view this figure in color.)

Suggestions for Further Reading

The following books clearly explain principles of graph design and provide examples of both effective and ineffective graphs and associated elements:

Kosslyn, S. M. (1994). *Elements of graph design.* New York: W. H. Freeman.

Miller, J. E. (2004). *The Chicago guide to writing about numbers.* Chicago: University of Chicago Press.

Robbins, N. B. (2005). *Creating more effective graphs.* Hoboken, NJ: Wiley Interscience.

Tufte, E. R. (1983). *The visual display of quantitative information.* Cheshire, CT: Graphics Press.

The following article is a good place to start if you are searching for empirical research on people's perceptions of graphs:

Shah, P., & Hoeffner, J. (2002). Review of graph comprehension research: Implications for instruction. *Educational Psychology Review, 14,* 47–69.

Selecting and Integrating Photography

James Maciukenas

This chapter describes how you can clearly communicate information, set the tone of a document, and capture a reader's attention using carefully selected photography. It describes photographic resources available to document designers that can help you select your photograph and briefly describes copyright issues involved in using photographs, and it offers advice to those who might want to begin or expand upon their own collections of photographs for use in their design work. It further offers guidelines to keep in mind when selecting photographs for use in print or Web documents. Lastly, this chapter discusses some issues to consider when determining the proper placement of a photograph as well as strategies for including captions with photographs. By the end of this chapter, you should be able to do the following:

- Understand the ways in which photography and text can work together so that you can make informed decisions about when and how to use photography
- Use commonly available resources for locating stock photography
- Work with a photographer to plan custom photography
- Integrate photography into a document's layout

Looking ahead, Chapter 10 takes you through some common editing tasks you may find yourself using frequently once you select your photographs.

OVERVIEW OF RELEVANT DESIGN CONCEPTS AND PRINCIPLES

As discussed in Chapter 8, "Displaying Information in Graphs and Charts," some information is conveyed more clearly by using visual language in conjunction with, or even instead of, verbal language. When the visual form is photography, the familiar phrase "a picture is worth a thousand words" comes to mind. For example, a combination of text and images can often convey information more efficiently and effectively than words alone, as

FEATURES & COMPONENTS:

Toddler tub

Fabric sling

Baby Bath Shower Components:

Removable top

Pump unit

Reservoir body

Sprayer handle

BATTERY INSTALLATION:

1 Twist lid of pump unit counter-clockwise.

2 Loosen screw on pump that holds the battery compartment cover in place.

3 Insert 6 new alkaline "AA" batteries into battery compartment. Be careful to install the batteries properly and in the right direction. The battery compartment is marked with + and -. Make sure the markings on the batteries match the markings in the battery compartment. Tighten and replace cover. DO NOT OVERTIGHTEN. Replace pump unit lid, turning clockwise.

4 Place pump unit into removable top as shown.

5 Turn unit over and twist clockwise until securely in place.

6 Place shower unit lid onto reservoir body. You are now ready to fill with water and use.

FIGURE 9.1 Illustrated instructions for installing batteries in a baby bath shower. Copyright Summer Infant Corporation. Used by permission. (Visit www.pearsonhighered.com/riley to view this figure in more detail.)

in the case of instructions for installing batteries into the pump unit of a baby bath shower (Figure 9.1). Similarly, a well-chosen and prominently placed photograph used in conjunction with other document elements (such as typography) can immediately orient the viewer to the tone, the emphasis, or the real or practical value of a document. For example, the Concordia alumni magazine cover in Figure 9.2 uses a bright green leaf. The image of the leaf has been modified using close *cropping*; that is, the subject in the image—the leaf— takes up much of the available space because other parts of the image have been removed. The photograph illustrates the university's focus on environmentalism—rather than, for example, choosing a photograph of an array of solar panels, which might illustrate the complexities of using sustainable materials in new building construction.

FIGURE 9.2 University magazine cover with environmental theme. Copyright Concordia University. Used by permission. (Visit www.pearsonhighered.com/riley to view this figure in color.)

WHY THESE PRINCIPLES ARE IMPORTANT

As described in Chapter 8, the value of including visuals such as photographs within your document layouts also derives from dual coding theory, articulated by Paivio (1986). Recall that dual coding theory proposes that people process words and images differently, through two different cognitive subsystems: "one specialized for the representation and processing of information concerning nonverbal objects and events, the other specialized for dealing with language" (p. 53). Thus, when you integrate visual elements with verbal elements, you give your readers two ways to process your message, which in turn fosters comprehension and recall. In Chapter 8, graphs and charts were the visual elements presenting explicit information. While photographs can also present explicit information, often they are used for another reason—to contribute to the tone of your document.

Manning and Amare (2007) argue that visual elements can be either decorative, indicative, or informative. A *decorative visual* element generates feeling in the audience. An *indicative visual* element provokes action. An *informative visual* element promotes understanding of an idea. Photographs fall into the decorative or indicative realm, while more diagrammatic representations fall into the indicative or informative realm. Manning and Amare argue that "Decorative/indicative photographs or descriptions would be particularly useful in a promotional brochure" (p. 69), that is, in a genre whose aim is more persuasive.

On the other hand, diagrams are more useful in genres whose aim is more instructional. Manning (1998) makes a similar argument, namely, that photos are less useful than cartoons (i.e., sketches and diagrams) for helping readers generalize about the nature of the item being displayed: "Most well-written technical writing manuals recognize that sketches have fewer distracting details than photos and that this can be an advantage . . . . cartoons amplify new ideas by simplifying them and cartoonlike sketches embody general concepts in a way that no photo-realistic image of an actual

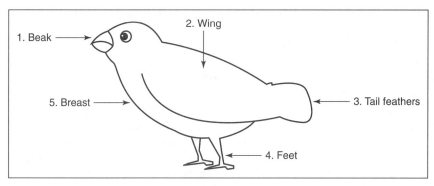

FIGURE 9.3   Line drawing illustrating anatomy of bird. Drawing by James Maciukenas. Used by permission.

thing can. A photograph is the imprint of one and only one object. A sketch potentially represents all objects of a general conceptual type" (pp. 67–68).

Along the same lines, Walsh (1998) argues that photographs are preferable for focusing on content, whereas diagrams are preferable for focusing on form. So, for example, a diagram such as Figure 9.3 would be more suitable if the writer's goal were to illustrate the parts of a bird—for example, in a discussion of bird morphology, or form, that applies to birds in general rather than to just one bird or species of bird. A purpose such as helping readers recognize a more specific object (e.g., a particular species of bird) may sometimes be better served by a drawing or diagram and other times by a photograph. A pair of drawings would be better suited to help readers focus on (say) details about beak length and tail-feather shape that distinguish two species of birds. In contrast, a photograph such as Figure 9.4 would be more suitable if the writer's goal were to enable beachgoers to recognize gulls on a holistic level.

In a different context, images in general and photographs in particular are effective in attracting readers (Decrop, 2007; Reichert, Heckler, & Jackson, 2001). So, for example, the photo in Figure 9.4 might be appropriate if the writer were creating a brochure designed to attract potential buyers to a beachfront property. Photographs and other images can be especially effective in psychological and emotional (as opposed to rational) persuasive appeals: "Many print ads that combine texts with photographs or other pictures use the text to convey an overt argument, thereby disguising the fact that the visuals serve up the affective, psychological identification, and thus do the real selling job. It's a clever shell game: suspicious of a non-rational sell, we get an

FIGURE 9.4   Photograph of gull. Copyright iStockphoto. Used by permission. (Visit www. pearsonhighered.com/riley to view this figure in color.)

(apparently) rational sell [i.e., through the text], which disarms us, thus leaving us vulnerable to the covert non-rational sell [i.e., through the image]" (Blair, 1996, p. 33; see also David, 2001, and Poynter Institute, 2004).

Drawing on previous research, Schriver (1997, pp. 412–430) identifies five types of relationships that images may have with prose: (1) redundant, (2) complementary, (3) supplementary, (4) juxtapositional, and (5) stage-setting.

A *redundant relationship* is one where image and text repeat or paraphrase one another. The idea of redundancy builds on Paivio's dual coding theory (1986), since it involves presenting the same information in more than one way. For example, in Figure 9.3, the combination of the diagram of the bird and text labels identifying specific parts of the anatomy of the bird presents a detailed surface description as well as a familiar illustration of an object. The inherent redundant relationship presents both an explanation of a object and a diagram of that object.

A *complementary relationship* is one in which the verbal and visual modes each provide different information about a concept or object, and thus "the two modes [together] render the idea more fully than either does alone" (Schriver, 1997, p. 415). At the same time, however, both the visual and verbal information are needed to fully understand the concept or object. Like redundant relationships, complementary relationships are often used in instructional documents, although they are not limited to those uses. An example of complementary verbal and visual information might be seen in a newsletter story that includes a photograph of student team that has won a competition (see, for example, Figure 9.13). The story text might simply narrate events, while the photograph supplies information about the team members' emotions.

A *supplementary relationship* describes a case in which either text or image is dominant, while "the other shores up and elaborates the points made in the dominant mode" (Schriver, 1997, p. 419). Again, this strategy may be useful in instructional or educational materials, where a photograph or other image might be used to reinforce the reader's understanding of an especially difficult point or to add visual interest at intermittent stages in the text (i.e., to keep the reader from being overwhelmed and bored by text-heavy pages). However, as Schriver points out, "randomly added pictures may inappropriately lead readers to believe that the topics with pictures are more important than those without pictures" (p. 421). An example of a supplementary relationship between text and image can be found in a traditional unabridged print dictionary or instruction manual. In the instructions in Figure 9.1, text is important, but images—photographs—constitute the predominate mode.

A *juxtapositional relationship* is one in which the text and image are at odds with each other—a strategy associated more with advertising and other persuasive genres than with instructional or informative documents. Such a juxtaposition may create a sense of irony. For example, an antismoking leaflet might carry a photograph of an extremely wrinkled smoker with nicotine-stained teeth, combined with a caption such as "Smoking. It's So Glamorous." In a different way, text and image may be juxtaposed to create a kind of visual pun. *New Yorker* covers often use this strategy by putting together a cover image with a title (not revealed until the table of contents page) that combine to create a kind of "aha" moment for the viewer. In Figure 9.5, the juxtaposition between image and text can be found between an image of a children's swing set and the title of a talk dealing with government environmental policies that can be seen as promoting death. A viewer's attention might initially be drawn by the swing set and idyllic mountain scene. Only after reading the text will the viewer realize the full impact of the image, that the only remnant of the children playing are shadows cast on the ground.

Finally, a *stage-setting relationship* occurs when a photograph (or other image) and text interact in a way such that "one mode provides a context for the other mode by forecasting the content or soon-to-be presented themes" (Schriver, 1997, p. 424). The

FIGURE 9.5 Poster illustrating a juxtapositional relationship in which text and image are seemingly at odds with each other. Design by James Maciukenas. Used by permission. (Visit www. pearsonhighered.com/riley to view this figure in color.)

idea of an image or text serving as an advance organizer for subsequent material relates to the concept of schema discussed in Chapter 3: Such a strategy helps to facilitate users' understanding of a document by preparing them mentally or psychologically for the subsequent material. So, for example, each chapter in an instructional manual for a piece of equipment might begin with a photograph forecasting the focus of that chapter. Or for Figure 9.3, a heading such as "Anatomy of Bird" might prepare the reader to understand the relationship between the text labels and the associated diagram.

You will quickly find that photography offers a seemingly endless number of subjects available for you to include in your document layout. Your challenge will be to discover photographs and strategies for using those photographs within your layouts to present information in a way that supports the message your document is conveying to its audience rather than distracting from or confusing your message. In short, the contribution of the image should be to provoke (in a positive sense) viewers' imaginations and engagement with a document and to move beyond or reinforce what is verbally stated in a document (Birdsell & Groarke, 1996; Douglis, 2007; Phillips & McQuarrie, 2002).

Exercise A

Examine textbooks (especially those in technical areas) and find examples of at least three of the types of text-image relationships identified previously.

RESOURCES FOR FINDING PHOTOGRAPHS

This section describes photographic resources available to document designers, addresses copyright issues involved in the use of photography, and offers advice about beginning or expanding on your own collections of photographs for use in your design work.

Fee-based Stock Photo Services

Stock photo services, also called *image banks*, are archives of photographs that can be licensed for use in specific document design projects. The term *stock photo* simply refers to the fact that the document designer is choosing from existing photos rather than having a photo custom-created for a specific purpose or client. Unlike in the past, when including a photograph in a document might have required hiring a photographer, determining a location, and scheduling a *photo shoot* (an event where a photographer takes the requested photograph), many online resources now provide searchable databases of images available for purchase. (They also usually offer nonphotographic illustrations as well as video images.) Services such as corbis.com, gettyimages.com, iStockphoto.com, and Adobe's Stock Photo service (to which Adobe's Creative Suite software offers access) provide a combined total of millions of images that can be purchased, with fees based on variables such as the intended use of the image and the required *resolution* (pixels or dots per inch, explained further in Chapter 10). A quick search of "stock photo service" using Google.com or another Internet search engine will lead you to numerous other online stock photo services. You may also find that the communications department at your university or place of employment maintains an archive of photographs available for use in your documents.

Stock photography services allow you to search available photographs using keywords, orientation (portrait or landscape), and categories (e.g., people, style, composition, dominant colors). CopySpace™, an advanced search feature found on iStockphoto.com, allows you to view a 3 × 3 grid dividing the photographs you will be searching into nine areas (upper left, upper middle, upper right, middle left, etc.). By clicking on one or more of the grid areas, you can limit your search to photographs on which text or a graphic (such as a logo mark) could be placed in the defined area (Figure 9.6).

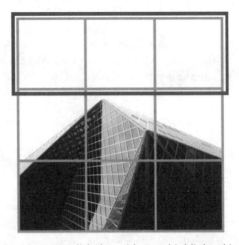

FIGURE 9.6 When using CopySpace™, click the grid areas highlighted in red to search for images with area at the top for text or a logo. Copyright iStockphoto. Used by permission. (Visit www.pearsonhighered.com/riley to view this figure in color.)

Your search results will display numerous photographs that meet your search criteria, from which you can then pick the photograph(s) that you would like to purchase, download them, and use them in your document layout. (The following section on selecting photographs provides more details about aesthetic and design criteria to consider.)

A secondary benefit of searching stock photography Web sites is that the process of skimming dozens or even hundreds of photographs can be a useful tool in the invention, or brainstorming, stage of designing a document. Whether you are trying to decide what image would best suit your project or you know what type of image your project needs, the act of searching for images exposes you to many alternative images that can inspire you and perhaps lead your project in unexpected directions.

A common feature on stock photo sites is a *lightbox*. The term alludes to the physical lightboxes used by photographers; these contain a surface of frosted glass lit from underneath, allowing the photographer to view and sort slides. An online lightbox is simply a folder that you create within your account on the stock photography site and in which you organize images by criteria that you create—for example, by project, subject matter, color, theme, and so on. For example, if you have three design projects going at once (a brochure, a newsletter, and a book cover), you might set up three different lightboxes to compartmentalize photos so that you, your collaborators, or your clients can survey them before making a final decision about which ones to purchase. Or, you might have lightboxes sorted according to subject matter (e.g., animals, people, buildings) or colors.

A commercial stock photo service usually offers a choice between *royalty-free* and *rights-managed photos*. Royalty-free images, despite what the name suggests, are not free. Royalty-free means that instead of paying the artist or service a royalty (i.e., a per-use payment), the user simply pays a one-time flat fee for the right to use the image. Typically you are given a choice of fees that vary depending on size (height and width dimensions), file type (e.g., .jpeg or .tiff), and resolution. For example, Figure 9.7 shows a pricing table for a particular image from iStockphoto.com. (One "credit" is approximately $1.50, so downloading the medium size of this particular image would cost about $7.50.)

For your purposes as a document designer, you will most often be dealing with images with a resolution of 300 DPI (the standard minimum resolution for quality printed documents) or 72 PPI (the standard resolution for images in Web or screen-based documents). DPI and PPI are discussed further in Chapter 10.

Sizes	Resolution	File Size	Credits
XSmall:	425 × 282 px 5.9″ × 3.9″ @ 72 DPI	81.75 KB	1
Small:	849 × 565 px 11.8″ × 7.8″ @ 72 DPI	230.32 KB	3
Medium:	1698 × 1131px 5.7″ × 3.8″ @ 300 DPI	800.18 KB	5
Large:	2716 × 1810 px 9.1″ × 6.0″ @ 300 DPI	2.22 MB	10
XLarge:	4368 × 2912 px 14.6″ × 9.7″ @ 300 DPI	5.60 MB	15

FIGURE 9.7   Example of price options for an image from iStockphoto.com.

A different type of price structure is used for rights-managed photos. The price for using a rights-managed photo is determined by how the image will be used, based on variables such as the kind of document (e.g., brochure versus Web site), the *print run* (i.e., how many copies of the document will be reproduced), where the document will be distributed (e.g., within one country versus worldwide), the length of time it will be used, and the industry in which the purchaser will be using it (e.g., commercial versus educational). Therefore, to get a quote on the fee for using a particular rights-managed photo, you will typically have to supply such details about the intended use of the photo.

Exercise B

Create an account in corbis.com or another site that offers rights-managed photos. Then explore the process of determining the fee for the same photograph, based on different usage variables (medium, print run, geographical distribution, and so on).

No-fee Image Banks

If you search for an image to use in Microsoft Word, you will be directed to the Office Online Clip Art site at http://office.microsoft.com/en-us/clipart/, where (despite the name) you can find not only clip art but also photographic images. While images of 150-DPI resolution are free, the Microsoft site will direct you to the (fee-based) iStockphoto site for higher resolution images, which, as explained next, are needed for certain print purposes.

More recently, alternative image banks have been developed that allow users to download images without paying a fee. Examples include the Flickr Creative Commons site at http://www.flickr.com/creativecommons/ and everystockphoto.com, a photography search tool for freely licensed photographs that was launched in 2006. As you might expect, the selection and search tools on such sites tend to be somewhat uneven compared to more established commercial sites, but such sites do represent an alternative that you may prefer for reasons of finances or principle. Sites such as everystockphoto.com are beginning to simplify the process of discovering and selecting photography for use in your documents. As of March 2010, the site search results are drawn from almost 5 million freely available photos, with license information included along with your found photography.

Copyright Considerations

Even on no-fee sites, you must be aware of the different types of use licenses by which photographers restrict the use of their photographs. Often Creative Commons licenses allow you to use photographs freely for educational uses, as long as attribution for the original work is provided. Other Creative Commons licenses limit the ways in which you can edit, crop, or modify the photograph for use within your document, as well as requiring compensation to the photographer for its use. The Creative Commons Web site, http://creativecommons.org/about/licenses/, is a valuable resource for information about the different licenses pertaining to digital photographic content. Restrictions on using Microsoft clip art are defined by the End-User License Agreement.

Students often use Google Image search to locate images for use in documents and then copy and paste the images into their assignments. This practice should be avoided for the following reasons (as well as for others):

- Copyright restrictions may not be explicitly detailed on the Web site hosting the image to allow for fair use of the photograph.
- Even if copyright restrictions are detailed on the site hosting the image, there is no easy way to confirm that the host site hasn't copied and pasted the image from another site or source without attribution.
- Most images that turn up in Google Image search are optimized for fast downloading and viewing over the Internet and are too low-quality to be used in print documents (see Chapter 10 for more discussion of digital photograph quality). Even though the images may look fine on screen, the effects of their low resolution will be apparent once the document is printed.

Custom Photography

Whether fee-based or not, online stock photo services are convenient and offer a seemingly infinite number of possible photographs for you to choose from, but even an extensive search may not provide you with exactly what you or your clients are looking for or may hinder your selection with copyright restrictions that you or your clients are unwilling to work with. Another issue that may arise with online stock photo services is that your search may lead you to a photograph that has proven popular with other users of the service. iStockphoto.com and many other image banks display information about the number of times a photograph has been downloaded (i.e., the rights to use it have been purchased) and, therefore, potentially used in other documents. You may want to consider this information when selecting your photograph. If a photograph has been purchased hundreds of times, there are potentially hundreds of other ad campaigns or corporate reports using the same photograph. Therefore, if you or your clients are looking to establish a unique identity within the document, you may want to turn to a photographer to capture an original photograph for you.

Identifying a photographer to use can be a complicated process, but perhaps your company already has a working relationship with a photographer or has a photographer on staff for custom photography. The benefit of working with a photographer is that you will have more control over the type of photograph you will end up with, as well as having more control over the copyright issues that might apply to your photo. In order to work with a photographer, you will need to present the following basic information:

- Concept (the idea for the photograph)
- Subject (the person, object, or scene that will be photographed)
- Location (where the photograph should be taken)
- Theme (further definition of the concept for the photograph)
- Intended use (the type of document where the photograph will be used)
- Type (conventional or electronic; see below for more discussion about electronic photograph requirements)
- Other information the photographer might inquire about during discussions about the photo shoot.

Once provided with this information, the photographer will go about the necessary steps to provide you with the requested photograph and then provide you with the photograph or photographs for your document layout.

Exercise C

For a brochure, newsletter, or other project that you have worked on in this class or another one, write up a one-page photographer's information sheet that covers the items just discussed and that you could use to coordinate a photography shoot.

Personal Photography Archives

The last type of photographic resource available to you is your own personal collection of photographs. With the proliferation of high-quality, compact, and affordable digital cameras, it is now easier than ever to develop a library of photographs that you can have at the ready when your documents require a photograph. Opportunities for photographs can happen at any time, so carry your camera with you, and take lots of pictures. Being indiscriminate about your subjects can provide you with many different types of photographs that may in whole or in part be useful for you in the future. Keep in mind to always take photographs at the highest quality and resolution possible (see Chapter 10 on image size and resolution). You can always reduce the quality and resolution of a photograph if the project requires it, but attempting to increase the resolution of a photograph using software such as Adobe Photoshop will not provide good results.

Because the photos are taken personally by you, copyright issues will not apply unless you are using them in work for a client and determine that you would like to retain copyright for them. Copyright law, especially in this digital age, is too complicated to fully address in this textbook, but you should be aware that if your photographs include people (especially children or minors), you must obtain their permission through a photo *release form* if you will use the photograph in a publication (print or electronic) or other public display. Your company most likely will have photo release forms available, and a search on Google.com for "photo release form example" yields many templates that can be downloaded, modified for your requirements, and printed.

Exercise D

If your organization or university has a standard photographic release form, obtain a copy of it and examine the conditions that it states.

Even if you do not consider yourself a photographer, digital photography has made it quite easy to build and expand upon a collection of images that can be used as you design your documents. As you design your documents, you will develop your individual design aesthetic through the choices that you make in regard to typography, color, graphic elements, and conventional or unconventional layouts. Photography is yet another element that is available to you and that will also inform your developing design aesthetic. Therefore, you will find photography very useful to you as you begin to think more consciously about the documents that you design and the world within which those documents will reside.

Use your digital camera (even an inexpensive one) to capture the world you find yourself in, finding which subjects you are drawn to photograph, and discovering subjects that you may not have imagined you would be interested in. As your library of photographs builds, find photo management software such as iPhoto for Macintosh or Microsoft Picture Manager for PC to manage your collection. These applications will allow you to use folders and/or *keywords* (terms that can be used to classify and search for an image) so that you can quickly find an image that might be suitable for use in your document.

SELECTING PHOTOGRAPHS

This section describes guidelines to keep in mind when selecting photographs for use in print or digital documents. After visiting the previously mentioned photography resources available to you on the Internet (or while compiling a collection of your own photography), you will realize the seemingly endless array of possible photographic subjects to select from for your document. Photographic resources offer photographs covering as many subjects as the world in which they are taken.

Portrait, *landscape*, and *documentary photography* often favor realism and present scenes or people in their natural state. (These terms refer to photojournalistic content and should not be confused with *portrait orientation* and *landscape orientation*, terms that refer, respectively, to whether the shape of the image is predominantly vertical or horizontal.) Figures 9.8, 9.9, and 9.10 illustrate these styles. On the other

FIGURE 9.8   Example of portrait photography. Copyright iStockphoto. Used by permission. (Visit www.pearsonhighered.com/riley to view this figure in color.)

FIGURE 9.9 Example of landscape photography. Copyright iStockphoto. Used by permission. (Visit www.pearsonhighered.com/riley to view this figure in color.)

FIGURE 9.10 Example of documentary photography. Copyright iStockphoto. Used by permission. (Visit www.pearsonhighered.com/riley to view this figure in color.)

hand, closely cropped photography such as the leaf image shown in Figure 9.2 favors abstractness by limiting the field of view, focusing on a texture or color rather than on the whole of a scene.

Some photography uses filters to enhance the color of a naturally occurring scene or uses *sepia tones* (warm brown colors) to make a recent photograph seem to have been taken in the distant past (mimicking the color tone of *tintypes* and *daguerreotypes*, which were early forms of photography developed in the 19th century). Black-and-white photography also remains popular, providing a cultured, artistic feel to a photographic subject. Figures 9.11 and 9.12 illustrate these photographic styles.

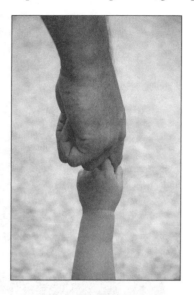

FIGURE 9.11   True daguerreotype (top left) and modern sepia-toned photographs. Copyright iStockphoto. Used by permission. (Visit www.pearsonhighered.com/riley to view this figure in color.)

Each style of photography provides a different feel to your photographic subject and will therefore affect the mood or tone of the document in which you use the photograph. Therefore, when choosing a photograph, carefully consider the audience for which your document is being designed. A communications company would most likely not use sepia-toned photography to illustrate a document in which they profess to be on the cutting edge of the latest technology. An accounting firm would probably want to avoid anything but realistic photography to represent their honesty and integrity in business to potential clients. In contrast, an artistic design firm might turn to enhanced photographs to demonstrate their distinctive view of the world and valuable creative talents.

Regardless of the purpose and resulting use of a photograph in your document layout, the photograph you choose should enhance the message you are presenting to your audience rather than competing with your message.

FIGURE 9.12 Black-and-white photos can be visually arresting because they present a unique view of the world, using contrast rather than color. Copyright iStockphoto. Used by permission.

Exercise E

Find two or three full-page advertisements that use black-and-white photography and where it appears to be a deliberate choice (i.e., not one dictated by budget limits or production constraints). Likely places to look include magazines such as the *New Yorker*, *Vogue*, *Harper's*, and the *New York Times Magazine*, but you may find others. Can you draw any generalizations about the visual effects, subject matter, and tone for which black-and-white photography is most effective? In other words, can you speculate on why the designer chose a black-and-white photo instead of a color photo?

INTEGRATING PHOTOGRAPHY INTO A LAYOUT

In addition to the theories mentioned previously in this chapter, Williams (2008) offers the following guidelines to document designers when designing their layouts. These guidelines should also be considered when choosing and placing photographs within your layout.

Proximity means that you should group related items together so the related items are seen as one cohesive group rather than as unrelated items (Williams, 2008, p. 15). In the case of document design and photography, this means placing the photograph that illustrates or supports a part of the text close to the relevant text.

Similarly, *alignment* (as discussed in Chapter 5) states that nothing should be placed on the page arbitrarily. Every item should have a visual connection with something else on the page rather than just being placed "wherever there happens to be space" (Williams, 2008, p. 33). Williams says, "Lack of alignment is probably the biggest cause of unpleasant-looking documents. Our eyes *like* to see order; it creates a calm, secure feeling" (p. 43). Therefore, the photographs within your layout should not only be placed be near related textual elements but should also be visually connected to those elements in some way. Strategies include using textual elements such as figure titles, graphical elements such as fields of color, or the underlying grid structure of the page to create a logical order of elements, including the photography you are placing within your layout. For example, you can see in Figure 9.1 that the photographic and textual elements adhere to both vertical and horizontal alignment.

Williams's principle of *repetition* suggests that you "repeat some element of the design throughout the entire piece" (2008, p. 51). Repetition can be thought of as "consistency" resulting from "a conscious effort to unify all parts of a design" (p. 51). The purpose of repetition is to unify and to add visual interest, thus making the page more likely to be read (p. 52). In the case of photography, a photograph can be used to visually reinforce a concept mentioned in the text. Likewise, using a photograph in the header of a multipage document can orient the reader of a document to its provenance, whether they read consecutive pages or peruse random pages of an annual corporate report. Likewise, a dominant color from a photograph might be repeated by using it for spot color in the text area (e.g., as the color of a headline or rule).

Exercise F

Analyze Figure 9.1 for its use of proximity, alignment, and repetition, especially with respect to the photographs used in the design.

Lastly, the principle of *contrast* states that "if two items are not exactly the same, then make them different. Really different" (Williams, 2008. p. 65). Our eyes are drawn to contrast, and contrast is created when two elements are different. When considering contrast and which photographs to use within your document layouts, an anecdote from my first photography class might be useful. One of the first things that happened in my basic black-and-white photography class was that all of the photographs from our first assignment looked basically the same. They all featured large areas of black and large areas of white (e.g., the shadow stripes of a stair railing on a washed-out wooden floor). In other words, our photographed compositions all featured the strongest of contrast. Our instructor explained that our eyes actually feel pleasure when experiencing strong contrast and, therefore, it was not surprising that our assignments each featured strong contrast. He went on to advise us that balancing the contrast of the play of light within the scene with the content of the scene being photographed would develop as we became more sophisticated with our photographic choices.

Similarly, contrast within the photographs you place within your layout and the contrast created by placing images within your layout will become more sophisticated as your document design approach becomes more balanced. You will develop a more balanced approach for selecting photographs to use within your document layouts by carefully considering the placement of photographs using the principles of design developed by Williams while also incorporating the theories mentioned previously in the introductory section of this chapter.

WRITING AND FORMATTING CAPTIONS

Part of effectively using photography in a newsletter, report, or article involves writing *captions* (also known as *cutlines*)—short pieces of text, usually placed under a photograph, that help the reader interpret the photograph and relate it to the surrounding story. Although the task of writing captions may not be your primary responsibility as a designer, it is one that you may be asked to provide help with or ideas about in consultation with an editor or other collaborator who is preparing the text. In addition, you should be sensitive to strategies for locating and formatting captions in relation to photographs and the main text of a story.

First, we can distinguish between captions for a technical or academic document, in which a photograph serves as a figure, versus captions for photographs in feature writing such as newsletters and annual reports, in which a photograph may be used more for visual interest than for instructional or explanatory purposes. For guidelines on how to label figures in technical or academic documents, review Chapter 8 ("Displaying Information in Graphs and Charts").

In feature writing, first and foremost, captions must be accurate, especially when they identify people. This means double-checking the spelling of names and making sure that name forms are consistent between the main text and the caption (e.g., *James* in the main text should not become *Jim* in the caption). Second, captions should identify the main people in the picture and do so in a way that helps the reader. Usually this involves including directional information if there is more than one person in the picture (e.g., "Dean F. R. McMorris, left, presents the CSL Faculty Research Award to Pat Conroy"). Even if the identification seems too obvious to you to be necessary, include it. Captions for pictures of groups (e.g., members of a team) should likewise include signals about which row is being identified, with names listed from left to right within each row—for example (see Figure 9.13):

> STC Award Winners. Front row, left to right: Michael Merkley, Matthew Ephraim, Almond Loh, Dr. Susan Feinberg. Back row, left to right: Keith Olsen, Yun Tan, Michael Slone, Joseph Lloyd, Konrad Branicki, Kurt Olson, Deborah Kimnach, Abdi Shabihul.

Conventionally, captions that include a verb are written in the present tense—for example:

> The IIT group gathers in front of BIT's logo, which symbolizes an eagle transforming into a dove.

Additional pointers for writing effective captions are summarized in Irby (2000), among them the following: "Check the facts. Be accurate!"; "A photograph captures a moment in time. Whenever possible, use present tense. This will create a sense of immediacy

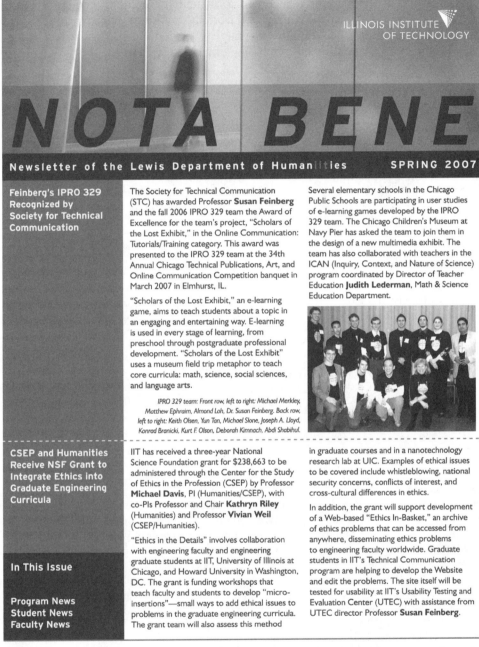

Newsletter content shown in figure:

ILLINOIS INSTITUTE OF TECHNOLOGY

NOTA BENE

Newsletter of the Lewis Department of Humanities   SPRING 2007

Feinberg's IPRO 329 Recognized by Society for Technical Communication

The Society for Technical Communication (STC) has awarded Professor **Susan Feinberg** and the fall 2006 IPRO 329 team the Award of Excellence for the team's project, "Scholars of the Lost Exhibit," in the Online Communication: Tutorials/Training category. This award was presented to the IPRO 329 team at the 34th Annual Chicago Technical Publications, Art, and Online Communication Competition banquet in March 2007 in Elmhurst, IL.

"Scholars of the Lost Exhibit," an e-learning game, aims to teach students about a topic in an engaging and entertaining way. E-learning is used in every stage of learning, from preschool through postgraduate professional development. "Scholars of the Lost Exhibit" uses a museum field trip metaphor to teach core curricula: math, science, social sciences, and language arts.

Several elementary schools in the Chicago Public Schools are participating in user studies of e-learning games developed by the IPRO 329 team. The Chicago Children's Museum at Navy Pier has asked the team to join them in the design of a new multimedia exhibit. The team has also collaborated with teachers in the ICAN (Inquiry, Context, and Nature of Science) program coordinated by Director of Teacher Education **Judith Lederman**, Math & Science Education Department.

IPRO 329 team: Front row, left to right: Michael Merkley, Matthew Ephraim, Almond Loh, Dr. Susan Feinberg. Back row, left to right: Keith Olsen, Yun Tan, Michael Slone, Joseph A. Lloyd, Konrad Branicki, Kurt F. Olson, Deborah Kimnach, Abdi Shabihul.

CSEP and Humanities Receive NSF Grant to Integrate Ethics into Graduate Engineering Curricula

IIT has received a three-year National Science Foundation grant for $238,663 to be administered through the Center for the Study of Ethics in the Profession (CSEP) by Professor **Michael Davis**, PI (Humanities/CSEP), with co-PIs Professor and Chair **Kathryn Riley** (Humanities) and Professor **Vivian Weil** (CSEP/Humanities).

"Ethics in the Details" involves collaboration with engineering faculty and engineering graduate students at IIT, University of Illinois at Chicago, and Howard University in Washington, DC. The grant is funding workshops that teach faculty and students to develop "micro-insertions"—small ways to add ethical issues to problems in the graduate engineering curricula. The grant team will also assess this method

in graduate courses and in a nanotechnology research lab at UIC. Examples of ethical issues to be covered include whistleblowing, national security concerns, conflicts of interest, and cross-cultural differences in ethics.

In addition, the grant will support development of a Web-based "Ethics In-Basket," an archive of ethics problems that can be accessed from anywhere, disseminating ethics problems to engineering faculty worldwide. Graduate students in IIT's Technical Communication program are helping to develop the Website and edit the problems. The site itself will be tested for usability at IIT's Usability Testing and Evaluation Center (UTEC) with assistance from UTEC director Professor **Susan Feinberg**.

In This Issue

Program News
Student News
Faculty News

FIGURE 9.13   Example of caption use for image in newsletter article. Copyright Illinois Institute of Technology. Used by permission. (Visit www.pearsonhighered.com/riley to view this figure in color.)

and impact"; and "Conversational language works best. Don't use clichés. Write the caption as if you're telling a family member a story."

Caption placement is typically under or adjacent to the photograph. When captioning a cluster of photographs, make it clear which caption goes with which photograph by using proximity strategies such as closing up space between a caption and the photograph it goes with while increasing space between the same caption and an unrelated photograph. Another strategy you may want to consider is numbering each photograph in the cluster and using the numbers in the captions as well.

Caption formatting should be handled consistently, usually by setting the caption in a font and size that is easily distinguished from the main text. For example, you may want to use a variant of a headline font as your caption font, thereby creating both contrast with the main text and repetition with another design element.

Conclusion

This chapter has discussed issues surrounding the use of photography within your document layouts. It has offered strategies that you can use to select and place photographs and has identified sources for acquiring photographs. Working with photographs (especially digital photographs) has become increasingly less complicated as document-layout software becomes more sophisticated as well as easier to use. Therefore, experimenting with photographs within your document layouts is easier than ever. Guidelines such as those offered by Williams (2008) should inform your experimentation, as should the description of common photographic editing tasks that you will find in Chapter 10.

Summary of Key Concepts and Terms

alignment
caption
complementary relationship
contrast
cropping
cutline
daguerrotype
decorative visual
documentary photography

image bank
indicative visual
informative visual
juxtapositional relationship
keyword
landscape orientation
landscape photography
lightbox
photo shoot

portrait photography
portrait orientation
print run
proximity
redundant relationship
release form
repetition
resolution
rights-managed photo

royalty-free photo
sepia tone
stage-setting relationship
stock photo
stock photo services
supplementary relationship
tintype

Additional Exercises

1. iStockphoto.com is a great resource for finding images or for use as a brainstorming tool. Yet, discovering the right image for your project among the more than 5 million files available on the Web site (as of March 2010) can be a challenge. Select a keyword and enter it into the search box on the Web site's home page. Do the image search results match your expectations? If not, how can you revise your search to refine your results? Select one of the image search results and view the keywords associated with the image and retry your search with one of the keywords associated with that image.

2. Explore the variety of image-text relationships (redundant, complementary, supplementary, juxtapositional, and stage-setting) by selecting images for famous first lines of novels found on the American Book Review Web site (located at http://americanbookreview.org/100BestLines.asp). Discuss whether obvious images versus less obvious images suit certain image-text relationships more successfully.

3. Many business or educational newsletters avoid using photography due to costs incurred in the printing process. Find opportunities in newsletters for integrating photography. Identify the strategy used when integrating a photograph with text (i.e. decorative, indicative, or informative).

Editing Photography

James Maciukenas

Chapter 9 discussed strategies for choosing which photographs to use and how to place them within your document layouts. These strategies were discussed within the context of principles specific to photography and those more generally applicable to document design. When using photographs in your print and online document layouts, it will also be helpful to have an understanding of some of the technical issues surrounding their use. This chapter offers a brief description of conventional and digital photography and then details some of the technical terms and processes you will encounter when incorporating images into your document design layouts. By the end of this chapter, you should be able to do the following:

- Understand the differences between film and digital photography
- Use appropriate technical vocabulary for talking about digital photography
- Understand file formats for digital photography, as well as the appropriate uses for each format
- Understand principles of color as they relate to the use of photography
- Edit photographs to modify the file size, image size, and visual features such as brightness and contrast

OVERVIEW OF RELEVANT DESIGN CONCEPTS AND PRINCIPLES

Generally speaking, there are two ways of creating photographs, conventional film-based photography and digital photography. Conventional photography uses light to expose film contained within the body of a camera, creating a negative of the desired subject on the film. This film negative is then used to develop a photograph on light-sensitive, emulsion-coated paper through a multistep chemical process performed inside a darkroom. Digital photography uses an image sensor within the camera to create digital files. These digital files are instantly viewable as images on the display found on most digital cameras or when imported onto a computer.

Despite the continued increase in quality of images captured by digital cameras, professional photographers may have many reasons for preferring film-based photography. Yet for many document designers, the relative ease of use of digital cameras and related imaging software allows us to easily capture and incorporate images into documents. Digital photography also allows us to prepare images for publication without using the messy, chemical-based processes needed to develop conventional film-based photographs or waiting for the film to be developed by a lab. In addition, digital files allow for relatively fast and easy editing. Therefore, given that working with digital photography is part of the everyday life of most document designers, much of this chapter focuses on digital photography and the terminology surrounding this medium.

In order to begin to understand the process of working with digital photographs, it is helpful to understand digital photography as a technological progression from conventional film photography.

Conventional film-based photography yields a high-quality, original photograph. The quality of the photograph is due both to the process used to capture a negative of the image on film and the process used to create the photographic print. Depending on the type of film used to capture an image and the paper used to print the photograph, conventional photography allows the production of a crisp, clean image, one close to the quality with which the human eye views the world.

If a photographic print is selected for reproduction within a print document layout, it must be prepared for the printing process. Usually, this preparation involves breaking the photo up into tiny dots using the halftone process. This process allows the printer to print only certain shades of gray or of the four colors cyan (C), yellow (Y), magenta (M), and black (K)—hence CMYK. See Chapter 11 for more information about color processes.

In much the same way, the goal of capturing and processing a digital photograph is to produce a high-quality original photograph, which can then be used to prepare derivatives for print layouts or screen display. For instance, you may use a digital camera with a 10-megapixel image sensor to capture a photograph at the highest settings the camera offers and then use digital-imaging software such as Adobe Photoshop to reduce the resolution, dimensions, and file size of the image for use in a print or Web document.

WHY THESE PRINCIPLES ARE IMPORTANT

Although the technical aspects of digital photography may seem complicated, taking the time to understand each of the following concepts and how each influences your document-layout decisions will save you much time and frustration when incorporating photographs in your documents. It may also be helpful to breathe a sigh of relief that this chapter is not asking you to mix dangerous chemicals in exacting measures while spending hours in a darkroom developing photographs taken days or weeks ago, only to discover an out-of-focus image with no opportunity to retake the photograph, each an all-too-common pitfall of conventional photography.

SOME TECHNICAL ASPECTS OF DIGITAL PHOTOGRAPHY

The preceding introduction raises some technical terms related to digital photography, such as megapixels, image resolution, and file size. One of the most confusing things that you will discover when working with digital photography is that these (and other) technical terms all seem to measure or refer to the size of a digital image. Your confusion may be further compounded when you realize that it is the balance of the unique qualities of each of these technical aspects that will allow you to choose the right digital image for your document. This section describes each of these terms and others related to digital photography in more detail in order to reduce the confusion that surrounds the "size" of a digital image. This section also discusses choosing one image size over another for your document layout.

Megapixels

One measure of a digital image is the number of pixels high and wide captured by the light-sensitive digital image sensor of the camera. One *pixel* is the smallest unit of color a sensor can detect. The image sensor performs the work of capturing a digital photograph. The sensor is measured by the number of pixels wide and high it captures. The greater the number of pixels captured by the image sensor, the greater the amount of information made available to reproduce the image. Because the number of pixels wide and high of these sensors measures into the thousands, multiplied together these sensors can run into the millions of pixels (or megapixels). One *megapixel* is 1 million pixels.

Viewed alone, one pixel looks like a small square of color. Viewed together, millions of pixels create a digital image (see Figure 10.1). Early consumer digital cameras, such as the Canon PowerShot S100, captured images using a 2-megapixel sensor able to capture 2 million individual units of color. As of the date of the publication of this book, current professional digital cameras (such as the Canon EOS-1Ds Mark III) capture images using up to a 21.1-megapixel sensor able to capture 21.1 million individual units of color.

While this discussion has explained what a megapixel is, you may still be wondering how this information impacts your decisions as a document designer. There are three points to keep in mind about megapixels.

- First, an image with more pixels will offer more detail, resulting in a better quality image for your document. It is always better to start with an image with more pixels, which you can reduce using software such as Adobe Photoshop, than to start with an image with fewer pixels and discover that you would like more detail.
- Second, understanding the difference between a 21-, 10-, or 5-megapixel camera is much like the difference between choosing tabloid-, legal-, or letter-size paper for your document: The larger the piece of paper, the more information you can put on it.

FIGURE 10.1   Comparison of one pixel of color (greatly enlarged), a group of 25 pixels (greatly enlarged), and a digital image containing millions of pixels. (Visit www.pearsonhighered.com/riley to view this figure in color.)

- Third, you most likely won't deal with megapixels on a daily basis. Megapixels are most often used when referring to the camera taking the digital image and would be considered only when either purchasing a camera or ensuring that a photographer has the proper equipment for the job.

Therefore, when thinking of megapixels, a document designer should know that the highest quality digital photography would be taken by a camera with an image sensor with the highest number of megapixels (as of early 2010, the Canon EOS mentioned previously is the highest quality digital camera available to consumers). However, you should also know that digital cameras with fewer megapixel counts are more than adequate for most print and Web uses of digital photography. Lastly, you should know that it is always better to start with an image with more pixels (i.e., more detail) rather than starting with fewer pixels and wishing for more detail in your image.

Exercise A

Pick a digital image and use Photoshop CS4 (or other image-editing software) to zoom in as far as you can to notice the individual pixels of color making up that image. Use Figure 10.1 as a reference. *Note:* As there are many different types of image-editing software, this and the other exercises assume that you are familiar with the software available to you. If you are not, start by referring to the software's help sections and/or search Google.com for assistance as necessary. A suggested format for your queries on Google.com is the following: "task name + image-editing software name + tutorial" (e.g., save image + photoshop CS4 + video tutorial). You may be surprised to find that there are many free tutorials on YouTube and other places on the Internet.

Resolution

Generally, *resolution* can be thought of as the ability of an image to represent what we actually see with our eyes. The highest image resolution available to us is the quality with which we are able to view the world with our eyes. As digital images are taken with ever-increasing numbers of megapixels, they come closer to capturing what our eyes actually see and, therefore, to capturing the image quality of the film cameras they are replacing.

More specifically, when describing the resolution of a digital image, you will notice the terms *dots per inch (DPI)* and *pixels per inch (PPI)* are often used interchangeably. However, these terms do indeed mean different things. The difference between these terms can be found by investigating the context from which these terms arose, which will help you better understand resolution and its relation to digital photography.

DPI The term DPI arose from the world of print documents and the dots used to create color separations (both gray-scale and CMYK) discussed previously in this chapter and in Chapter 11. Think of an old dot-matrix printer, which produced a printed document using a matrix of dots. A dot is the smallest unit of color that can be generated by the device, and therefore DPI describes the output generated by a printer or similar device. The higher the DPI count of your printer, the better document quality your printer will be able to produce. Even though dot-matrix printers have by and large been replaced by inkjet or laser printers, these new printing technologies continue to produce documents with small dots of ink, which when viewed together display image or textual content.

PPI.   The term PPI arose from the monitors used to display information generated by computers. The term PPI identifies the number of pixels per inch a computer monitor can display. The greater the number of pixels displayed in 1 inch, the higher the image or display quality experienced by the viewer. Simply stated, a computer monitor with more pixels per inch displays more information or detail about the image within that inch.

For example, when purchasing a computer monitor, you may have encountered a 20-inch monitor for almost the same price as a 21-inch monitor. If you look closely at the technical specifications of both monitors, the seemingly inexpensive 21-inch monitor's display area may actually have the same number of pixels high and wide as the 20-inch monitor display area. In this case, the 21-inch monitor actually has fewer pixels per inch and will display a poorer quality image.

For your purposes as a document designer, you will most often be dealing with images with a resolution of 300 DPI (the standard minimum resolution for quality printed documents) or 72 PPI (the standard resolution for images in Web or screen-based documents).

300 DPI   The standard minimum resolution for quality printed documents produced by a professional printer is 300 DPI. High-quality printing devices can print documents at a variety of DPI, yet 300 DPI is the standard for ensuring that images used in print documents will reproduce the original image without the noise or reduction in quality that results from using lower DPI photographs.

72 PPI   A standard resolution for images for Web or screen-based documents is 72 PPI. Many computer monitors are capable of displaying only 72 PPI, which is why you may have encountered the rule that any image saved for the Web should be saved at 72 PPI. When saving an image for use in screen-based documents at 72 PPI, you are saving an image at the highest resolution possible for the medium displaying the document. In this case, the medium is the screen. Another consideration when saving an image for use in screen-based documents is to minimize file size, ensuring that the Web page containing the image will load quickly. For a comparison of images using 300 DPI and 72 PPI, see Figure 10.2.

Although all the numbers and terms in this discussion may seem complicated, when choosing an image for your document you should remember three points:

- First, it is most important to identify the medium presenting your information to your audience. Essentially, you have two choices: print or screen. Each medium can display a variety of image resolutions, yet all you need to remember is that PPI and DPI are often used interchangeably and that the optimal resolution for each medium is 300 DPI for print-based documents and 72 PPI for screen-based documents.
- Second, resolution can be thought of as the ability to fit more information onto the "page" you have chosen for your document. If you have decided on a letter-size document using 12-point type, you might be able to fit 500 words on a page. If you instead decide to use 9-point type on the same letter-size document, you might be able to fit 800 words on the page. Therefore, with the same page dimensions, you could fit much more information on that page. To complete this analogy, if you choose to use an image that is 1 inch by 1 inch square at 72 PPI, your image will have only 72 pixels of color information. If you choose to use the same 1 inch by 1 inch image at 300 PPI, your image will be made up of 300 pixels of color information. Each image will be the same size (1 inch by 1 inch), but the 300 PPI image will contain 228 more pixels and therefore will contain more detail or information about the image.
- Third, resolution differs from megapixels in that megapixels measure the width and height of a digital image in pixels, while resolution measures how much detail is present within those dimensions.

72 PPI

300 DPI

FIGURE 10.2 Comparison of printed document using 72 PPI vs. 300 DPI. Notice the reduced image quality on the left portion of the image. (Visit www.pearsonhighered.com/riley to view this figure in color.)

File Size

When working with digital photographs, the concept of image size may quickly prove confusing. The previous sections of this chapter have detailed two aspects of image size, megapixels and image resolution, which influence the dimensions and detail of a digital photograph. This section focuses on a third aspect of the image size of a digital photograph—namely, file size—and the considerations you will need to make in order to choose the proper photograph for print or Web documents.

File size refers to how large or small a digital file must be to store information about your image in order to be displayed on your camera or computer. Traditional film-based photography consists of physical objects storing both the negative used to make the photograph (a roll of film) and the photograph itself (the paper coated with emulsions displaying the image). Digital photography stores the information as bytes, a series of data made up of ones and zeros. The data would make little sense to you if viewed, but a computer uses the data to display the image. A small image might use 100,000 bytes to store the necessary information, while a large image might use 30,000,000 bytes or more to store the necessary information. A shorthand is used to describe the number of bytes in a computer file, with kilobyte (KB) referring to 1,000 bytes and megabyte (MB) referring to 1,000,000 bytes.

As a document designer, you will encounter file-size issues quite often as you decide on the proper image for your document layouts. For print documents, you need to remember two points:

- First, whichever image you choose should have a resolution of at least 300 DPI.
- Second, if you are using many images in your document and each possesses a large megapixel count and a large DPI count, your document file size can quickly become quite large. You will need to define a procedure for delivering your print-ready documents to your printing company, as the files containing images will not be easy to send by e-mail due to the large file size.

For Web or screen-based documents, you will need to consider other issues regarding digital image file size:

- First, especially for images delivered using the Web, file size is very important. You will need to balance the visual quality of your image with the number of bytes or kilobytes necessary to store the information to display the image on a Web page or multimedia CD or DVD. In the case of screen-based documents, it is always best to strive for the smallest possible file size and the lowest quality image that still manages to illustrate the subject or scene you would like to share with your audience. I think we have all shared the experience of visiting a Web site, only to witness a page of broken-up text with images slowly loading from top to bottom, like shades being drawn slowly down over a window. By taking the time to *optimize* your images for display on the Web—that is, to reduce the file size while maintaining image quality—you will ensure a pleasant user experience with quick page rendering and the display of both image and text at the same time.
- Second, the standard rule of thumb for images optimized for displaying on the Web is 72 PPI. Many consumer computer monitors do not display at resolutions higher than 72 PPI (Mac) or 96 PPI (PC); therefore, there is no need for most screen-based documents to use images with higher resolutions. By saving your images at 72 PPI, you will be taking into account the environment your audience will use to view your document, and you will also be ensuring that your image will be able to be viewed quickly in a Web-based environment.
- Third, software such as Adobe Photoshop CS4 has relatively easy-to-use tools for optimizing your images for use on the Web. Either use the Image Size tool within the main Photoshop CS4 user interface or select File > Save for Web or Devices, which guides you through the image-optimization process. Save for Web or Devices offers image comparisons at different resolutions and file sizes so that you can decide which degree of optimization will best suit your document needs.

Exercise B

With the image chosen for Exercise A, use your image-editing software to create two files. Save the first file at 72 PPI. Save the second file at 300 PPI. Open each file and print. Compare the image quality of each. (For example, is one printed image blurrier than the other? Is one printed image more detailed than the other?)

FILE FORMATS AND DIGITAL PHOTOGRAPHY

The previous sections introduced you to a few of the terms that will help you understand some of the technical aspects of digital photography. This discussion concluded with the Save for Web or Devices feature of Adobe Photoshop CS4. Whether or not you decide to use Photoshop to modify and optimize your digital photographs, whenever you save a digital image, you will have to choose one of many possible file formats. Before you click "Save" and finalize any changes you made to the image, you will see many choices in any "Save As" dialog box, including .gif, .jpeg, .tiff, and others. If you are unfamiliar with these choices, they are similar to the choices you make when saving a Microsoft Word document, such as .txt (for plain text), .rtf (for rich text), .doc or .docx (for standard Word format), or .pdf (Adobe's portable document format). This section details some of the more common digital image file formats. This section also provides a guide for selecting the appropriate formats for your document layouts.

File Formats and Compression

You most likely noticed that the previous sections advised you to always start with the largest pixel width and height image as well as the highest image resolution possible from your digital camera. Yet, in the file-size section, you were then advised to optimize your image for print or for the Web, often involving the reduction of the width and height of the image as well as the reduction of the resolution of the image. Whenever a digital image is optimized for print or the Web, you will have to choose a file format to save your image. You may already be familiar with the file format options for saving your image, options such as GIF, PNG, JPEG, and TIFF, yet you may not be familiar with what each of these file formats means or does. Each of these file formats is actually a way of compressing your image in order to reduce its file size while optimizing the resulting image quality to best suit your document requirements. The following sections describe each of these common compression formats and mention the types of documents in which they are most commonly used.

PRINT-FILE FORMATS

TIFF

Tagged Image File Format (*TIFF*) is the most commonly used file format for print documents. For the purpose of this textbook and your future print-document layouts, all you need to know about TIFF files is that if you are designing a document that will be sent to a printer, all images must be saved in the TIFF file format. The TIFF file format is uncompressed and retains all information and image detail your original image file contained. Because print documents are often produced in a professional environment using the latest technologies and no requirements for the quick delivery of a file over the Internet, file optimization and compression are not required.

WEB OR SCREEN-BASED FILE FORMATS

GIF

Graphics Interchange Format (*GIF*) is often used for graphics or illustrations to be delivered and displayed on Web pages. GIF files use a type of compression with up to 256 colors for the display of an image or graphic. When saving an image as a GIF file, you are given the option to choose how many colors to use to display the image or graphic. By choosing fewer colors, you will create a smaller optimized file. If, for example, you are saving a black-and-white illustration and you choose 2 colors, black and white, your

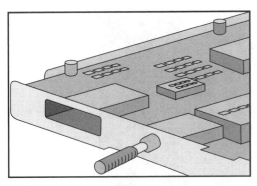

FIGURE 10.3   Examples of art similar to clip art using the GIF file format. (Visit www.pearsonhighered. com/riley to view this figure in color.)

resulting file will be relatively smaller as it is using only black and white to display the illustration. If you choose 256 colors, your resulting file will use 256 shades of gray to display the illustration, resulting in a relatively larger file. Due to the limited number of colors available to render your file, GIF compression is not ideal for use with detailed photographic imagery. Clip art (see Figure 10.3) is a familiar use of GIF compression to users of Microsoft Office applications such as Word and PowerPoint.

PNG

Another file format for graphics—one that is replacing the GIF format—is the Portable Network Graphic (*PNG*) format. For the purposes of this textbook, the main difference between the GIF and PNG formats is that the PNG format is nonproprietary, meaning that developers of image-editing software or Internet browsers do not need to pay for a license in order to support this type of compression. Therefore, the use of the PNG format is advocated by the open-source community, which offers alternatives to image-editing software such as Photoshop CS4 (GIMP; see www.gimp.org) or to Microsoft Office (Open Office; see www.openoffice.org).

JPEG

When working with detailed photographic imagery for display on the Internet, Joint Photographic Experts Group (*JPEG*) is the most commonly used file format. The mysterious name of this file format is due to its being named for the group that created this compression type for images. Unlike TIFF files, the JPEG file format offers five levels of compression, ranging from low to maximum. And unlike GIF files, the JPEG file format can render millions of colors, making it an ideal format for displaying images on the Internet (see Figure 10.4). Another benefit of the JPEG file format is that it is widely supported by browsers used to view content on the Internet. A variation on the JPEG file format, JPEG 2000, is able to compress image files into much smaller sizes while still maintaining a high-quality image. Yet, the JPEG 2000 file format is not widely supported by modern Web browsers. Therefore, only users who have installed the extensions for their browsers to view the JPEG 2000 file format will be able to view your content.

These are just a few of the many possible file formats available for use with digital images. When deciding which format to use with your document layouts, you first need to determine whether the image will be used in a print document or in a Web or screen-based document. If your document will be printed on paper, you will need to use the TIFF file format. If your document will be displayed on a screen, you will need

FIGURE 10.4 Example of an image rendered with the millions of colors displayed when using the JPEG file format. (Visit www.pearsonhighered.com/riley to view this figure in color.)

to use one of the various compression file formats, of which GIF and JPEG are just two of the most commonly used formats. Your decision will need to take into account whether your image is detailed photographic imagery or a simpler graphic. Your decision will also need to take into account if the compression type is available on common modern Web browsers or if your image will be viewed in a more specialized environment requiring another compression file format.

Exercise C

Often you may find yourself asked to use the source file of a high-quality printed document to publish a companion piece on the Internet. In order to do so, you will need to optimize the file for use online. Propose a strategy to optimize one of the images found in the document by stating first the type of file the image would be in the source file and by stating the type of file it would be following your optimization strategy.

COLOR SPACE AND DIGITAL PHOTOGRAPHY

As discussed briefly earlier in this chapter as well as in Chapter 11, a color space should also be assigned to your digital image. In order to properly prepare a photograph taken by a digital camera for your layout, you will need to determine whether the photograph will be used for a print or Web or screen-based document. Your decision will determine which color space (CMYK or RGB) should be assigned.

PRINT COLOR SPACE

CMYK

The CMYK color space is derived from the four colors of ink professional printers use (in combination) to create the seemingly infinite variety of colors necessary to reproduce a high-quality image on paper. Rather than requiring a printer to have on hand millions of possible colors to match whatever color might be contained within an image, the printer needs only cyan (C), magenta (M), yellow (Y), or black (K).

WEB OR SCREEN-BASED COLOR SPACE

RGB

The RGB color space is derived from three colors used (in combination) to display the variety of colors for screen-based media. You may recall early video projectors, which appeared to have three lenses focused on a screen. Each of the three lenses projected the same image, except one lens projected the image using red color information, another green color information, and another blue color information. Each lens was focused on the same location on the screen and when viewed together, combined to offer a realistic full-color image. Today, your color monitor (whether it is a more conventional CRT type monitor or modern LCD monitor) still relies on this type of technology to display color.

Selecting a color space, which can easily be done in image-editing software such as Adobe's Photoshop CS4, will be a task that you will need to perform when working with digital images. Depending on the type of digital camera used to capture your image, the CMYK or RGB color space may already be assigned. If you do not assign the appropriate color space to your image, you may end up sending an RGB image to your printer, who will attempt to reproduce that image using the CMYK color space. Or you may display a CMYK image on an RGB screen display. Either way, allowing the end user's technology to display an inappropriate color space will result in a lack of control over what the image will look like in the end. Taking a moment to select the color space while the image is still in your hands will allow you to see if the choice results in a change in the image quality and to make any color adjustments before your audience views your document.

EDITING PHOTOGRAPHS FOR USE IN YOUR DOCUMENT LAYOUTS

Just as personal computers have found their way into all aspects of office environments, the development of desktop publishing and image-editing software has affected the nature of document designers' work. In the past, document designers may have been responsible for writing content, selecting images, and creating layouts ready for print, but specialists were responsible for performing the various activities that would ensure a quality printed document. Today, due to the availability of personal computers and desktop publishing software, many document designers will find themselves preparing their documents from the concept stage all the way through to the delivery of print-ready packaged files.

This section does not detail all of these activities but instead focuses on the most common tasks related to working with digital images in your document layouts. These include cropping images, resizing images, and adjusting images for color, brightness, and contrast. This section identifies why these tasks are useful, providing you with a vocabulary of tools that you can investigate more fully through help offered by your image-editing software or any number of digital imaging resources that can be found using the Internet.

Cropping Images

Before a photograph is taken, often the subject of the photograph will be framed by a viewfinder or display screen found on the back of many a digital camera. In ideal circumstances, the viewfinder or display screen shows exactly what you are attempting to photograph, yet often when the image is viewed in the context of the document layout in which it will appear, you will notice that an element is out of place or should be more prominent. Rather than gathering all of the resources necessary to reshoot the image, you may instead take advantage of tools offered by image-editing software such as Adobe Photoshop CS4.

One tool available to you in image-editing software is the *crop* tool. The crop tool allows you to select only the desired area of an image, thereby focusing your viewer's attention rather than leaving your intent undefined. The crop tool has origins in conventional photography. The procedure for developing a photograph in a darkroom involved mounting paper in an easel with an adjustable frame, allowing you to print only the desired area of the photograph. The frame and easel combination allowed the cropping operation to be performed systematically multiple times during printing rather than by carefully cutting the photograph with scissors following printing.

Cropping is a useful image-editing tool for document designers because you may find that your library of images to select from may be provided through stock photo agencies or libraries of images you or your company uses as resources. Notice that each of these resources would contain images that were not originally taken with your project in mind. Therefore, you may find in your image resources an image that meets 85% of the requirements of your project. Removing the 15% of the image that doesn't meet your project's requirements can be performed through cropping your image (see, for example, Figure 10.5).

Exercise D

Pick a digital image and use Photoshop (or other image-editing software) to crop the image to focus attention on a specific element within the image. (In Photoshop you would select the Crop tool from the Toolbar and click and drag across the image to make your crop selection.) Use Figure 10.5 as a reference.

Figure 10.5(a)

Figure 10.5(b)

FIGURE 10.5 Example of (a) uncropped and (b) cropped image, focusing audience attention on a specific element of the image. (Visit www.pearsonhighered.com/riley to view this figure in color.)

FIGURE 10.6   Cropped image from Figure 10.5b resized to a larger image. (Visit www.pearsonhighered. com/riley to view this figure in color.)

Resizing Images

Image size can be a hard-to-define aspect of digital imaging. In your digital image requests, you should specify requirements about the future use of the image. Your photographer will need to modify the technique used to capture the image if it is destined for a billboard in Times Square rather than as a header image on a corporate report printed on letter-size paper. If you want a high-quality source image that can be adapted to a wide variety of future uses, your image requests should yield images containing as many pixels as you can afford and may have unspecified image dimensions. Most often, these large images will need to be resized for your document layout.

Digital image-editing software is well suited to this task, with most software offering an Image Size adjustment within the main interface selections. This tool allows you to select dimensions in pixels and inches as well as to set the PPI of the resulting image (see Figure 10.6). Although image-editing software makes it easy to resize images, it is also easy to inadvertently change the *aspect ratio* of an image when resizing it. The aspect ratio of an image refers to the height and width dimensions of an image. If you resize an image without maintaining its aspect ratio, the image will become distorted by squeezing or stretching its original proportional dimensions (see Figure 10.7). Most image-editing software makes it easy to avoid this by offering an option when resizing called "maintain aspect ratio." Another way of avoiding changing the aspect ratio of an image is to use a keyboard shortcut such as the Shift key when clicking and dragging an image boundary when resizing an image in Photoshop CS4 or Microsoft Word. Review the Help sections of your image-editing software to determine the best way to avoid changing the aspect ratio of images when resizing.

FIGURE 10.7   Cropped image from Figure 10.5b resized to a larger image without maintaining the aspect ratio of the original image. The resulting image is distorted, since the width of the image has been stretched. (Visit www.pearsonhighered.com/riley to view this figure in color.)

Resizing images is a task you will find yourself performing over and over, especially in the current media environment, where the variety of possible destinations—print, Web, mobile devices, and so on—all require adjustments to image size in order for them to properly display. Also, research into how images attract audience attention points to reasons why their use and your knowledge in properly using images in your documents will prove invaluable.

For example, research by Poynter (2004) about online photos indicates that a larger photo size (at least 210 × 230 pixels for online photos) increases the percentage of users seeing photos and the time they spend looking at them, on both home pages and article-level pages. Further observations from this study include the following:

1. Faces in photos draw users' eyes.
2. Multiple faces in photos attract more viewers.
3. A minority of users routinely click on photographs.

Taking research such as this into account, you can begin to determine what size your image should be as well as which elements you might want to focus your audience attention on through the use of the crop tool described in the previous section.

Exercise E

Pick a digital image and use Photoshop CS4 or other image-editing software to resize the image by selecting the appropriate tool for your software and adjusting the image following the process described by your software. (In Photoshop CS4, select Transform from the Edit Menu, click on the bounding edges of the image, and click and drag to resize.) Make sure to maintain the aspect ratio of the original image in your resized image. Use Figure 10.6 as a reference.

Exercise F

Pick a digital image and use Photoshop CS4 or other image-editing software to resize the image by selecting the appropriate tool for your software and adjusting the image following the process described by your software. (In Photoshop CS4, select Transform from the Edit Menu, click on the bounding edges of the image, and click and drag to resize.) Deliberately distort the aspect ratio of the original image in your resized image. Use Figure 10.7 as a reference. Compare your results from Exercises E and F.

Adjusting Image Color, Brightness, Contrast, and Other Features

Image-editing software provides tools for modifying digital images, including color, brightness, and contrast, among many others. Each tool has been developed out of some need defined by developers or users or arose out of the transition from conventional to digital photography.

FIGURE 10.8   Demonstrations of before and after adjustments to color, brightness, and contrast. (Visit www.pearsonhighered.com/riley to view this figure in color.)

Some tools may prove quite useful to document designers, such as color adjustment that allows you to remove the color information so that an image can be used in a black-and-white document when a budget is reduced and full-color printing is no longer possible. Image-brightness adjustment is often useful when cropping an image and focusing user attention on what was once a secondary element of the image. Because the secondary element was not the primary focus of the original image, it may not have been properly lit for its new role. A quick adjustment of image brightness can easily add the needed highlight required to catch the viewer's eye. Adjusting contrast, another common modification of digital images, can provide an ultra-real look to an otherwise conventional image, thereby attracting your viewer's attention (see Figure 10.8 for examples of image adjustments).

Exercise G

Pick a digital image and use Photoshop CS4 or other image-editing software to automatically adjust the brightness and contrast settings of the image. (In Photoshop CS4, select Auto Contrast from the Image Menu.) Notice the effect the Auto Contrast selection had on your image. Discuss whether the Auto Contrast selection produced acceptable results.

Exercise H

Pick a digital image and use Photoshop CS4 or other image-editing software to resize the image by selecting the appropriate tool for your software and adjusting the image following the process described by your software. (In Photoshop CS4, select Adjustments from the Image Menu and click on Brightness/Contrast.) Notice the different effect on the image that the brightness or contrast adjustments make. Reassess whether the Auto Contrast selection produced acceptable results.

Exercise I

Repeat Exercises G and H using Tone adjustments and Color adjustments. Discuss whether the automatic adjustments provided by your software produce acceptable results.

Conclusion

This chapter has introduced only a few of the many tools offered for image manipulation when using digital imaging software such as Adobe Photoshop. In order to become comfortable using these tools, it is best to select some images for experimentation and witness the effect on your image that each tool offers. Many tools will seem useless to you and your responsibilities as a document designer, but it may be helpful to know that of the many tools available, the six briefly described in this chapter are those that are most often used. Through practice with these tools, you will be able to learn quite quickly the fundamentals of working with digital imaging software and will be prepared to learn the nuances of other available tools.

Summary of Key Concepts and Terms

aspect ratio	GIF	optimize	PNG
crop	JPEG	pixel	resolution
dots per inch (DPI)	megapixel	pixels per inch (PPI)	TIFF
file size			

Review Questions

1. When choosing an image to be used in a document, which of the following strategies is better? Explain your choice.
   a. Start with an image with more pixels that you can reduce using software such as Adobe Photoshop.
   b. Start with an image with fewer pixels.
2. For a digital image to be used on a Web site, which resolution would you choose? Explain your choice.
   a. 300 DPI
   b. 72 PPI
   c. 72 DPI
3. For a digital image to be used in a high-quality printed document, which file type would you choose? Explain your choice.
   a. TIFF at 150 PPI
   b. TIFF at 300 DPI
   c. JPEG at 300 PPI
4. For a digital image to be used in a high-quality printed document, which color space would you choose? Explain your choice.
   a. RGB
   b. CMYK
5. Describe why a printer would require your source file for a high-quality printed document to be formatted in the CMYK color space.
6. Which of the following tasks would you use to focus attention on a selected area of a digital image? Explain your choice.
   a. Resize the image
   b. Crop the image
7. Which of the following tasks would you carry out to provide a larger image for your document or Web page? Explain your choice.
   a. Resize the image
   b. Crop the image

Additional Exercise

This chapter discussed powerful software allowing you to modify and edit images for use in your documents. This ability to edit images opens the door to ethical issues you may not have considered. For example, on June 27, 1994, *Time Magazine* and *Newsweek Magazine* ran the same image of O. J. Simpson's mug shot. *Time Magazine* digitally altered the image, resulting in criticism from many sources. Locate the cover images (search online or in your university library's archives) and discuss the ethical issues that arise. Also discuss the motives behind the decision of *Time Magazine* to digitally alter the image. Review Harris (1991) and Lowrey (2003) to inform your discussion.

Using Color

To use color effectively in your print or online documents, you should know something about color's properties, the psychological and physiological responses it generates, and its cultural association. You should also know its effects on accessibility, that is, the effects it has on users' ability to perceive and comprehend your documents. This chapter explains basic color theory, particularly color properties and color systems. It discusses how you can employ color to increase usability, including accessibility. In addition, it discusses color management and offers advice from an art director, a graphic artist, and a printer to explain what technical communicators should know about color to work effectively with professional printers.

By the end of the chapter, you should be able to do the following:

- Understand color properties and color systems
- Use color to increase document readability and accessibility
- Use color to focus users' attention, associate elements of a document, prioritize different elements of a document, and signal organization
- Manage color effectively
- Communicate with printers about the printing process

OVERVIEW OF RELEVANT DESIGN CONCEPTS AND PRINCIPLES

On a very basic level, we can divide our understanding of color into two categories: theory and practice. Knowing something about color theory can help you understand the underlying, universal principles that will govern the rhetorical situations of your print and online documents. Understanding color theory—at least the basics—will help you in your practice of using color effectively. Figure 11.1 diagrams theoretical and practical knowledge about color that is of interest to technical and professional communicators. In an important article about using color in technical documents, White (1991/2003) focuses mainly on four branches of this diagram; these four fall under the "creating

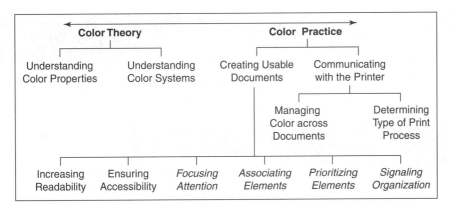

FIGURE 11.1 Theoretical and practical knowledge about color.

usable documents" node (and appear in italics in Figure 11.1). In this chapter, we examine all the branches.

WHY THESE PRINCIPLES ARE IMPORTANT

Used carefully and thoughtfully, color can substantially contribute to effective design. Color can be used to enhance the clarity and usability of a document, for example, by calling attention to important information and making it easier for readers to find. Color can be used to unify the internal elements of a document; for example, when the same color is used for similar elements in the document, readers will understand that those elements share something in common. In addition to its functional uses, color has a powerful emotional effect and can, therefore, be an effective tool for creating the desired tone and aesthetic appeal. For all these reasons, it is critical to understand the fundamentals of using color in document design.

UNDERSTANDING BASIC COLOR THEORY

It is easy to be put off by mention of theory, but in this case, a little bit of theory can go a long way. For example, understanding the properties of color could help you choose a more accessible color combination and then explain that choice to others.

The Properties of Color

Essentially, as Sir Isaac Newton showed when he split a beam of white light with a spectrum, colors are wavelengths of light. Objects around us absorb and reflect different wavelengths of light, and we perceive the reflected ones as color. These visible wavelengths—the visible light spectrum, as opposed to ultraviolet light and infrared light—are the wavelengths to which we attach names: red, orange, yellow, green, blue, indigo, and violet. You have, of course, heard these color terms before, but what you may not know is that these terms refer to just one of three color properties that together create the different colors we perceive. That is, color has three properties: hue, value, and saturation. Terms such as *red* and *green* refer to a color's *hue* (also called pigment). Nonspecialists tend to use the terms *color* and *hue* interchangeably, but when you begin differentiating between color and hue and using the terms correctly, you will be able to discuss your rhetorical and design intentions more precisely. Figure 11.2 displays a spectrum of hues.

Differentiating between color and hue is important because two different colors can have the same hue. For example, Figure 11.3 shows an array of colors, all with the same hue. These colors differ not in hue, but in *value*. Value is a property of color that is

FIGURE 11.2 A spectrum of hues. (Visit www.pearsonhighered.com/riley to see this figure in color.)

FIGURE 11.3 Colors with identical hue but different value. (Visit www.pearsonhighered.com/riley to see this figure in color.)

FIGURE 11.4 Colors with identical hue and value but different saturation. (Visit www. pearsonhighered.com/riley to see this figure in color.)

also called *lightness,* or *luminance.* Value is related to the amount of light a color reflects. Low-value colors appear more blackish, and higher value colors appear whitish; therefore, pastels are high-value colors.

The third property of color is *saturation* (also called *chroma*). Saturation is the degree to which a hue is present. In conceptualizing saturation, it helps to think of ink being absorbed into paper. The more ink, the more saturated the paper becomes. Saturation is usually measured as purity in relation to gray. Figure 11.4 shows colors with identical hue and value but varying saturation (from more gray to more green).

By understanding these three properties—hue, value, and saturation—you will be able to specify and analyze differences among colors and communicate better with printers (and other designers too) because you understand their language.

Exercise A

How do the colors in each set below differ—in hue, saturation, or value?

1.

2.

(Visit www.pearsonhighered.com/riley to see this figure in color.)

FIGURE 11.5   Itten's color wheel. (Visit www.pearsonhighered.com/riley to see this figure in color.)

Widely Used Color Systems

Understanding the basics of color theory also means knowing a bit about color systems. Color systems are tools for understanding relationships among colors and color combinations. You are probably familiar with one useful tool for systematizing color already: a color wheel. One of the most popular color wheels was developed by Johannes Itten and later published in his popular book *The Art of Color* (1963). Itten's color wheel displays how colors contrast in hue (see Figure 11.5).

Itten's color wheel, often called the mixing color wheel because of its use to painters, contains 12 hues and is based on the primary hues red, yellow, and blue. Itten's wheel is particularly useful for analyzing combinations. For example, hues across from each other on the wheel are *complementary colors*. Two complementary colors contrast, making each other look brighter and, thus, more aesthetically pleasing. Complementary colors such as blue and orange often appear together in corporate logos because they contrast so well.

Itten's color wheel also helps in understanding why *analogous colors*, colors next to each other on the color wheel, are attractive together. Analogous colors such as the three colors at the bottom of Itten's wheel in Figure 11.5 are similar and, thus, harmonize. Myriad other relationships among colors exist, and the wheel helps explain why some combinations are aesthetically pleasing and others are not.

Though Itten contributed enormously to our understanding of color, his system is not the one most professionals in graphic and online design use today. Itten based his wheel on red, yellow, and blue, but two other color systems are more common (and likely more important to you). The first, the *RGB* (red, green, blue) color system, applies to documents viewed on screen. As it turns out, all the colors that human beings see can be produced from red, green, and blue. These three hues are this system's primaries. The RGB system is also called the direct color system because it systematizes colors produced by light we see directly, as opposed to colors we perceive based on light that is absorbed. In this system, red and blue together create magenta, red and green together create yellow, and blue and green together create cyan. Red, green, and blue together create white, as shown in Figure 11.6.

If you design documents for online display, you will definitely need to understand the RGB color system. Even if you intend to produce mainly print documents, you will still need to understand the RGB color system because you will write and design

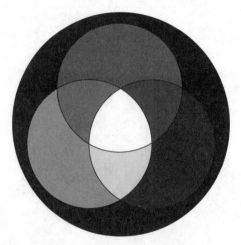

FIGURE 11.6 The RGB color system, in which red, green, and blue together create white. (Visit www.pearsonhighered.com/riley to see this figure in color.)

documents on a computer screen before printing them on the desktop or packaging them for professional printing.

If you intend to design documents for print, it's equally important that you have an understanding of the *CMYK* (cyan, magenta, yellow, black) color system. This system, based on hues secondary to red, green, and blue, is based on light that is absorbed (i.e., subtracted). Cyan absorbs red light, magenta absorbs green light, and yellow absorbs blue light. In this system, adding one hue to the other makes a darker hue. So, adding magenta and cyan together creates blue. All three hues together, in theory, absorb all light and generate black, as shown in Figure 11.7.

We have to say that cyan, magenta, and yellow added together create black "in theory" because in practice (in real-world print shops, for instance) the three do not necessarily make a black that is black enough for the printer's and the client's purpose. Therefore, printers and designers reconfigured the system to accept additions of more black (the K in CMYK represents "black" but stands for *key)* to achieve the dark black they want. In addition, using black ink makes it possible to use just one ink to create black rather than mixing cyan, magenta, and yellow to get the same or even less satisfactory results.

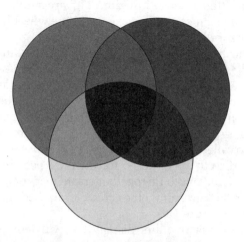

FIGURE 11.7 Cyan, magenta, and yellow together create black (in theory). (Visit www.pearsonhighered.com/riley to see this figure in color.)

Exercise B

What hues combine to make green in the CMYK color system?

One reason that it is important to understand basic differences between the RGB and the CMYK systems, particularly differences in our perception of color from light within the two systems, is the difference in the range of colors—the *gamut*—each produces. Monitors display a gamut of RGB colors, and inks and toners on print documents display a gamut of their own, but these ranges are not identical. When you use color in your print documents, you need to account for the difference between RGB colors that you see on your screen and the CMYK colors that you want to achieve in print. That is, moving from online to print or from print to online may generate color shifts. For example, an online yellow may look quite different in print.

Exercise C

Explain in your own words the difference between the RGB and the CMYK color systems.

INCREASING READABILITY WITH CONTRASTING COLORS

When you choose background color for your print and online documents, one of your main concerns will be readability, especially the degree to which verbal and visual elements show up in relation to the colors "behind" them. Readability research makes clear that a document's background and its foreground elements, particularly its verbal elements, must contrast. That is, for foreground elements to be salient, they must be salient in relation to their background. Readability research shows that regardless of color combination, more contrast equates to greater readability in print (Bruce & Foster, 1982; Radl, 1980) and online (Hill & Scharff, 1999).

It is possible to be more specific about background-text color choices, however, by turning to research on online documents. In studies of Web pages, *positive polarity*, the contrast of dark text on a light background, has been found to be more readable than *negative polarity*, or light text on a dark background (Shieh & Lin, 2000; Wang, Fang, & Chen, 2003). See Figures 11.8 and 11.9 for examples.

That said, to employ contrast effectively, you can do more than eyeball different hues for contrast; instead, you can put your knowledge about color and its components— hue, value, and saturation—to work in choosing contrasting background and foreground elements. Indeed, differentiating the properties of color is important in light of research that makes it clear that value accounts for readability as much or even more than hue, as was previously thought (Lin, 2003). For example, two versions of negative polarity design, white text on a black background and light blue text on a dark blue background, were found to be equally readable, even though the light blue on dark

Ethanol, when produced correctly, performs effectively. It can be made from any biological feedstock that contains appreciable sugar or materials that can be converted into sugar, such as starch or cellulose. Corn is a popular feedstock for creating ethanol because it contains a large amount of starch that can be easily converted to sugar.

FIGURE 11.8 Positive polarity. (Visit www.pearsonhighered.com/riley to see this figure in color.)

Ethanol, when produced correctly, performs effectively. It can be made from any biological feedstock that contains appreciable sugar or materials that can be converted into sugar, such as starch or cellulose. Corn is a popular feedstock for creating ethanol because it contains a large amount of starch that can be easily converted to sugar.

FIGURE 11.9 Negative polarity. (Visit www.pearsonhighered.com/riley to see this figure in color.)

blue version contrasted in value rather than hue (Hall & Hanna, 2004, p. 192). On the other hand, as Figure 11.10 shows, two colors may contrast starkly in hue but may not generate readable text if they do not contrast in value.

Saturation plays a role in readability as well. More saturation in foreground text can generate greater contrast, as Figure 11.11 shows.

In short, taking all three components of color into consideration will enable you to create maximally readable documents.

Ethanol, when produced correctly, performs effectively. It can be made from any biological feedstock that contains appreciable sugar or materials that can be converted into sugar, such as starch or cellulose. Corn is a popular feedstock for creating ethanol because it contains a large amount of starch that can be easily converted to sugar.

FIGURE 11.10 Contrasting hues in text and background. (Visit www.pearsonhighered.com/riley to see this figure in color.)

Ethanol, when produced correctly, performs effectively. It can be made from any biological feedstock that contains appreciable sugar or materials that can be converted into sugar, such as starch or cellulose. Corn is a popular feedstock for creating ethanol because it contains a large amount of starch that can be easily converted to sugar.

FIGURE 11.11 Violet text (with more saturation) against light violet background (with less saturation). (Visit www.pearsonhighered.com/riley to see this figure in color.)

Exercise D

1. Rank the readability of these four text boxes (A–D).
2. How do your answers compare to the research findings just discussed?

A. Ethanol, when produced correctly, performs effectively. It can be made from any biological feedstock that contains appreciable sugar or materials that can be converted into sugar, such as starch or cellulose. Corn is a popular feedstock for creating ethanol because it contains a large amount of starch that can be easily converted to sugar.

B. Ethanol, when produced correctly, performs effectively. It can be made from any biological feedstock that contains appreciable sugar or materials that can be converted into sugar, such as starch or cellulose. Corn is a popular feedstock for creating ethanol because it contains a large amount of starch that can be easily converted to sugar.

C. Ethanol, when produced correctly, performs effectively. It can be made from any biological feedstock that contains appreciable sugar or materials that can be converted into sugar, such as starch or cellulose. Corn is a popular feedstock for creating ethanol because it contains a large amount of starch that can be easily converted to sugar.

D. Ethanol, when produced correctly, performs effectively. It can be made from any biological feedstock that contains appreciable sugar or materials that can be converted into sugar, such as starch or cellulose. Corn is a popular feedstock for creating ethanol because it contains a large amount of starch that can be easily converted to sugar.

(Visit www.pearsonhighered.com/riley to see this figure in color.)

INCREASING USABILITY WITH COLOR

Certainly, good readability is critical to document usability, but by making good choices about color, you can improve usability in other ways.

Attracting Attention and Facilitating Searches

Prior research attests to the ability of color to attract attention (D'Zmura, 1991; Wickens & Hollands, 2000). In a study of people's ability to locate target words in a list of colored target and colored nontarget words, text color significantly affected search time, and not surprisingly, when participants knew the target color, their search times significantly decreased (Nes, Juola, & Moonen, 1987). Clearly, because human beings are limited in the amount of stimulus that they can process at one time, they must be selective in what they focus on, and they must ignore, or filter (Ashcraft, 1998), competing stimuli. Used effectively, color can help them in the process.

You can employ color, in addition to text size, shape, and weight, to attract readers' attention and to help them find information. For example, Figure 11.12 shows a newsletter that employs color to attract attention and to facilitate readers' searches for information. Color facilitates readers' searches for information in the newsletter in Figure 11.12 in that the color of the "faculty" watermark is echoed in the background color of the left-hand column. The blue used for the word "faculty" in the vertically

faculty

Hamid Arastoopour

Hamid Arastoopour (M.S. GE '75, Ph.D. '78), director of the Wanger Institute for Sustainable Energy Research, was invested as the Henry R. Linden Endowed Chair in Engineering at a ceremony held on April 30.

Alan Cramb

Alan Cramb, provost and senior vice president for academic affairs, has been named an honorary member of the American Institute of Mining, Metallurgical, and Petroleum Engineers (AIME). An AIME past-president, Cramb was recognized for being a member who is outstanding in his respective field and/or who has performed unusual service to the institute. Cramb was also named a 2009 fellow of the American Society for Metals International for his efforts in advancing the science and technology of modern steelmaking.

Martin Felsen

Martin Felsen, studio associate professor at IIT College of Architecture, was awarded the 2009 Latrobe Prize from the American Institute of Architects' College of Fellows.

Judith Gregory

Judith Gregory, assistant professor at IIT Institute of Design, was appointed to a multi-year visiting scholar position at the University of Denmark.

Taking Sustainability on the Road

IIT and Chicago are natural partners who share a strong commitment to serving the city's people and communities. Now the university hopes to build upon those shared goals by focusing its unique resources—including architecture, engineering, and design—on projects that will benefit IIT's neighbors, further strengthening the university's ties with the city.

As a collaboration between IIT College of Architecture and the Chicago Park District shows, the results can be stunning.

Project Nomad, a mobile learning center, is serving as a testament to the possibilities of eco-friendly living and modern architecture. Specifically, it's an interactive exhibit that takes cues from Mies van der Rohe's iconic Farnsworth House and showcases green technologies ranging from photovoltaic solar panels (a set of them is mounted on Project Nomad's roof, providing the exhibit's electricity) to recycling. Nomad will rotate among city parks, educating Chicagoans on the benefits of sustainability.

"The primary goal is to reach low-income urban families who aren't really thinking about living green or experiencing nature," says Alan Bell, the Chicago attorney whose company, The Elements Group, is spearheading the project. "Some of the areas where these people live aren't the most beautiful, architecturally. We want to bring them something modern, innovative, and exciting that will brighten up their communities and get them thinking about experiencing nature and the environment in a whole new way."

Bell explained his vision to Eva Kultermann, assistant professor of architecture, who loved the idea and suggested making it a student project. Bell agreed, and during the 2008–09 school year teams of students worked on developing and refining a design that would be striking, functional, and portable. In addition to the solar panels, the design incorporates recycled, Earth-friendly materials.

The students' design was a hit with Bell, the Chicago Park District, and the audience at Modern Earth, the Earth Day 2009 event where the project was unveiled. Project Nomad then moved to Krueck + Sexton Architects, which will oversee the exhibit's final design and construction. The firm hired one of the IIT student leaders for a summer internship to work on the project.

"The project provided our students with experience in the complete process of building design and construction in a more comprehensive and real-world setting than is possible in traditional academic studios," says Kultermann. "Additionally, it provided an educational platform for the ethical practice of architecture by serving the needs of the local community."

Construction should be complete in late 2009, and Project Nomad is on track to begin its tour of Chicago's parks in spring 2010.

—*Steve Hendershot*

MVOV RESEARCH AND CHICAGO

http://airwaterearthsun.com/html/community/project_nomad.php

FIGURE 11.12 A newsletter that effectively employs color. Source: *IIT Magazine*. Copyright Illinois Institute of Technology. Used by permission. (Visit www.pearsonhighered.com/riley to see this figure in color.)

Overview	Policies	Car title

Overview

Vehicle insurance is a contract between an individual and an insurance company. It protects against loss in the case of an accident. Individuals make payments to insurance companies on a regular basis, and these companies agree to pay for individuals' losses when accidents occur. Insurance on vehicles covers the following losses: (1) damage to the vehicle, (2) theft of the vehicle, (3) damage an individual causes to another person's property, (4) legal responsibility of an individual for bodily injury to another person, and (5) lost wages.

TIP:
Remember low-cost insurance isn't? always (or even usually) best.

Policies

TIP:
Check with your insurance agent about the duration of your policy.

Insurance: An agreement with a company that periodic payment will guarantee a large payment when necessary, such as an accident.

An insurance policy is a legal document that manages risk of loss. Insurance distributes potential risk from an individual to a group of individuals in exchange for a payment. Individuals pay to avoid a large loss.

Car title

Title: A document distributed by the city that shows ownership of a particular make and model.

A car title relates to the person or business that legally owns a vehicle. Car titles are issued in the United States by a state's Department of Motor Vehicles Car titles are not standardized across different states in the United States. However, they do relate the same basic information. For example, they state the vehicle's identification number, make, and the year of manufacture. They also state the license plate number, the vehicle's weight, and the vehicle's price.

FIGURE 11.13 Use of color in level-one and level-two headings and in text boxes. Source: http://en.wikipedia.org/wiki/Insurance. (Visit www.pearsonhighered.com/riley to see this figure in color.)

oriented text is also used for the names of individual faculty members in the left-hand column. The use of blue for the faculty names also serves to separate them visually from the surrounding text and helps readers quickly locate each faculty member's news item.

Unifying and Organizing Document Elements

White (1991/2003) points out that coloring verbal elements such as headings and visual elements such as text boxes or icons allows readers to comprehend relations among document elements more efficiently. As Figure 11.13 shows, you could use one color (e.g., purple) for a first-level heading, such as "Overview," and another color (e.g., blue) for second-level headings, such as "Policies" and "Car title" in Figure 11.13. You could use a light yellow background in all text boxes that provide tips for using a product and a light blue background in all text boxes that display a definition.

This strategy visually signals the kind of content in front of the reader and unifies the document as a whole visually, connecting different content in different chapters or sections of your document.

White notes that user manuals—which can be quite lengthy—become less daunting if their authors use color to subdivide them into segments (1991/2003, p. 487). Winn (1991) says that "color cueing" (exploiting color to group information) can clarify a document's structure (p. 183). Figure 11.14 illustrates how you could use color in headings to signal that all pages belong to the same section. The same strategy would work with level-two and level-three headings, too.

Using color in headings signals the level of generality of the text and, therefore, eases readers' comprehension of the text. Similarly, color also allows sections of a document to be associated, or grouped together. For example, you can use colored tabs to group content and make a document more searchable as well. Figure 11.15 also shows how the authors used *bleed tabs*. In these tabs that group content, color meets the edge of the page, or in other words, "bleeds" off the page. Figure 11.15 shows the use of bleed tabs in a telephone directory, a strategy that helps users to find alphabetical listings more quickly.

Chassis maintenance

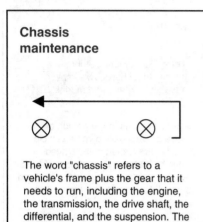

The word "chassis" refers to a vehicle's frame plus the gear that it needs to run, including the engine, the transmission, the drive shaft, the differential, and the suspension. The body of the vehicle is built on the chassis. You'll need to take several steps to maintain the chassis.

Chassis maintenance

All parts of the chassis require thorough, periodic cleaning. You should clean all parts, including the rod ends, A-arms, coil-over dampers, and so on, with WD-40 or some other water-displacing spray throughout the life of the vehicle. You should clean these parts by hand with a soft towel.

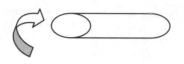

Chassis maintenance

You should also check the torque of the bolts and nuts on a regular basis (about every 15,000 miles). You should pay particular attention to checking the torque of the bolts and nuts if you use your vehicle on roads kept in poor conditions. For example, after the winter in northern Wisconsin and Minnesota, roads are generally in poor condition and warrant a check of the bolts and nuts. Also, use of the vehicle on dirt roads with washboard surfaces warrants a check.

FIGURE 11.14 Using (purple) color to unify a document section. Source: www.jblmotor.com/JBLmaint.html. (Visit www.pearsonhighered.com/riley to see this figure in color.)

PSYCHOLOGICAL AND PHYSIOLOGICAL RESPONSES TO COLOR

It has long been a standard practice to discuss people's color perceptions and preferences in terms of temperature, particularly warm—red orange, and yellow—and cool—blue, green, and violet (Sutherland & Karg, 2003). Discussing colors in terms of temperature—warm and cool—harkens back to "archetypal human experiences" (Gage, 1999, p. 22). As Wierzbicka (1990) points out, we think of yellow as warm because of the sun, and we think of red as warm because of fire. In fact, in a cross-cultural study of color meanings, red was rated as "hot" by participants from diverse cultures (Madden, Hewett, & Roth, 2000, p. 98). In 1810, Johann Wolfgang von Goethe published

FIGURE 11.15 Bleed tabs used to group sections of a telephone directory. (Visit www.pearsonhighered.com/riley to see this figure in color.)

Theory of Colors, in which he discussed warm and cool colors. In using such terms, Goethe, unlike Newton, considered the role of psychology—the mind's perception of and reaction to color—as opposed to thinking about color solely in terms of wavelengths. Empirical research shows that different colors generate different psychological and physiological responses.

Research suggests that warm colors generate quite different psychological responses than cool colors. Warm colors are considered more arousing (Bellizzi & Hite, 1992; Cahoon, 1969) and active (Aaronson, 1970; Madden et al., 2000; Richards & David, 2005). They lead to higher levels of anxiety (Jacobs & Suess, 1975; Profusek & Rainey, 1987) and greater levels of distraction (Gerard, 1957).

Warm colors also appear to have greater ability than do cool colors to draw attention (Danger, 1969), which is the reason behind advice to use warm colors to emphasize and to make main points (Jones, 1997). You need only think of a highlighting pen—often bright yellow—or danger warnings—usually incorporating red with black—to understand how warm colors attract attention and, consequently, lend emphasis. That said, a study of color's effect on people's ability to search for different shapes in an onscreen array showed that green shapes were located most quickly; beige and peach generated the slowest search times (Jansson, Marlow, & Bristow, 2004, p. 187). In addition, green and blue targets were most accurately located. The researchers note that culture likely played a role in their results. Their participants were from the United Kingdom, and thus the results may not be generalizable to non-Western cultures. Regardless of the colors you use to attract attention, remember to contrast their hue, value, and saturation.

Cool colors like blue and green, on the other hand, are perceived to be peaceful and calm (Bellizzi & Hite, 1992; Madden et al., 2000; Sharpe, 1974) and relaxing and pleasant (Bellizzi & Hite, 1992). For example Gorn, Chattopadhyay, Sengupta, and Tripathi (2004) studied the effect of color on Web users' perceptions of download times. They found that screen hue (blue or red) had a significant effect on perception of download time: A blue hue correlated with perception of a quicker download time, as opposed to red screens (p. 219). Such responses are likely part of the reason that cool colors were found to be more attractive than warm colors in retail environments (Bellizzi & Hite, 1992).

Physiological research correlates with that on people's psychological perceptions of color. Measures of moisture on the palm of the hand, called palmar conductance (Wilson, 1966), as well as blood pressure, respiratory rate, eye blink frequency, and galvanic skin response (Gerard, 1958), show that the warm colors yellow and red generate a less relaxed state than blue. According to Clynes (1977), red may be inherently exciting to the human brain, and human evolution could be responsible for these physiological responses.

CULTURAL ASSOCIATIONS OF DIFFERENT HUES

Cross-cultural research on color shows that blue is well liked universally (e.g., Guilford & Smith, 1959; Karpowicz Lazreg & Mullet, 2001; Valdez & Mehrabian, 1995). In fact, people respond so positively to blue that there exists what is called a *blue phenomenon* (Choungourian, 1968; Madden et al., 2000; Simon, 1971). For example, when high school students from 20 countries were asked to evaluate 7 colors, blue was most highly evaluated (Adams & Osgood, 1973). Another study of perceptions of 80 colors by participants from 8 countries found that blue was rated "most liked" by participants from 5 of the 8 countries (Madden et al., p. 95).

Researchers have also examined the meanings that diverse cultures assign to different hues. In a meta-analysis of cross-cultural color research, Aslam (2006) found that blue is associated with "high quality," "corporate," and "masculine" in Anglo-Saxon cultures, but in other cultures it conveys different meanings. For instance, in Malaysia it conveys "evil." Green means "good taste" and "envy" in Anglo-Saxon cultures, but it means "pure" in China and Korea and "love" in Japan (p. 19).

People also assign strong meanings to warm colors. In Anglo-Saxon cultures, yellow conveys "happy," and in Chinese cultures it conveys "pure" and "royal." In Germanic, Slavic, and Japanese cultures, it conveys "envy" and "jealousy" (Aslam, 2006, p. 19). Red means "lucky" in China, Denmark, and Argentina, but "unlucky" in Chad, Nigeria, and Germany (Neal, Quester, & Hawkins, 2002; Schmitt, 1995).

Exercise E

Search for the Web sites of the following banks: Bank of Chile, Bank of Ireland, Bank of Mongolia, Bank of Thailand, and Reserve Bank of Australia. What similarities and differences in color do you see among the Web sites of these banks?

ENSURING ACCESSIBILITY WITH COLOR

Our discussions of contrasting colors and emphasizing information with color allude to the need to make documents—print and online—maximally usable. Yet another component of usability is accessibility, making sure that all users are able to perceive and comprehend all the information from your documents. Your use of color can threaten document accessibility if you do not consider the needs of people who have visual impairments such as partial sight and impairments brought on by aging and congenital deficits. Indeed, some people's impairments may lessen their ability to distinguish among all three color properties. For example, people with deuteranomaly, a difficulty differentiating red and green, may have trouble using a manual that employs colored tabs to group and organize sections and trouble matching a pie chart's wedges to its legend if those visual elements are red and green.

An important step in maintaining the accessibility of all information in your color documents is to ensure that color is not "the only visual means of conveying information, indicating an action, prompting a response, or distinguishing a visual element the information" (Caldwell, Cooper, Reid, & Vanderheiden, 2007). In other words, color should be a redundant or reinforcing means of conveying information. For example, you can design Web site navigation links and tabs in printed manuals so that the information they convey with color is conveyed via other means as well. You could make navigation links both weightier and a different color than other text. And, in addition to using color on a manual's tabs to signal discrete sections, your manual's colored tabs could show an icon or state section names explicitly. In these examples, providing the information conveyed with color through another visual means ensures that users who cannot see color can still perceive the information.

Another important strategy in designing for accessibility is contrasting foreground elements with background, paying attention once again to value. A background and a foreground color that are of equivalent value, even if they differ in hue and saturation, can be less accessible to people who have visual impairments. To distinguish

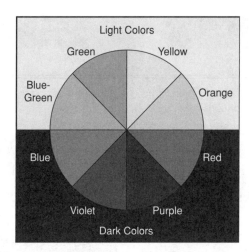

FIGURE 11.16   Arditi's (2005) illustration of "light" and "dark" colors to contrast for accessibility
Copyright Lighthouse International. Used by permission. (Visit www.pearsonhighered.com/riley to see
this figure in color.)

background from foreground color in a manner that enhances accessibility, Aries Arditi,
a researcher with Lighthouse International, recommends first choosing colors that contrast in hue. His illustration of colors that should be contrasted against each other is
shown in Figure 11.16. The hues blue-green, green, yellow, and orange should be contrasted against blue, violet, purple, and red.

The second step in creating contrast is to "lighten the light colors and darken the
dark colors" (Arditi, 2005). Figure 11.17 illustrates how light colors (yellow background
on the left and green background on the right) can be made lighter, and dark colors
(dark blue text on the left and dark purple text on the right) can be made darker to create more contrast.

Among the myriad resources to help Web designers ensure the accessibility of
their sites are the Web Content Accessibility Guidelines 2.0 (WCAG 2.0, 2007). These
guidelines call for designers to "ensure that text and graphics are understandable when
viewed without color" and that colors provide "sufficient contrast." That is, the main
points to remember about using color and maintaining accessibility are these: Use color
redundantly, and use color contrast.

Ethanol, when produced correctly,
performs effectively. It can be made from
any biological feedstock that contains
appreciable sugar or materials that can
be converted into sugar, such as starch
or cellulose. Corn is a popular feedstock
for creating ethanol because it contains
a large amount of starch that can be
easily converted to sugar.

Ethanol, when produced correctly,
performs effectively. It can be made from
any biological feedstock that contains
appreciable sugar or materials that can
be converted into sugar, such as starch
or cellulose. Corn is a popular feedstock
for creating ethanol because it contains
a large amount of starch that can be
easily converted to sugar.

FIGURE 11.17   Examples of Arditi's (2005) accessible color contrasts. (Visit www.pearsonhighered.
com/riley to see this figure in color.)

Exercise F

Rate these text-background color combinations (A–D) in terms of accessibility. Explain your ratings in terms of Arditi's recommendations

A. Color or colour is the visual perceptual property corresponding in humans to the categories called red, yellow, blue, and others. Color derives from the spectrum of light (distribution of light energy versus wavelength) interacting in the eye with the spectral sensitivities of the light receptors. Color categories and physical specifications of color are also associated with objects, materials, light sources, etc., based on their physical properties such as light absorption, reflection, or emission spectra (http://en.wikipedia.org/wiki/Color).

B. Color or colour is the visual perceptual property corresponding in humans to the categories called red, yellow, blue, and others. Color derives from the spectrum of light (distribution of light energy versus wavelength) interacting in the eye with the spectral sensitivities of the light receptors. Color categories and physical specifications of color are also associated with objects, materials, light sources, etc., based on their physical properties such as light absorption, reflection, or emission spectra (http://en.wikipedia.org/wiki/Color).

C. Color or colour is the visual perceptual property corresponding in humans to the categories called red, yellow, blue, and others. Color derives from the spectrum of light (distribution of light energy versus wavelength) interacting in the eye with the spectral sensitivities of the light receptors. Color categories and physical specifications of color are also associated with objects, materials, light sources, etc., based on their physical properties such as light absorption, reflection, or emission spectra (http://en.wikipedia.org/wiki/Color).

D. Color or colour is the visual perceptual property corresponding in humans to the categories called red, yellow, blue, and others. Color derives from the spectrum of light (distribution of light energy versus wavelength) interacting in the eye with the spectral sensitivities of the light receptors. Color categories and physical specifications of color are also associated with objects, materials, light sources, etc., based on their physical properties such as light absorption, reflection, or emission spectra (http://en.wikipedia.org/wiki/Color).

(Visit www.pearsonhighered.com/riley to see this figure in color.)

MANAGING COLOR

Understanding color theory, responses to color, and color usability is useful only to the extent that the colors you intend to use in your document—the ones you see on your screen—are consistent across your documents or with the ones that the printer produces.

To achieve consistency in your color choices, you should manage color carefully throughout the document production process into the *prepress* stage—the stage at which files are checked before they are sent to the printer. An important part of managing color is carefully checking the specific RGB (e.g., R = 89, G = 131, B = 103) or CMYK numbers (e.g., C = 75, M = 24, Y = 65, K = 14) that you choose when using software such as In-Design (in this case, to create a greenish-gray color). Those numbers encode the amount of colorant that you intend. (You can find RGB color settings in Word 2007 when you choose the More Colors option, for example, when you want to change the color of a font or of a text-box border. Then, you should select the Custom tab.)

In relation to documents accessed via monitors and other electronic devices, you should try to control settings within your own organization; however, it is impossible to control how users outside your organization will calibrate their monitors and other devices. Therefore, it is impossible to control exactly how the online document will appear for them. You can manage color on your end, though, by assigning consistent RGB numbers.

Even after carefully choosing CMYK colors for print documents, getting those colors to appear in print can be tricky. This is because the CMYK model is device dependent. For one thing, the gamut of colors that most printers can produce is far more limited than the gamut of color combinations that you can create with a given software application. In addition, the type of press that a professional printer uses and the type of paper that you choose for your document (heavy card stock versus light newsprint, for example) will affect the outcome, even when you have supplied your printer with specific numerical values for your colors. As Fraser, Murphy, and Bunting (2003) write, "CMYK printers still deal with the idiosyncrasies of . . . mashed wood pulp that we call 'paper'" (p. 57).

You can increase your chances of getting the colors that you intend by following the guidelines delineated by Kelly (2007), the president of PDF-specializing Apago Inc. First, prepare your PDF files (as well as your other file types) to common standards. For example, to ensure seamless exchange of color visual elements, use the PDF/X type of PDF rather than the "standard" one that Word produces by default. PDF/X certifies compliance with standards set by the International Organization for Standardization (ISO). Kelly also recommends that you standardize the preferences of the software applications across all computers involved in the creation of your documents. To find other guidelines for ensuring that colors appear as you want them to and that they remain constant across different output devices, consult the sources listed at the end of this chapter.

Exercise G

Use Microsoft Word (or document design software such as InDesign) to determine the colors (e.g., light green) indicated by each combination of numbers.

a. R = 229, G = 138, B = 43
b. R = 97, G = 69, B = 43

TALKING TO PRINTERS ABOUT COLOR

You may be responsible at some point for your organization's document production. To maintain effective workflows and to generate the publication products that you want, you need to speak the language of the people who work in the printing industry. In being able to discuss the printing process, you decrease the likelihood of inconsistent and incorrect colors, as well as print runs that cost more than they should.

Spot Color Versus Process Color

An important factor in creating quality publications is determining whether a document would be better printed with *spot color* or with *process color* (i.e., CMYK color). In contrast to *digital printing*, in *offset printing*, both choices are possible. Digital printing involves layering toner on the surface of the paper; toner, digital printing's "ink," does not absorb into the paper. With digital printing, only process color is possible. Offset printing involves transferring ink from a plate to a rubber blanket and, finally, to the paper.

Spot color refers to inks that are mixed prior to the printing run; they are created according to formulas for specific colors, usually in relation to widely used color systems like *Pantone® Matching System* or *Trumatch®*. For this reason, spot colors are often called "custom colors." Pantone 3258, a shade of green, is one example. Because spot colors are mixed prior to printing, they ensure that important and specific colors, such as colors in corporate logos, appear in print as intended. They are also useful for getting vibrant colors to appear in print. They are necessary for generating fluorescent and metallic colors.

In terms of cost, using spot color may be the better choice when a document contains just one or two colors, including black. (That is, black counts as one color.) Figure 11.18 shows an example of a newsletter that employs two spot colors: black and brown. Besides showing the use of two spot colors, Figure 11.18 also shows the use of a duotone image (the newsletter's photograph of the building). Duotone images use two inks; black and some other color. Such images are more complex than two colors on distinct areas of a page, but

december 2006

our history

In the winter of 2004, I was walking down 31st Street in the Bridgeport neighborhood of Chicago, when I noticed a FOR LEASE sign in the window of a beautiful, old, corner storefront. I thought, "What a great spot for a coffee shop!" My best friends Tom and Ed agreed. Over the next few months, we converted this amazing space into the Bridgeport Coffee House and opened the cafe early in spring.

The coffee house features outdoor seating from April 1st to November 1st, as long as weather permits.

We roast our own coffee daily, and we also serve pastries, toasted sandwiches, ice-cream, shakes, and a good variety of loose leaf teas.

In 2005, we added our wholesale facility which is presently supplying restaurants, cafes, and boutiques in the Chicago area with fresh roasted coffee, Adagio teas, and related equipment. We presently offer equipment manufactured by Wilbur Curtis and Brasilia.

Even though our neighborhood is a little bit off of the beaten path, we are often asked how we will react when large coffee house chains arrive in Bridgeport. Our response is part of our mission statement. We will strive to be more than merchants, rather part of the community and the history of our surroundings. ⤎

featuring:

coffee from Tanzania

music by Chase Faber

art by Kate Perryman

our neighborhood

When visiting a new place, people often wonder about its origins. Where did the name come from? How was the area settled? Who lives here? Well, there is no reason to keep these questions a mystery. Bridgeport's story is rich in Chicago's history, and should be shared with all who visit it.

The name "Bridgeport" originated from the location of the neighborhood. Bridgeport lies next to a bridge which crosses the Chicago River. However, the bridge is too low for boats to pass underneath it, so instead, the cargo from the boats has to be unloaded, loaded on to carts, and then re-loaded back on to bardges, which are waiting on the other side of the bridge.

The neighborhood is bordered on the north by the Chicago River, south by 39th Street, east by the Dan Ryan Express Way (I90) and west by Ashland Avenue. All together, Bridgeport is approximately 3.9 sq. miles.

Other notable trivia about Bridgeport includes the fact that it has been the home of Chicago's 46-year dynasty of mayors from 1933 to 1979 (Edward J. Kelly, Martin Kennelly, Richard J. Daley and Michael Bilandic).

Mayor Richard J. Daley lived his entire life in this neighborhood. When he died, he was living in a modest brick bungalow at 3536 S. Lowe Avenue, in the same block as the house he was born in. His son, Richard M. Daley, the present Mayor of Chicago - is in his 3rd term in office. ⤎

BRIDGEPORT
coffee company

FIGURE 11.18   A newsletter with two spot colors (brown and black) and a duotone image. Design by Rachael Winter. Used by permission. (Visit www.pearsonhighered.com/riley to see this figure in color.)

they do indeed require only two colors. In fact, sepia-toned images, the kind associated with photography from the 1800s, are duotone images.

If a document contains full-color photographs or multicolored graphics, it requires process color. Process refers to the process of combining cyan, magenta, yellow, and black (CMYK) together to create a multicolor image. With process color, a document containing a wide range of colors gets the benefit of CMYK's ability to produce thousands of colors. Figure 11.19 shows an example of a newsletter that contains full-color pictures and employs process color.

december 2006

our history

In the winter of 2004, I was walking down 31st Street in the Bridgeport neighborhood of Chicago, when I noticed a FOR LEASE sign in the window of a beautiful, old, corner storefront. I thought, "What a great spot for a coffee shop!" My best friends Tom and Ed agreed. Over the next few months, we converted this amazing space into the Bridgeport Coffee House and opened the cafe early in spring.

The coffee house features outdoor seating from April 1st to November 1st, as long as weather permits.

We roast our own coffee daily, and we also serve pastries, toasted sandwiches, ice-cream, shakes, and a good variety of loose leaf teas.

In 2005, we added our wholesale facility which is presently supplying restaurants, cafes, and boutiques in the Chicago area with fresh roasted coffee, Adagio teas, and related equipment. We presently offer equipment manufactured by Wilbur Curtis and Brasilia.

Even though our neighborhood is a little bit off of the beaten path, we are often asked how we will react when large coffee house chains arrive in Bridgeport. Our response is part of our mission statement. We will strive to be more than merchants, rather part of the community and the history of our surroundings.

our neighborhood

When visiting a new place, people often wonder about its origins. Where did the name come from? How was the area settled? Who lives here? Well, there is no reason to keep these questions a mystery. Bridgeport's story is rich in Chicago's history, and should be shared with all who visit it.

The name "Bridgeport" originated from the location of the neighborhood. Bridgeport lies next to a bridge which crosses the Chicago River. However, the bridge is too low for boats to pass underneath it, so instead, the cargo from the boats has to be unloaded, loaded on to carts, and then re-loaded back on to bardges, which are waiting on the other side of the bridge.

The neighborhood is bordered on the north by the Chicago River, south by 39th Street, east by the Dan Ryan Express Way (I90) and west by Ashland Avenue. All together, Bridgeport is approximately 3.9 sq. miles.

Other notable trivia about Bridgeport includes the fact that it has been the home of Chicago's 46-year dynasty of mayors from 1933 to 1979 (Edward J. Kelly, Martin Kennelly, Richard J. Daley and Michael Bilandic).

Mayor Richard J. Daley lived his entire life in this neighborhood. When he died, he was living in a modest brick bungalow at 3536 S. Lowe Avenue, in the same block as the house he was born in. His son, Richard M. Daley, the present Mayor of Chicago - is in his 3rd term in office.

BRIDGEPORT
coffee company

FIGURE 11.19   A process color (four-color) newsletter. Design by Rachael Winter. Used by permission. (Visit www.pearsonhighered.com/riley to see this figure in color.)

FIGURE 11.20 Halftones in process color. Design by Rachael Winter. Used by permission. (Visit www.pearsonhighered.com/riley to see this figure in color.)

Sometimes a document might require both process and spot color. For example, to increase the intensity of a particular process color, a printer may suggest adding a spot color.

In process color printing, an image is converted to *halftones*, tiny dots of color. Figure 11.20 shows halftones up close. Set in different angles and overlaid on top of each other, halftones trick our perception. They combine to create color, such as the light blue background color in Figure 11.20.

In process color printing, the halftones of each of the CMYK colors are layered on paper; the CMYK halftones combine to create the appearance of thousands of colors. Figure 11.21 shows how halftones in CMYK combine to create a process color image.

Exercise H

Using about 50 words, explain the difference between spot color and process color.

FIGURE 11.21 CMYK combined to create a process color image. Design by Rachael Winter. Used by permission. (Visit www.pearsonhighered.com/riley to see this figure in color.)

Advice from Printing Professionals

This section reflects the advice of three experts:

- Steve Johnson, president of the Glen Ellyn, Illinois, printing company Copresco, who has worked for more than 35 years in printing
- Mike Mackiewicz, a digital graphic artist with Mark-It Graphics in Osceola, Wisconsin, who has worked for 30 years in graphic production
- Nancy Schoon, who often works with professional printers on her university's publications and has been working in publishing and higher education for 32 years

These experts had some advice for better communication with printers. First, they all made clear that you should explicitly state your priorities for your documents. Schoon, for example, pointed out that if your images have flesh tones, making sure those tones are realistic will likely be your priority (personal communication, January 14, 2007). Johnson exemplified the point this way: "On a fashion print, flesh tones are critical, whereas on a bar graph, exact matching of a shade of green is less important than that the green sufficiently contrast with the red and the blue" (personal communication, January 28, 2008).

Second, these experts also stressed the benefits of showing the printer a hard copy of the publication. According to Mackiewicz, this hard copy will show the printer "your expectation of the final product" (personal communication, November 1, 2007). Schoon agrees, noting that a hard copy "gives the printer something to match" (personal communication, January 14, 2008). Showing a hard copy to the printer can also mitigate discrepancies between the copy the printer at the office produced and one the printer will be able to produce. For example, Johnson said that he cautions clients that "'muddy' inkjet prints, as often produced on a writer's printer, show greater contrast than final high-quality digital or offset prints" (personal communication, January 28, 2008).

Conclusion

This chapter covered color properties and color systems so that you can analyze the components of color—hue, value, and saturation—to employ color effectively in your online and print documents, no matter the rhetorical situation. We considered ways to use color contrast to focus attention, associate elements of a document, prioritize different elements of a document, and signal organization. We discussed how to manage color. Finally, we examined some of the terminology that is important when working with professional printers, such as the difference between spot color and process color.

Summary of Key Concepts and Terms

analogous colors	digital printing	luminance	process color
bleed tabs	gamut	negative polarity	RGB
blue phenomenon	halftone	offset printing	saturation
chroma	hue	Pantone® Matching System	spot color
CMYK	key	positive polarity	Trumatch®
complementary colors	lightness	prepress	value

Review Questions

1. What are the three properties of color? How are these properties different from each other?
2. What is the difference between color and hue?
3. What do the abbreviations RGB and CMYK stand for? What is the main difference between these color systems?
4. What are two strategies for making color accessible?
5. What is the difference between process color and spot color? When should you use one instead of the other?

Additional Exercises

1. In 1929, when William Faulkner completed his novel *The Sound and the Fury,* he told his publisher that he would like to see the first chapter, the Benjy chapter, printed in ink of various colors. Faulkner wanted the ink to indicate Benjy's time shifts, giving readers a visual reinforcement of how Benjy's thoughts slip back and forth from one time to another. Faulkner's publisher (Jonathan Cape and Harrison Smith) said no to his request, saying that using colored ink in such a way would be too complex an endeavor (Padgett, 2000). If the publisher had granted Faulkner's request, the strategy might have facilitated readers' comprehension.

   Use color to organize an excerpt of text from the first chapter of Faulkner's *The Sound and the Fury.* An online version of the text is available at http://www.usask.ca/english/faulkner.

2. Use a search engine like Google to explain why black is called "key" in CMYK color.

3. Use a search engine like Google to explain the difference between "plain black" and "rich black."

4. In what ways does color make the Budapest metro map more usable? In relation to its use of color, to what extent is the map accessible?

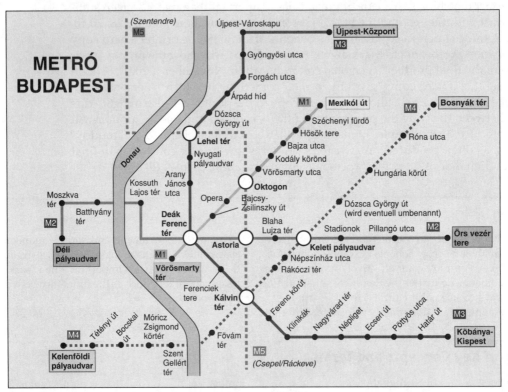

Source: http://commons.wikimedia.org/wiki/File:Budapest_Metro_map.svg. (Visit www.pearsonhighered.com/riley to see this figure in color.)

5. Compare the use of red and yellow in a Web site localized for the United States (http://www.mcdonalds.com/usa.html) and one localized for Japan http://www.mcdonalds.co.jp). What does cultural research on color say about these two countries? To what extent are these colors used differently in the two sites? To what extent should organizations modify the colors they use in their documents when localizing for different cultures?

6. Check to see whether your personal Web site, your organization's Web site, or your university's Web site displays sufficient contrast by using a site like Vischeck (http://www.vischeck.com), which shows how a page would look to people with visual impairments such as colorblindness.

7. The following is a diagram for guiding railway traffic. If you were bringing this diagram to a professional printing company, would you ask that the company use spot color or process color? What factors would you consider?

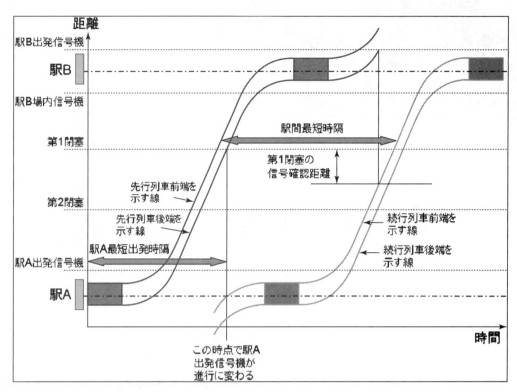

Source: http://commons.wikimedia.org/wiki/File:Train_headway_diagram_ja.png. (Visit www. pearsonhighered.com/riley to see this figure in color.)

Acknowledgments

Thanks to Rachael Winter, a talented designer who created Figures 11.2 through 11.7 and Figures 11.18 through 11.21.

Thanks also to Steve Johnson, Mike Mackiewicz, and Nancy Schoon for their advice.

Suggestions for Further Reading

Readers interested in using color in technical documents should certainly read White's (1991/2003) "Color: The Newest Tool for Technical Communicators." Those interested in using color while maintaining accessibility should read Arditi's (2005) "Effective Color Contrast." A good meta-analysis of perceptions of color and culture is Aslam's (2006) "Are You Selling the Right Colour?"

Creating Presentation Materials

Although a variety of software for creating presentations exists, PowerPoint (PP) is the choice of many professionals, probably because it comes with the widely used Microsoft Office suite. It is the software that we discuss by name in this chapter, but the relevant design principles hold no matter what software you use to create presentations. By the end of this chapter, you should be able to do the following:

- Understand the debate about PP
- Balance text and images to help enhance audience comprehension of PP slides
- Incorporate visual elements into slides
- Select readable and legible text for slides
- Use color to unify slide content
- Use organizational signals to help your audience follow your content
- Incorporate multimedia effectively into your slides
- Use the Slide Master and Slide Sorter to help unify and organize your slides

OVERVIEW OF RELEVANT DESIGN CONCEPTS AND PRINCIPLES

This chapter returns to the idea of dual coding theory to support the use of PP slides to enhance and clarify what you say in your oral presentation, that is, your spoken words. Drawing on current empirical research and practitioner advice, it delineates some strategies for creating clear and attractive slides and organized slide presentations that enhance, elaborate, and clarify your message.

WHY THESE PRINCIPLES ARE IMPORTANT

Before delving into strategies for creating slides that enhance your message, we want to give you a heads-up about the debates that PP has generated. For several years now, researchers, business professionals, and journalists have criticized presentation software, with PP—because of its ubiquity in business and academic organizations—receiving the bulk of the criticism. Mainly, people debate whether presentation software leads presenters to oversimplify the content of their message or, worse, to fail to develop a coherent and substantive message. The most vocal critic of PP is Edward Tufte, whose opinion matters because his work in visual design is so well respected and widely known. Besides arguing that PP leads presenters to simplify their messages and to generate slides that hinder meaning, rather than support and enhance it, Tufte (2003) claims that PP leads to "conspicuous decoration" and "a preoccupation with format not content" (p. 4).

In responding to Tufte's criticism of PP, Doumont (2005) says that Tufte's fault-finding is justified insofar as "many slides . . . contain much noninformation . . . unnecessary colors . . . and overdecorated graphs" (p. 68). However, Doumont points out that slides are meant to be viewed while the presenter is speaking; thus, they are one component (albeit an important one) of a presentation that contains many other considerations. Even so, Doumont acknowledges that slides should be able to convey their main points on their own—they just don't need to include "all the details" (p. 66).

Many criticisms of PP arise from the fact that presenters overrely on default settings in the software rather than looking for ways to apply rhetorical and design principles to slides (just as people must use sound principles when creating print documents). For example, relying on PP's defaults can easily lead a presenter to employ one of PP's bullet-list layouts, which often leads presenters to use "excessive, dysfunctional body text" (Farkas, 2005, p. 26). According to Farkas (2005), slide titles and bulleted text should mark the explicit structure of a presentation, acting as a skeleton for what the speaker says (p. 26). Thus, we have a central problem arising from a default setting: text slides that compete for the audience's cognitive resources for verbal processing.

To make matters worse, ineffective design arising from default settings may become the norm, leading presenters to maintain such designs rather than break from convention: "Young professionals, trying their best to fit in, learn by imitation; those who deviate from the norm, for example by designing their slides markedly differently may be frowned upon by middle or even upper management, who implicitly set expectations for poor slides even if they suffer the consequences" (Doumont, 2005, p. 68).

Many people who use projected slides end up distracting their audience from the intended focus of the presentation because the audience focuses on sound effects, animation, or clip art. In a survey of business students' perceptions of PP presentations, Blokzijl and Naeff (2004) found that students named clip art, busy background images, and animations as some of the worst design choices that presenters could make. Similarly, they found that students rated (animation) effects and poor layout/wrong color combination as the most annoying design choices (p. 75). In contrast, students appreciated use of diagrams, pictures, and graphs. These findings suggest that you should be wary of PP's busy slide templates, useless clip art, and distracting animations.

PP presentations are most effective when they take advantage of human cognitive processing, rather than fighting against it. That is, an effective presenter designs slides so that they do not compete with the presenter's spoken words, but instead support and enhance that auditory input with nonverbal, visual input. In other words, slides that display nonverbal language such as photographs, diagrams, and graphs are more likely to support and clarify the presenter's oral presentation.

HELPING YOUR AUDIENCE COMPREHEND YOUR MESSAGE

As detailed in Chapter 8, dual coding theory proposes that people process words and images through two different cognitive subsystems: one specialized for nonverbal objects and events, the other for language (Paivio, 1986, p. 53). Thus, by integrating visual and verbal elements, you give your audience two ways to process your message, which in turn fosters comprehension and recall. As a corollary, research has found that audiences have difficulty processing verbal information that is presented simultaneously through auditory and visual channels. This means that if you display text on a PP slide and simultaneously speak to your audience, you may actually be impeding their comprehension rather than aiding it (e.g., Mayer & Moreno, 2003). Figure 12.1 shows a text-heavy slide that would impede audience comprehension of the presenter's message.

There is no definitive answer to the question of how much text on a slide is acceptable. Common guidelines include the rule of "no more than six words per line, and no more than six lines per slide." Figure 12.2 shows a slide that adheres fairly closely to the *six-by-six rule*. The six-by-six guideline is well intended, aimed at keeping people from creating slides filled with paragraphs of text.

However, even a slide with relatively limited text, such as that in Figure 12.2, can be improved by using visual elements rather than verbal elements. While the presenter is talking about why diodes are classified as semiconductors, an audience member may be thinking about diodes' insulating state. Displaying bullet points sequentially rather than all at once keeps audience members from reading upcoming bullet points, but it cannot keep them from focusing on previous points. In short, text-only slides overtax the audience's limited capacity to process verbal language.

Rather than following the six-by-six rule to decide how much text is acceptable, you can determine how long it will take your audience to read the text on your slides. For at least that amount of time, your audience will not be attending fully to your spoken words. That's because the audience members will be receiving two streams of verbal input (visual and auditory), rather than verbal auditory input and nonverbal

---

LED Facts

A light-emitting diode (LED) is an electronic light source. The LED was first invented in Russia in the 1920s, and introduced in America as a practical electronic component in 1962. Oleg Vladimirovich Losev was a radio technician who noticed that diodes used in radio receivers emitted light when current was passed through them. In 1927, he published details in a Russian journal of the first ever LED.

All early devices emitted low-intensity red light, but modern LEDs are available across the visible, ultraviolet and infra red wavelengths, with very high brightness. LEDs are based on the semiconductor diode. When the diode is forward biased (switched on), electrons are able to recombine with holes and energy is released in the form of light. This effect is called electroluminescence and the color of the light is determined by the energy gap of the semiconductor. The LED is usually small in area (less than 1 mm^2) with integrated optical components to shape its radiation pattern and assist in reflection.

LEDs present many advantages over traditional light sources including lower energy consumption, longer lifetime, improved robustness, smaller size and faster switching. However, they are relatively expensive and require more precise current and heat management than traditional light sources.

FIGURE 12.1   Example of a slide with far too much text.

Source of text: http://en.wikipedia.org/wiki/LED

What is a diode?

- A diode is a semiconductor.
- A semiconductor conducts current.
- Diodes conduct current in one direction.
- When a diode receives no voltage,
  it returns to an insulating state.
- In its insulating state, current cannot flow.
- Diodes are, therefore, efficient.

FIGURE 12.2 A slide that follows the six-by-six rule but causes other comprehension problems. (Visit www.pearsonhighered.com/riley to view this figure in color.)

visual input. Also, your audience will need a bit longer to read the text because they won't be as familiar with the content as you are.

Your slides should definitely not look like the text-heavy slide in Figure 12.1. If you create a slide that contains paragraphs of text, such as that in Figure 12.1, you can be sure that you audience will not fully attend to and, thus, not comprehend your oral presentation. If you create slides that follow the six-by-six guideline like the slide in Figure 12.2, you should still try to cut text and take advantage of human cognitive processing by incorporating visuals like photographs, diagrams, and graphs, such as the revised slide in Figure 12.3.

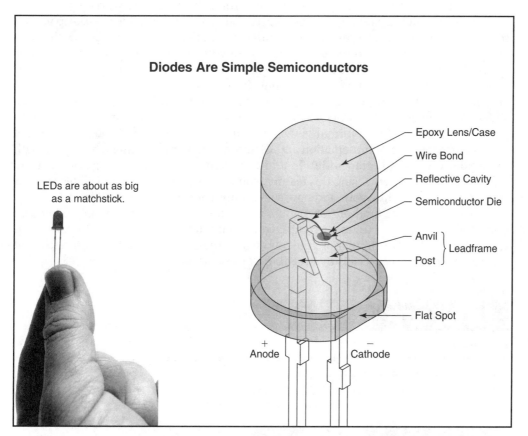

FIGURE 12.3 Diode slide that uses a photograph and labeled drawing. Photograph copyright iStockphoto.com. Used by permission. (Visit www.pearsonhighered.com/riley to view this figure in color.)

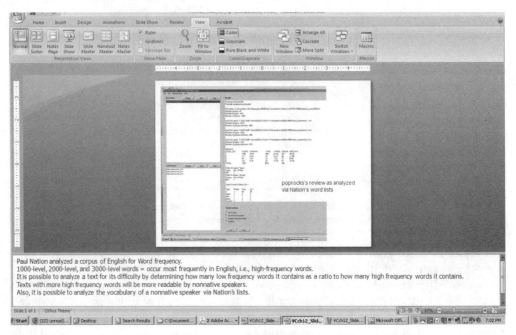

FIGURE 12.4   A PP slide with associated notes. (Visit www.pearsonhighered.com/riley to view this figure in color.)

It is worth acknowledging, though, that you might want easy access to written text—text you might be tempted to include on your presentation slides—to keep you on track during your presentation and to ensure that you remember all the points that you want to make. But that written text should be in your presentation notes, not on your slides. The good news is that PP lets you easily create notes for your presentation. (It will even generate the content of your notes for you, although such automatically created notes will be of little use to you if you take our advice and create visual-heavy slides.) You can associate particular notes—points you want to remember to say—with particular slides. In PP's Normal view, you will see a window for notes. Figure 12.4 shows a screenshot of a presentation and its accompanying notes (the white space with text under the visual-laden slide). In addition, you can take advantage of a feature called the *Presenter View*. Using this feature, you can view your notes and slides on your computer's screen while your audience views only your presentation slides.

No matter what kind of notes you use and how you view them, remember that you should use your notes as a prompt; you should not read your notes to your audience. Nothing bores people more quickly than a speaker who reads long stretches of written text out loud and calls that reading a "presentation."

Exercise A

1. What is dual coding theory? Briefly define it.
2. What is the six-by-six rule for PP slides?
3. What options do you have for creating and viewing presentation notes?

INTEGRATING VERBAL AND VISUAL ELEMENTS

When creating slides that emphasize visuals rather than text, one of your main challenges will be integrating thoughtfully chosen verbal elements with visual elements. Besides simply using visual elements to convey your message, you will use text in headings, callouts, captions, tables, and diagrams. In other words, you will use text, but you will minimize your use of it.

Before leaving the topic of minimizing slide text, it is important to discuss one potential slide element that might call for more—not less—text: slide headings. Current research suggests that creating a *sentence heading (headline)*, rather than a phrasal title (e.g., "Diodes are simple semiconductors" rather than "LED Facts"), generates "more potential than a phrase headline at orienting the audience to both the topic and purpose of the slide" (Alley & Neeley, 2005, p. 419). Alley and Neeley claim that sentence headlines are more persuasive because they explicitly state the presenter's assertions and assumptions (p. 423). In a later study, Alley, Schreiber, Ramsdell, and Muffo (2006) found that using succinct, complete sentences as slide headlines, rather than phrases, significantly improved study participants' recall of the information presented on the slides.

Exercise B

Which of the following qualify as sentence headings (headlines) for slides?

a. Bactericide factor.
b. How are potholes formed?
c. Ability to reduce auto emissions.
d. With optical media backup, burning is permanent.
e. Teaching with technology evaluation.
f. Possible frame materials.
g. Solid axle suspension is inexpensive but corners poorly.

USING VISUAL ELEMENTS

Taking advantage of PP's ability to display visual elements, such as illustrations, photographs, diagrams, charts, and graphs, is arguably the most effective choice you can make for compounding the information your audience receives from your presentation. So what kind of images should you use? The visuals that you choose should be "representative" of the topic, not simply decorative (Alley & Neeley, 2005; Carney & Levin, 2002). Decorative images, such as template background art in PP, do not enhance recall of information and may actually hinder it (Alley & Neeley, 2005; Manning & Amare 2006). In this section, we discuss some of the visuals that you can use in your slides to enhance your oral presentation.

Graphs

If you are developing your presentation from an existing print or online document, you may be tempted to repurpose visuals such as graphs and tables and insert them directly into your slides. This is a natural impulse; after all, when you created the print document, you determined that those visuals conveyed your message effectively. Rather than simply inserting those visuals into your presentation, though, make sure that they

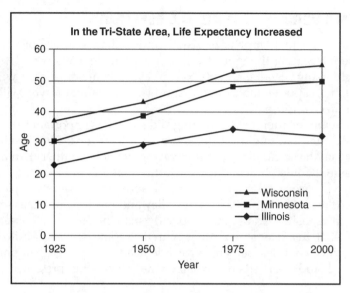

FIGURE 12.5 Example of a slide that displays a line graph. (Visit www.pearsonhighered.com/riley to view this figure in color.)

are comprehensible in the amount of time that they will be shown on screen. In other words, they should not be so detailed and complex that your audience will not be able to process the information they convey.

The line graph in Figure 12.5 tells a story: It clearly shows that life expectancy rose throughout the 20th century in all three states. Several design elements facilitate the audience's quick comprehension of that main message. The graph contains lines of different colors, and the line labels are placed nearby. It also uses a sans serif font and displays contrasting colors among its lines. As Doumont (2005) writes about graphs, "Complex graphs . . . may be perfect for silent analysis or, to a point, for a group discussion, but seldom for formal exposition of salient features to a large audience" (p. 66). Doumont's advice applies to all visual elements shown on screens, not just graphs.

Photographs and Other Representational Illustrations

A representational illustration depicts its subject matter realistically. For example, the computer-generated image in Figure 12.6 shows an exploded version of a gear pump. The exploded view allows the audience to see the internal components of the pump.

Similarly, photographs offer a representation of reality. Figure 12.7 shows a slide that uses a photograph to enhance the presenter's message about teamwork.

Just as in your print documents, you need to think about the kind of visuals that will best convey our message. It would be possible, for example, to show a photograph in Figure 12.6 rather than a computer-generated, exploded view of a gear pump. But photographs would bring other details, and those details might detract from the goal of showing only the critical components of the pump.

Charts

You can employ visual elements like flow and organizational charts when you need to explain a process or hierarchical structures. One important consideration with these charts is to pay attention to font size. It is easy to create charts with small fonts, but these small fonts decrease readability, especially if the audience is far from the

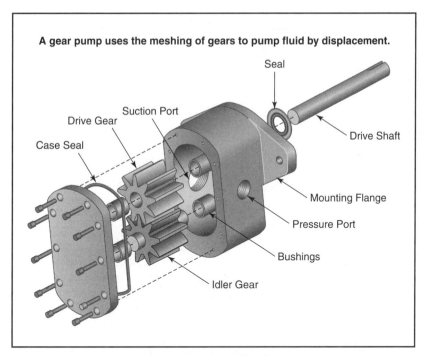

FIGURE 12.6   Example of a slide that uses a representational illustration. (Visit www.pearsonhighered.com/riley to view this figure in color.)

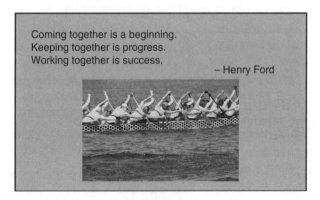

FIGURE 12.7   Example of a slide that uses a photograph. Photograph copyright iStockphoto.com. Used by permission. (Visit www.pearsonhighered.com/riley to view this figure in more detail.)

screen. Figure 12.8 shows a slide that helps explain the process of manufacturing ice cream.

In the flowchart in Figure 12.8, the labels in the rectangles that represent stages in the manufacturing process are large enough (at least 18 points) that the audience will be able to read them when the slide is projected onscreen.

Tables

When including a table in a slide, it is especially important to attend to the amount of information—either numbers or words—that your audience will have to process.

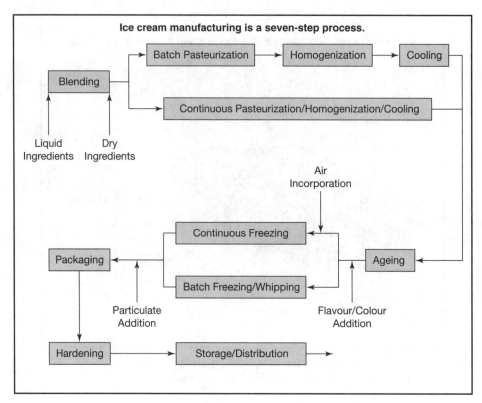

FIGURE 12.8 Example of a slide that shows a flowchart. Copyright University of Guelph. Used by permission. (Visit www.pearsonhighered.com/riley to view this figure in color.)

The temperature range of thermocouples must be 300 to 1250° F.

Type of thermocouple	Useful application range (F°)
E	200–1650
J	200–1400
K	200–2300
N	1200–2300
T	−330–660

Table I. Useful temperature range for thermocouples [3], [6-7].

FIGURE 12.9 Example of a table that displays numerals and integrates verbal elements. (Visit www.pearsonhighered.com/riley to view this figure in color.)

Figure 12.9 shows an example of a table that contains numerical information. The table is simple enough for the presenter to discuss all the data it contains.

Figure 12.10 shows an example of a table that contains textual information. Again, the table organizes the presenter's information, but the amount of information it organizes is not excessive. The presenter could discuss all the information about the syntax of compliments that appears in the table.

Tutors used a variety of **phatic** compliment syntax.

Compliments	Constructed Example
noun phrase + *is/looks* + (*really*) + adjective	The introduction is really good.
pronoun *is* (*really*) *a* adjective + noun phrase	It is a really good introduction.
You + verb + (*a*) + (*really*) + adjective + noun phrase	You wrote a really good introduction.
Adjective + noun phrase	Good introduction.
You + verb + (noun phrase) + (*really*) + adverb	You organized the introduction really well.
I + (*really*) + *like* + noun phrase	I really like the introduction.

FIGURE 12.10   Example of a table that contains verbal elements. (Visit www.pearsonhighered.com/riley to view this figure in color.)

You can use the guidelines in Chapter 7 to help you design tables for onscreen display, but you will need to keep your rhetorical purpose in mind. With tables in print documents, readers find specific data; with tables in PP slides, the presenter shows audience members selected, specific data—the difference in who is doing the finding or showing is important. Readers of print documents can scour tables looking for the specific information that they need, and they can search as long as they want. Viewers of a slide presentation do not have this luxury, so presenters should show simplified tables that are designed specifically for onscreen display.

USING LEGIBLE AND READABLE TEXT IN SLIDES

As when designing print documents, you need to think about the legibility and readability of the textual elements that you will use in your slides. Recall that legibility refers to the ease with which someone can identify a word. Readability, in contrast, is the extent to which someone feels comfortable when reading stretches of text. Text in presentation slides should be legible and readable, just like text in print documents. Indeed, Blokzijl and Naeff (2004) found that good legibility was the design element that students appreciated most. To create text that is both legible and readable, you should, at a minimum, consider typeface size and shape.

Text Size

Because audiences will view your slides from a distance (although the slides will be enlarged when projected on a screen), you need to use a relatively large font size. According to most manuals, all text on a slide, including labels of illustrations and graphs, should be at least 18 points (e.g., Finkelstein, 2003). Other slide text, such as body text, should be even larger, around 24 points. Slide headings can be even larger to indicate their more general level of hierarchy within the presentation.

Text Shape

In presentations, as in print documents, typeface shape plays a critical role in legibility and readability. As detailed in Chapter 1, shape characteristics that correlate with legibility include a large x-height, large aspect ratio, and lack of ornamentation (i.e., extraneous strokes on letterforms). Some typefaces that display these characteristics are Arial, Century Gothic, Franklin Gothic, Tahoma, Trebuchet, and Verdana.

You may be tempted to use display typefaces that are attention getting and convey strong personalities (e.g., Fette Fraktur and Western). Because they are designed to be read in large formats, display typefaces are likely to be more legible on a projected slide than on an 8.5 × 11 (or A4) sheet of paper. However, keep in mind that such typefaces still present readability problems over longer stretches of text and that unusual typefaces may actually distract viewers. If you are trying to convey a professional tone, offbeat display typefaces probably will not suit your presentation.

Exercise C

At a minimum, what size font (typeface) should you use in your slides?

USING CONTRASTING COLORS IN A CONSISTENT COLOR SCHEME

PP and other types of presentation software offer you a variety of ready-made *color schemes*, automatically selecting colors for background, headings, subheadings, and graphs. Of course, you can always modify one of these color schemes or create your own, perhaps using colors from your organization's logo. (For example, if you skip ahead to Figure 12.12, you will see a title slide that uses the color scheme of Illinois Institute of Technology, the affiliation of Kathryn Riley, whose name is on the slide.) Whether you use one of PP's default color schemes or create your own, you should keep a few guidelines in mind.

The most important point to keep in mind when selecting colors is to choose slide colors that will enhance the visibility of the slide content, particularly slide text. If you are giving your presentation in a fully lit room, you should use a dark hue for your verbal elements (e.g., black, blue, or brown) and a light-hued background (e.g., white, light yellow, light gray). Your dark-on-light design will help your audience read the text on your slides easily and comfortably. Figure 12.3 shows an example of a dark-on-light graph slide.

If you know that you will be able to control the lighting in the room where you will be giving your presentation, you may want to use light text on a dark background. Figure 12.11 shows an example of such a scheme.

It is important to make sure that you will be able to at least dim the lights of the room: When light hits a screen with a light-on-dark scheme, the text and the background fade, and the audience sees very little of the slide content.

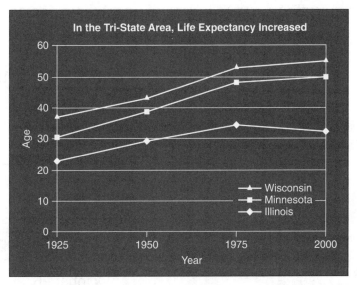

FIGURE 12.11   Example of a slide with a light-text–dark-background color scheme. (Visit www.pearsonhighered.com/riley to view this figure in color.)

Exercise D

In creating your PP slides, would you use dark text on a light background knowing the presentation room's lights will not be dimmed? Explain your answer.

SIGNALING ORGANIZATION IN YOUR SLIDE PRESENTATION

You can use slides to signal the structure of information in your presentation. When you signal the hierarchical level of content that you are addressing, you help your audience comprehend your message. Audiences expect title and conclusion slides, and presentation overview slides are becoming more common. These slide types signal the presentation's organization. According to Farkas (2005), slides should make clear the presentation's main point and the structure of the presentation and should help the audience understand the organization, thus enabling better comprehension. You can also use design elements such as a numbering system and color in your slides to help the audience follow the presentation.

Title Slides

Title slides, especially for presentations given to an audience external to your organization, should include some basic information to orient your audience to you and your topic. In addition, this information will help you identify the purpose of presentation if you return to the archived file at a later date. Your organization may have a slide template that "boilerplates" required information. Otherwise, Figure 12.12 illustrates essential points that your title slide should contain.

Overview Slides

An *overview slide* provides your audience with a "map" of your presentation, helping to orient listeners to the major sections of your talk and the order in which you'll be

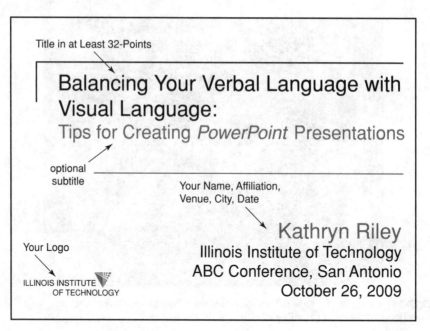

FIGURE 12.12   Example of a title slide with content labeled. (Visit www.pearsonhighered.com/riley to view this figure in color.)

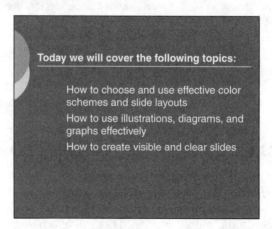

FIGURE 12.13   Example of a presentation overview slide. (Visit www.pearsonhighered.com/riley to view this figure in color.)

covering them. This strategy helps your listeners construct a schema, or mental picture, of the structure of your presentation, which in turn will aid in their comprehension. Figure 12.13 illustrates an overview slide.

Conclusion Slides

A *conclusion slide* serves several purposes. First, it summarizes the main points of your presentation and, thus, improves the chance that your audience will understand your main points. Second, by facilitating audience comprehension of the main ideas, the conclusion slide increases the chance that your audience will remember your main points later on. Third, by cuing the audience about the end of the presentation, it gives them a moment to gather their thoughts and prepare questions or comments. Figure 12.14 shows an example of a conclusion slide that explicitly invites questions from the audience.

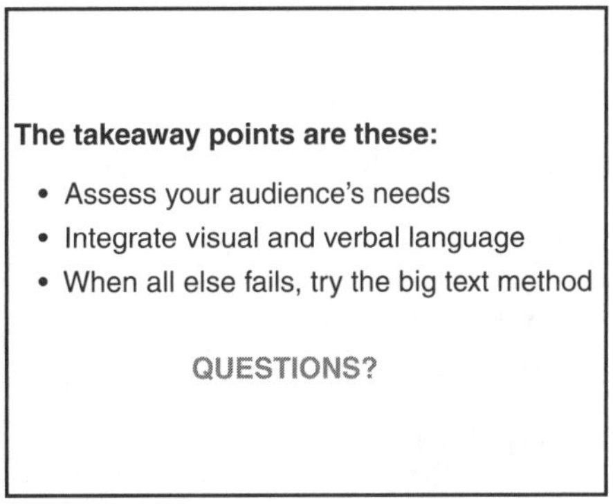

The takeaway points are these:

- Assess your audience's needs
- Integrate visual and verbal language
- When all else fails, try the big text method

QUESTIONS?

FIGURE 12.14   Example of a conclusion slide that cues audience questions. (Visit www.pearsonhighered.com/riley to view this figure in color.)

Exercise E

State reasons for using (a) a title slide, (b) an overview slide, and (c) a conclusion slide.

Numbering Systems

If your presentation follows an outline structure, containing sections and subsections, numbering the headings of your slides will help your audience follow along and understand where you (and they) are within the presentation. For example, the slide in Figure 12.15 tells the audience that they are in section 3 of the presentation.

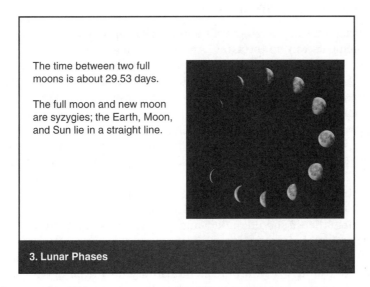

The time between two full moons is about 29.53 days.

The full moon and new moon are syzygies; the Earth, Moon, and Sun lie in a straight line.

3. Lunar Phases

FIGURE 12.15   Example of a body slide that is numbered for organization. Photograph copyright iStockphoto.com. Used by permission. (Visit www.pearsonhighered.com/riley to view this figure in color.)

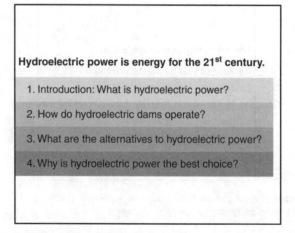

FIGURE 12.16 An overview slide that uses color to introduce presentation sections. (Visit www.pearsonhighered.com/riley to view this figure in color.)

Design Elements

You can help your audience understand the organization of your presentation by associating its sections or hierarchical levels with different colors, icons, edging, or borders. For example, you could introduce the sections of your presentation at the beginning, assigning each section a color. Then, you could reuse the assigned color in the titles of each section's slides. Figures 12.16 and 12.17 illustrate this strategy. Figure 12.16 shows an overview slide that associates each section of the presentation with a color. Figure 12.17 uses color to connect one section of the presentation back to the overview slide.

Note that if you are planning to create a handout for your audience, you can use the same colors to associate sections of your presentation with corresponding sections of the handout.

INCORPORATING MULTIMEDIA

Just as visual elements like photographs and graphs support and clarify your message, multimedia elements can do the same. Animations that you have created yourself (as opposed to PP's animations, such as the one that shoots text onto a slide like bullets from a gun), can help you show a process in a way that still drawings cannot. Embedded video clips have also become common in PP presentations. Figure 12.18 shows a still from a short video clip embedded in a presentation, aimed at organizational team managers, that illustrates common group behavior.

Besides supporting and clarifying what you want to convey, video clips and unique animations add interest. The trick to using video clips and animations is to keep them short relative to the duration of your presentation. After all, your audience wants to hear you what you have to say; they do not simply want to watch a video.

Also, your audience should understand the reason behind your use of the video or animation. Therefore, before you insert one of these items into your presentation, consider what it is that you are trying to show. In other words, use video and animation purposefully. For example, if you were an industrial safety expert giving a presentation about proper disposal of hazardous chemicals, you might include a short video to show the audience the procedure for packaging waste. If you determine that using multimedia during your presentation will make your message more understandable and, perhaps,

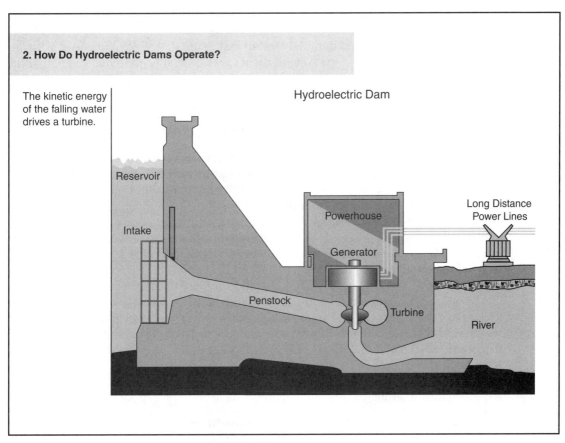

2. How Do Hydroelectric Dams Operate?

The kinetic energy of the falling water drives a turbine.

Hydroelectric Dam

Reservoir

Intake

Penstock

Powerhouse

Generator

Turbine

Long Distance Power Lines

River

FIGURE 12.17 A slide that repeats color from the overview slide in its heading. Source of illustration: http://en.wikipedia.org/wiki/File:Hydroelectric_dam.svg, (Visit www.pearsonhighered.com/riley to view this figure in color.)

Group behavior is often predictable.

FIGURE 12.18 A still image from a short video embedded in a presentation. (Visit www.pearsonhighered.com/riley to view this figure in color.)

more interesting, you should definitely test to make sure that slides embedded with audio and video work the way you intend them to work. You need to make sure that the audience will be able to hear the sound and that the video (or animation) does not play haltingly or skip.

CREATING HANDOUTS FOR YOUR PRESENTATION

Using PP's *Handout Master*, you can easily create handouts based on your slides. However, we recommend that you create your own handout instead of relying on PP's Handout Master to do it for you. The Handout Master will copy your slides (in various quantities per printed sheet, for example, six or nine), but it will not take advantage of print's ability to display greater detail than slides. As noted before, print documents allow for greater resolution than projected slides do, so you should take advantage of the opportunities that print offers for greater detail and complexity in information. In a handout, you can include large tables, multivariate graphs, complex diagrams, and lists of references—all sorts of details that you would not use on a projected slide because the information would be illegible or unusable. Figures 12.19 and 12.20 show the four panels of a handout created by folding an 8 × 14-inch (legal-size) piece of paper in half. This layout allows room enough for detailed tables and figures but has the added benefit of grouping information more than a two-sided handout with no fold would do. For example, if you wanted to include a reference list, you could place the reference list on the back of the folded handout.

When you create your own presentation handout, make sure that you include the following information:

Your name	Kathryn Riley
Your organization or academic affiliation	Illinois Institute of Technology
The title of your presentation	Formulaic Interactions with Engineering Students
The date of your presentation	July 12, 2005
The venue of your presentation	International Professional Communication Conference
The city and state or country	Limerick, Ireland
Your contact information	riley@iit.edu; 312–555-0000

With this information, members of your audience will remember when and where they saw your presentation and can contact you later. Such contact may very well be the goal of the presentation. For example, college recruiters need to ensure that their audience of high school students will be able to contact them later. Contact information on a presentation handout is also important when you need or want feedback on the ideas you discuss. Academic researchers, for example, want colleagues in their discipline to respond to their results and conclusions. Audience feedback is also useful if you intend to make the same or a similar presentation to another group.

Also, consider using color in your handout—especially the color scheme that you've used in your presentation slides. For example, if you have used dark blue type for slide headings, use the same dark blue for headings in your handout. In using color and other design elements such as typeface, borders, and icons consistently, you create a cohesive document set. (To see an example, look at how the handout displayed in Figures 12.19 and 12.20 matches the design of the slide in Figure 12.10.) You can go one step further, too; your advertisements or announcements for your presentation could contain the same colors placed in the same location.

Formulaic Interactions with Engineering Students: Compliment Form & Function

Jo Mackiewicz & Kathryn Riley

jomackiewicz@yahoo.com & riley@iit.edu

Illinois Institute of Technology

IPCC, Limerick, Ireland

Tuesday, July12, 2005, 2:00-3:30

The Research Questions:

1) To what extent are writing tutors' compliments to engineerig students formulaic in form?
2) What functions, other than a PHATIC function, do formulaic compliments serve?
3) What functions do non-formulaic compliments serve?

Methods.

Participantsinthetutoringinteractions: This study examined 13 interactions about engineering writing between 12 writing tutors (5 male, 7 female)who were working with 12 engineering students (9 male, 3 female). Each interaction lasted about 30 minutes and was transcribed in full.The 12 tutors were writing instructors whose teaching experience averaged 4.58 years.

Procedure for coding compliments: A total of **107** tutor compliments were coded according to the definition proposed by Holmes:

A compliment is a speech act which explicitly or implicitly attributes credit to someone other than the speaker, usually the person addressed, for some 'good' (possession, characteristic, skill, etc.) which is positively valued by the speaker and hearer (Holmes, 1988, p.446; see also Hyland & Hyland, 2001, p.186).

Two raters identified compliments in randomly chosen excerpts of transcripts. The excerpts comprised 260 participant turns, or 5,400 words. Raters' coded 31 of the same 34 utterances as compliments, suggesting that raters agreed on what constitutes a compliment. The utterances on which raters' coding diverged consisted of two tutors' one-word responses: *Cool* and *Perfect* (used twice).

The 107 compliments were then classified as either formulaic or non-formulaic according to whether their syntactic structure matched one of the nine SYNTACTIC FORMULAE Manes and Wolfson found in their seminal study of naturally occurring compliments (1981, pp. 120-121). A compliment that followed one of the formulae in Manes and Wolfson's (1981) study was counted as formulaic, but just six of those nine formulae were found in the data of the present study. A compliment that did not follow one of the formulae was counted as non-formulaic.

Compliments manifesting one of the formulaic syntactic structures were then analyzed for patterns in their SEMANTIC FORMULAE—common words like *good* and *nice*—as well.Specifically, they were analyzed to determine whether they carried their positive semantic load in an adjective and whether that adjective matched the semantic formulae that Manes and Wolfson found in their compliment data (1981, pp.116-119).

Conclusions

1. Tutors' compliments to engineering students tend t o be formulaic, both syntactically and semantically.
2. Formulaic compliments tend to be PHATIC in function, but they perform other functions as well:
    - Counter-balancing suggestions and criticisms
    - Offering instantaneous feedback
    - Closing the interaction
3. Non-formulaic compliments serve other functions:
    - Offering specific and individualized feedback
    - Focusing on students as writers
    - Focusing on students' expertise in the subject matter
4. These functions of non-formulai ccompliments could make them more instructive and can make them EXPLORATORYi nfunction, negotiating a change in the relationship.

References

Boyle, R. "You've worked with Elizabeth Taylor!": Phatic functions and implicit compliments. *Applied Linguistics, 1*: 26-46, 2000.

Brown, P. & Levinson, S.C. *Politeness: Some universals in language use.* Cambridge: Cambridge University Press, 1987.

Golato, A. Studying compliment responses: A comparison of DCTs and recordings of naturally occurring talk. *Applied Linguistics, 24:* 90-121, 2003.

Laver, J. Linguistic routines and politeness in greeting and parting. In F. Coulmas (ed.), *Conversational routine: Explorations in standardized communicative situations and prepatterned speech* (pp.289-304). The Hague: Mouton, 1981.

Mackiewicz, J. The effects of tutor expertise in technical writing: A linguistic analysis of writing tutors' comments. *IEEE Transactions on Professional Communication, 47:* 316-328, 2004.

Mackiewicz, J. & Riley,K. The technical editor as diplomat: Linguistic strategies for balancing clarity and politeness. *Technical Communication, 50:* 83-94,2003.

Manes, J. & Wolfson, N. The compliment formula. InF. Coulmas(Ed.), *Conversational routine: Explorations in standardized communication and prepatterned speech* (pp.115-132). The Hague: Mouton, 1981.

Schegloff, E.A. Reflections on quantification in the study of conversation. *Research on Language and Social Interaction, 26:* 99-128, 1993.

Tannen, D.*You just don't understand.* New York: Ballantine,1990.

Van Lancker, D. Is your syntactic component really necessary? *Aphasiology, 14:* 242-360,2001.

VanLancker-Sidtis, D. & Rallon, G. Tracking the incidence of formulaic expressions in everyday speech: Methods for classification and verification. *Language & Communication, 24:* 207-240, 2004.

Wray, A. *Formulaic language and the lexicon.* Cambridge: Cambridge University Press, 2002.

Wray, A., & Perkins, M.R. The functions of formulaic language: An integrated model. *Language & Communication, 20:* 1-28, 2000.

FIGURE 12.19 Page 4 (the back page) and page 1 (the front page) of a presentation handout designed to be folded in half. (Visit www.pearsonhighered.com/riley to view this figure in color.)

Results.

Table 1. Frequency and percentage of formulaic and non-formulaic compliments.

Compliment	Frequency	Percent
Formulaic	65	60.7
Non-formulaic	42	39.3
Total	107	100

Figure 1. Examples, frequencies, and percentages of formulaic compliments and non-formulaic compliments.

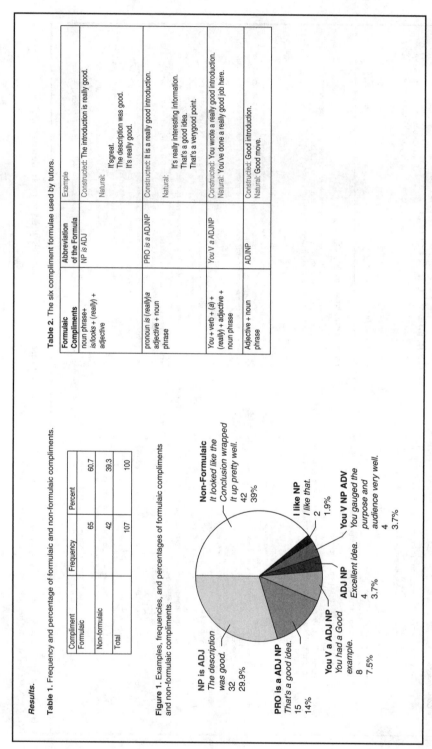

Non-Formulaic
It looked like the Conclusion wrapped It up pretty well.
42
39%

I like NP
I like that.
2
1.9%

You V NP ADV
You gauged the purpose and audience very well.
4
3.7%

ADJ NP
Excellent idea.
4
3.7%

You V a ADJ NP
You had a Good example.
8
7.5%

PRO is a ADJ NP
That's a good idea.
15
14%

NP is ADJ
The description was good.
32
29.9%

Table 2. The six compliment formulae used by tutors.

Formulaic Compliments	Abbreviation of the Formula	Example
noun phrase+ is/looks + (really) + adjective	NP is ADJ	Constructed: The introduction is really good. Natural: It'sgreat. The description was good. It's really good.
pronoun is (really)a adjective + noun phrase	PRO is a ADJ NP	Constructed: It is a really good introduction. Natural: It's really interesting information. That's a good idea. That's a verygood point.
You + verb + (a) + (really) + adjective + noun phrase	You V a ADJ NP	Constructed: You wrote a really good introduction. Natural: You've done a really good job here.
Adjective + noun phrase	ADJ NP	Constructed: Good introduction. Natural: Good move.

FIGURE 12.20 Page 2 and 3 (the inside spread) of a presentation handout designed to be folded in half. (Visit www.pearsonhighered.com/riley to view this figure in color.)

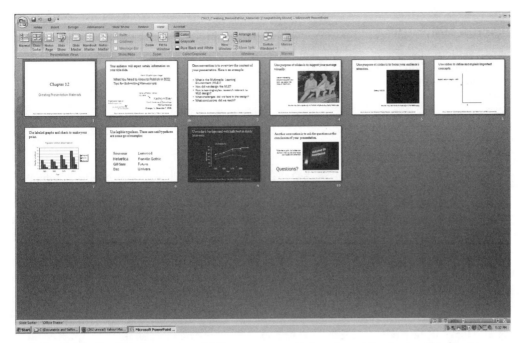

FIGURE 12.21   The Slide Sorter view. (Visit www.pearsonhighered.com/riley to view this figure in color.)

GETTING A HOLISTIC VIEW OF YOUR PRESENTATION

It is worth pointing out two features of PP that will help you create effective presentations. First, to create slides with consistent design, use the *Slide Master* feature, found under View > Slide Master. The Slide Master lets you create and modify design defaults, such as font size for headings and layout of verbal and visual elements. By using the Slide Master, you avoid replacing and resizing slide content on each individual slide.

Second, as you revise your slides to incorporate more visual elements, use PP's *Slide Sorter* view, shown in Figure 12.21. This feature, found under View > Slide Sorter, gives you a reduced-sized view of all of your slides at once and therefore is useful for organizing your presentation, checking the amount of text in the slides, and checking for visual consistency. For example, with the Slide Sorter view, you will be able to tell right away whether your images are consistent in size and placement in the slide layout. The Slide Sorter view will also help you organize your presentation because you will be able to see all of the slides' content at one time. (To return to the Normal view, which displays a one-at-a-time close-up view of each slide, select View > Normal.)

Conclusion

In this chapter, we have discussed PowerPoint (PP) by name, but the design principles we have covered hold regardless of the software you use. After reading this chapter, you know the importance of minimizing the amount of text in your slides and incorporating visual elements that you have designed for onscreen display. Also, you can use effective typefaces and color schemes and effec-

tively signal your presentation's organization. Finally, in using the strategies from this chapter, you can help end the controversy about PP by showing that PP does not necessarily cause a presenter to simplify his or her message, as PP critics have said. Rather, your presentations can use PP and other presentation software to enhance and clarify your message.

Summary of Key Concepts and Terms

color scheme	Handout Master	sentence heading (headline)	Slide Sorter
conclusion slide	overview slide	six-by-six rule	title slide
dual coding theory	Presenter View	Slide Master	

Review Questions

1. What are two main criticisms of PP?
2. What is the relevance of dual coding theory to PP slide design?
3. What is a sentence heading and how does it differ from traditional PP headings, such as "hydrogen fuel cell capacity"?
4. What characteristics of size and shape should text elements in slides have?
5. What are three ways to signal the organization of a presentation to the audience?

Additional Exercises

1. In PP, you can find templates for slide design under the Design tab; the templates are called themes. To what extent do the templates contain busy and distracting background images? Briefly describe three examples. Which templates do you think might be appropriate for professional presentations?
2. Analyze the following text slide, taken from a presentation on medical waste. Discuss three ways that the presenter could improve the slide.

Weaknesses in Medical Waste Management Processes

- Labs lack the capacity to do decon on-site
- Lack of awareness of key information:
  - State regulatory process and recommended decon methods
  - Transport and chain of custody issues
  - EPA registered chemicals for medical waste treatment (ListG)
    http://www.epa.gov/oppad001/chemregindex.htm
  - Autoclave operations
  - Infectious waste isnot hazardous waste

Sehulster, L. Centers for Disease Control and Prevention. Medical waste management in the bioterrorism era. Online at http://www.bt.cdc.gov/coca/ppt/wastemanagement _082305.ppt. (Visit www.pearsonhighered.com/riley to view this figure in color.)

3. Analyze the following table slide, from a presentation on selecting a digital camera. Based on what you learned in Chapter 7 and in this chapter, discuss three ways that the presenter could improve the slide.

Summary: Digital Camera Comparison

	Canon PowerShot	Casio Exilim EX-Z75	Sony Cyber-Shot
Price	$145.95	$124.68	$132.99
Star Rating	4.5	3.5	3.5
Megapixels	8.3	7.41	8.1

My Recommendation = Canon

(Visit www.pearsonhighered.com/riley to view this figure in color.)

4. Analyze the following graph slide, taken from a presentation on international agricultural trade. Based on what you learned in Chapter 8 and in this chapter, discuss three ways that the presenter could improve the slide.

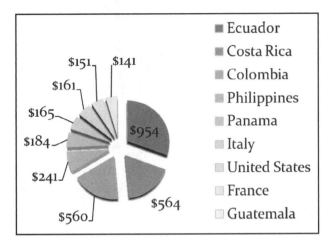

Source of data: http://www.nationmaster.com/graph/
agr_ban_exp-agriculture-banana-exports; (visit www
.pearsonhighered.com/riley to view this figure in color.)

5. Redesign the graph slide in Problem 4, taking into
account the design advice and principles covered in
Chapter 8 and in this chapter.
6. Evaluate the following slide, especially its visual elements. To what extent are the visual elements useful?

What kinds of visuals would improve the slide? In
what other ways might the presenter improve the slide,
depending on the audience for the presentation?

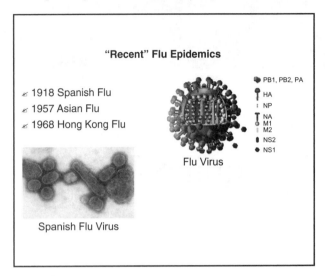

http://commons.wikimedia.org/wiki/File:Recon-
structed_Spanish_Flu_Virus.jpg; http://en.wikipedia.org/
wiki/File:Flu_und_legende_color_c.jpg. (Visit www
.pearsonhighered.com/riley to view this figure in color.)

Suggestions for Further Reading

The following articles are popular ones from the Power-
Point debate:

Keller, J. (2003). Killing me Microsoftly. *Chicago Tribune
Magazine* (5 January): 8–12, 28–29.
Thompson, C. (2003. December 14). The 3rd annual year in
ideas; PowerPoint makes you dumb. *New York Times*,
Sec. 6, p. 88.

These readings report empirical studies about PowerPoint:

Lowry, R. B. (1999). Electronic presentation of lectures—
Effect upon student performance. *University Chemistry
Education, 3*, 18–21.
Mackiewicz, J. (2007). Audience perceptions of fonts in projected PowerPoint text slides. *Technical Communication, 54*, 295–307.
Mackiewicz, J. (2007). Perceptions of clarity and attractiveness in PowerPoint graph slides. *Technical Communication, 54*, 145–156.
Mackiewicz, J., Mastarone, G., & Lee-Kim, J. (2006). What's
not to like? Business students' opinions about
PowerPoint slide design. Proceedings of the 2006
Association for Business Communication Conference. Retrieved January 18, 2010, from http://www
.businesscommunication.org/conventionsNew/
proceedingsNew/2006New/08ABC06.pdf
Susskind, J. E. (2005). PowerPoint's power in the classroom: Enhancing students' self-efficacy and attitudes.
Computers & Education, 45, 203–215.
Szabo, A. & Hastings, N. (2000). Using IT in the undergraduate classroom: Should we replace the blackboard
with PowerPoint? *Computers & Education, 35*,
175–187.

Designing for the Web

Karl Stolley

Printed documents and even certain digital documents such as those saved in Adobe PDF files provide their designers with a high degree of confidence that what the end user or reader will see is essentially identical to what the designer created. The design of Web pages is very different; part of the Web's strength and appeal is that a wide range of users can access pages on an equally wide range of devices, including adaptive technologies for people with low vision or limited motor skills (such as are required to use a mouse or other pointing device). Therefore, one of the most important ideas to keep in mind when designing for the Web is that, in contrast to print, how users experience Web pages varies widely, depending on the technology they have available and their own physical abilities.

Many of the principles and strategies discussed elsewhere in this book apply to Web page design. This chapter focuses on visual composing and design issues for the screen that are unique to the Web. By the end of this chapter, you should be able to do the following:

- Think about designing for the screen to maximize accessibility of Web pages on the screens of many different users.

- Choose appropriate, commonly available fonts for Web pages while allowing for generic font alternatives and considering the different ways users may see the effects of your font choices.

- Understand the use of color on the screen and in Web page design, particularly on text, borders, and backgrounds.

- Design layouts that maximize the use of screen space, keeping in mind the wide range of screen sizes and resolutions that users may have and how that range of screen sizes impacts choices in Web page layout and design.

- Prepare Web-appropriate images to display photographs while providing descriptive textual alternatives for users unable to experience images.

- Employ design choices that clearly indicate actionable areas on a page, including hyperlinks, navigation buttons, and other clickable page elements.
- Understand the need to design and test your pages for usability, keeping in mind the goals and needs of actual users.

Some of the exercises in this chapter encourage you to use the Web Developer Add-on (WDA, https://addons.mozilla.org/en-US/firefox/addon/60) created by Christopher Pederick for the Firefox Web browser (http://www.mozilla.com/firefox/). The WDA will allow you to disable images, resize the browser window, and simulate other conditions of access that impact how pages are viewed. Both the WDA and Firefox can be downloaded for free and are available on Windows, Mac OS X, and Linux.

For the production exercises in this chapter, you will need access to a Web editor such as Adobe Dreamweaver. If you do not have Dreamweaver, try downloading and installing KompoZer, which is a free, open-source Web editor available for Windows, Mac OS X, and Linux (http://www.kompozer.net). If you cannot install software but have access to a Windows computer, you can also try installing and running KompoZer Portable on a USB drive (http://portableapps.com/apps/development/nvu_portable).

OVERVIEW OF RELEVANT DESIGN CONCEPTS AND PRINCIPLES

Web design requires designers to think about *accessibility*: Even the most visually stunning, usable Web page imaginable must still be accessed before its visual features or use value and ease of use can be experienced by its intended user or reader. With print documents, such as books, it is often necessary to create additional versions to make them accessible: Look for the large-print section in your local public library, for example. Large-print books often require entirely different layouts and print runs.

By contrast, a single Web page can be built to suit the access needs of all users, regardless of their computer technology or physical abilities. While it is common to visit Web sites that offer links to text-only versions of their pages, *Web standards*, including *Hypertext Markup Language (HTML)* and *Cascading Style Sheets (CSS)*, make it possible to create a single page that can be viewed either graphically or in text-only forms. While advanced Web designers often write HTML and CSS by hand, it is possible to use a *what-you-see-is-what-you-get (WYSIWYG)* editor, such as KompoZer, to build very basic—but accessible—Web pages.

In technical communication circles and information design, creating one document that serves multiple media (e.g., screen viewing and printing) and multiple audiences or groups of users is called *single sourcing*. The benefits of single sourcing include having only one version of a document to update and maintain. If a Web site offers separate screen, print, and text-only versions of its pages, any revisions must be made in triplicate. A site with a handful of pages might be able to maintain multiple versions; a site with hundreds or thousands of pages cannot, unless it is staffed by a large team of people.

But single sourcing requires a very different way of thinking about page design. One approach that Web page designers can use as a guide when designing in a single-source style for the Web is *universal design*, which is outlined in seven principles by the Center for Universal Design (1997):

- **Equitable use:** "Provide the same means of use for all users: identical whenever possible; equivalent when not." Web design examples for this principle include providing font alternatives and creating a design that is still usable in the absence of color, images, or other visual components.
- **Flexibility in use:** "The design accommodates a wide range of individual preferences and abilities." For the Web, this principle helps designers to create page

layouts that do not "break" on different user-preferred fonts and font sizes or different operating systems, browsers, and screen resolutions.

- **Simplicity and intuitiveness:** "Use of the design is easy to understand." Web designers employ this principle by creating actionable areas that behave as expected and even by creating meaningful headings and scannable paragraph text.
- **Perceptible information:** "The design communicates necessary information effectively to the user." As with simplicity and intuitiveness, this principle emphasizes clear navigation, way finding, and communicating information redundantly (e.g., through images and alternate, or "alt," text)—while also avoiding designs that falsely make items appear actionable.
- **Tolerance for error:** "The design minimizes hazards and the adverse consequences of accidental or unintended actions." Web browsers have features that assist users in this principle, such as the ability to use the Back button to return to a page after mistakenly clicking a link. Error-tolerant features that designers can create include providing alternative fonts and high contrast and non-color-dependent visual features on actionable items.
- **Low physical effort:** "The design can be used efficiently and comfortably and with a minimum of fatigue." This principle is also addressed by Web browsers, which typically allow keyboard navigation (using the arrow, tab, and return keys) in lieu of a mouse. But designers can opt to make larger actionable areas, which are easier to click accurately than tiny areas, which require painstaking mouse pointing.
- **Size and space for approach and use:** "Appropriate size and space is provided for approach, reach, manipulation, and use." This principle encourages designers to build page layouts that display usably on a variety of screen sizes and at different font sizes.

WHY THESE PRINCIPLES ARE IMPORTANT

The idea behind universal design (UD) is to create the best experience possible for all users, not just those with alternative devices, such as a mobile or adaptive browser or other *assistive/adaptive technology*. UD principles, especially those aimed at accessibility, improve pages and sites for everyone.

Specifically, UD principles aim "to simplify life for everyone by making products, communications, and the built environment more usable by as many people as possible at little or no extra cost. Universal design benefits people of all ages and abilities" (Center for Universal Design, 2008). When UD is applied to page design, in other words, designers consider varying user needs and attempt to create a design that will work for all users.

It's still common, though, to see Web sites that present multiple versions of the same page. A Web page stored in triplicate for screen, print, and text-only versions represents its designer's attempt to address different audience needs. However, multiple versions may confuse site visitors as to which version to choose. Worse, the only links to text-only versions often appear on the graphical version of a page; if the graphical page is inaccessible, the text-only audience may not be able to find the link to the version intended for them.

By following UD principles, Web page designers can create a single page that better ensures that site visitors will automatically have the appropriate "version" of the document available to them. Some users may see a fully graphical version of the page or hear what seems to be a text-only version. Site visitors can even print the page and have it appear differently from the screen but appropriately for print.

UD requires Web designers to think about a range of users for every design decision. This includes thinking about users with low vision or alternative Web access, such as mobile devices or adaptive technologies. When we design for the Web, in other words, we have to get beyond our own screens and the way pages look to us as Web designers.

However, that does not mean that Web design has to be limited to "lowest common denominator" design decisions. Instead, as the principles in this chapter show, it is possible to design pages in a way that makes them flexible and fail-safe: Web pages can look and function well in a full-size desktop browser just as they can on a tiny, Web-enabled mobile phone screen. Web pages can also be printed, if a user wishes, or even read aloud to low-vision users.

DESIGNING AND TESTING FOR MANY SCREENS

Although many principles from print design carry over to designing for the screen, the screen has important advantages and limitations compared to print. For example, design and production constraints in print documents, such as the cost of large print runs or color printing, are obviously not issues in screen design, where color is no more expensive than black and white and transmitting or accessing a copy of a document is just a matter of Internet access. With print, though, we can examine a final copy of a document and ensure its quality before sending it to its intended readers. We can also be certain that the copy is the same thing that readers will receive. On screen, there are many conditions that affect page display, so assuring quality is a significant challenge.

One of the primary conceptual challenges in Web design, then, is to grasp that how your page will look depends in large part on your Web site visitor's computer and screen or adaptive device. Devices that can display Web pages will render the same page very differently, depending on the number of colors the device can display, the fonts available on the system, and even certain settings (such as font smoothing) that are part of the user's operating system.

The key to ensuring accessibility is to keep a variety of user access conditions in mind as you design. As the sections below on fonts, color, and layout show, the challenge for Web designers is that few of the variables of a user's visual experience of a page are knowable, and they cannot be fully controlled by Web design technologies. So when designing for the Web, rather than insisting that a page look a particular way, pages (and their designers) must have a high tolerance for different users and devices. For this reason, it is good practice to test your pages on many different devices and operating systems under many conditions (e.g., with images disabled).

All Web pages should be tested in the three most popular Web browsers: Internet Explorer, Mozilla Firefox, and Apple's Safari. All three browsers can be downloaded for free (though Internet Explorer is available only on Windows computers). It is also important to test pages on Windows and Mac OS X; sometimes this means visiting campus computer labs or public libraries to find machines different from your own.

Exercise A

Install Firefox and the Web Developer Addon (WDA), and visit some of your favorite Web sites. Try Images > Disable All Images to see how the page renders in an imageless environment, or try CSS > Disable Styles > All Styles to view the page without its visual styling, which is how the page would "appear" to a user with low vision who is having the page read aloud or to a user in a text-only environment. Are you still able to view and interact with the Web site? Also try viewing the sites on your mobile phone or using Miscellaneous > Small Screen Rendering on the WDA.

USING FONTS ON WEB PAGES

Certain digital formats, such as Adobe PDF, allow page designers to include or embed fonts with the document itself. This is not possible with Web pages, which can display text using only those fonts that are installed on a site visitor's computer.

Perez (2008) maintains a useful Web page that lists and displays all the commonly available fonts on Windows and Mac OS X. Beyond its use as a reference, Perez's page also demonstrates how the fonts look on your own system. It also includes links to screen shots that show how Perez's page appears on different browsers and operating systems.

As Perez's page shows, there are serif (Georgia, Palatino Linotype), sans serif (Arial, Verdana), and monospace (Courier New) fonts commonly available on both Mac and Windows. These are examples of *Web-safe fonts*. There are other font faces that appear roughly the same but have different names (Times New Roman on Windows, Times on Mac; Tahoma on Windows, Geneva on Mac; Lucida Console on Windows, Monaco on Mac); these are also Web-safe fonts but require a bit more care in their use.

In a Web editor such as KompoZer, there are multiple ways to add design elements to your page, so consult the online help or documentation that comes with your editor. Generally, you want to look for the option to use CSS. To specify fonts for text on a page, KompoZer offers a number of predefined font families; as you can see in Figure 13.1, these font families include the names of some of the Web-safe fonts just mentioned.

What is important to note, though, is that the family appears as a comma-separated list: Arial, Helvetica, sans serif. Providing a list of fonts, rather than a single one, reinforces UD principles: That list instructs a user's Web browser to use Arial on the page; if Arial is missing, the browser will try and use Helvetica; if Helvetica is not on the user's computer, the user's computer will display a generic sans serif font instead.

This is also how the differently named Web-safe fonts, such as Tahoma and Geneva, can be used. KompoZer and many other Web editors allow you to modify their set lists of font families; Figure 13.2 shows Tahoma and Geneva added to the list. (In

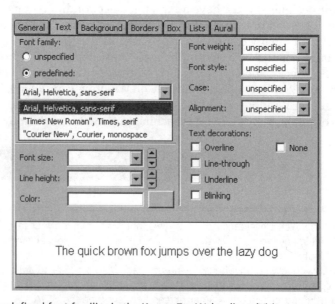

FIGURE 13.1 Predefined font families in the KompoZer Web editor. (Visit www.pearsonhighered .com/riley to view this figure in color.)

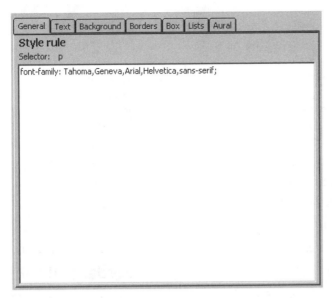

FIGURE 13.2   Modified font list in KompoZer. (Visit www.pearsonhighered.com/riley to view this figure in color.)

KompoZer, you can do this just by accurately typing additional font names in the box; be sure you have not made any spelling or typographical errors.)

With Tahoma and Geneva added to the list, Windows computers will display this page with Tahoma; Macs will skip Tahoma and use Geneva instead. But the appearance to Windows and Mac users will be basically the same. And, as before, if Tahoma or Geneva is missing, the browser will move through the other fonts until it finds a match or will use a generic sans serif font instead.

Designing for alternative fonts is a prime example of universal design. As a designer, you may prefer Tahoma on your page rather than Arial. And, indeed, users who have Tahoma installed will see Tahoma. At the same time, users without Tahoma will see something other than the default browser font (which is usually a form of serif font, typically Times or Times New Roman). Using this scheme, you could even specify a more unusual font, such as Futura, which will benefit users who have the font installed while still providing Web-safe alternatives for everyone else.

However, even computers that have a particular font installed, such as Verdana, may display it very differently, depending on the size of the font and whether font smoothing is enabled on the system. Figure 13.3 shows the Verdana font on Windows XP at different sizes, with font smoothing turned both on and off. While it is good practice to specify type in points for print, accurate display of font sizes onscreen relies on the pixel (px) unit (though see Rutter, 2007, for advanced, alternative means of sizing text on Web pages).

At very small sizes, the smoothed font is somewhat more readable (though not by much). Note, though, that on a screen without font smoothing, Verdana at 17 pixels displays as though it were in boldface. On a font-smoothed screen, there is little difference between 16 and 17 pixels.

The lesson here is that, even though a font might appear one way to you, it is important to check it on different systems and under different viewing conditions. If you need text to appear in bold, such as for a heading, specify it as bold. Do not simply rely on the quirks of one display (e.g., Verdana at 17 pixels on a nonsmoothed Windows screen).

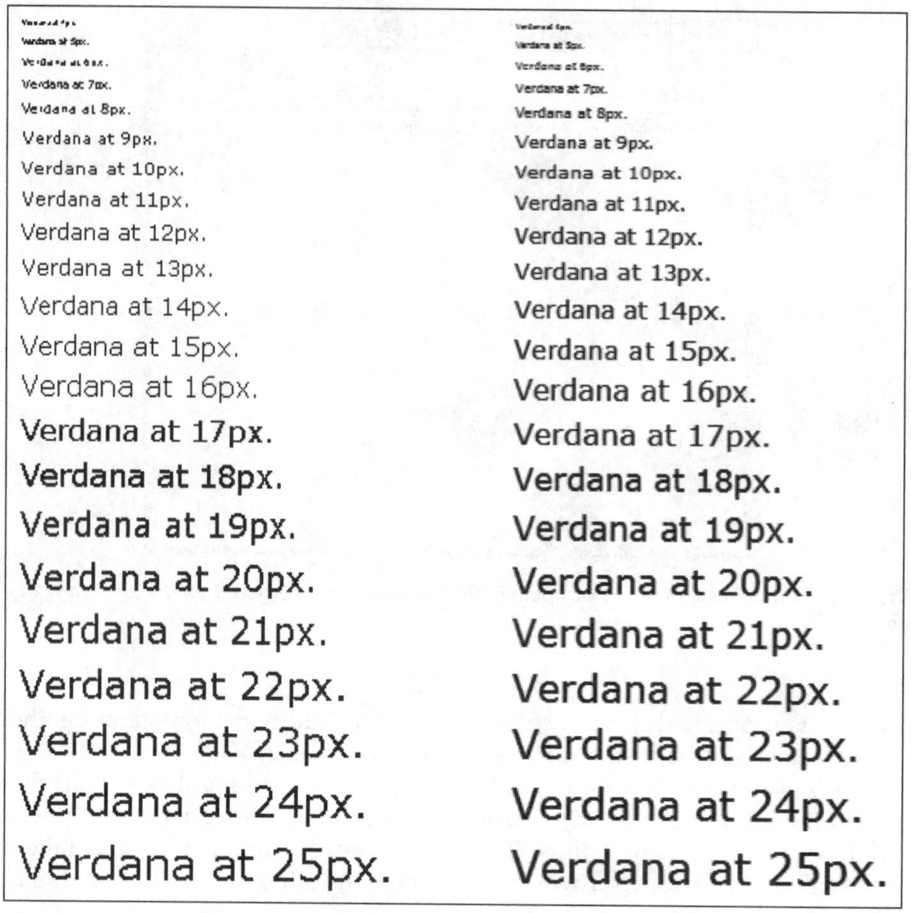

FIGURE 13.3   Verdana on Windows, normal (left) and smoothed (right). (Visit www.pearsonhighered. com/riley to view this figure in more detail.)

USING IMAGES FOR SPECIAL FONTS

Print designers are used to having a very large selection of fonts available for document design. By any measure, there are few Web-safe fonts, and none of them convey much personality.

One approach to using unique or unusual fonts for headings or page branding is to use an image-editing program such as Adobe Photoshop or Fireworks to create the text and then save it as a JPEG or PNG image and load it onto the Web page. Note the text in Figure 13.4, which has a non-Web-safe font and has also taken advantage of the ability to lay out the heading text in a way that would be difficult or impossible with HTML and CSS alone.

The trouble with images, of course, is that neither search engines nor screen readers for users with low vision can access the text the images contain. (When you do an "image search" on a Web search engine, you are actually searching text on Web pages that contain images, not the images themselves.)

This is where alternative text, or *alt text*, comes in. Most Web editors allow page designers to specify alt text for the image; in the case of an image that contains only text, use the same text as appears in the image. Figure 13.5 shows the same Web page as Figure 13.4, but with images disabled. The alt text is provided to the user instead, as it would be on a text-only device.

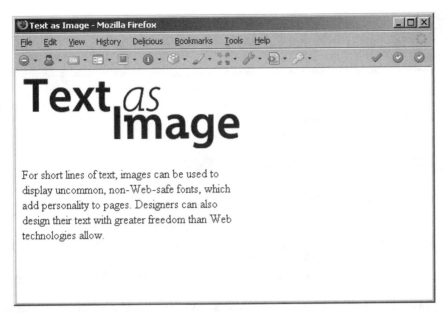

FIGURE 13.4   "Text as Image" run as an image, not as HTML text. (Visit www.pearsonhighered.com/ riley to view this figure in color.)

However, it is best to use images for special fonts only on short bits of text, such as site branding, headings, and so on. Alt text is limited to 1,024 characters (Clark, 2002), so while alt text is an important accessibility feature, it is not intended for long passages of text. Also, if the text must ever be revised, it is much easier for designers to open a Web editor to revise text than it is to open an image editor, retype or recreate the text image, and then save it in JPEG or PNG format.

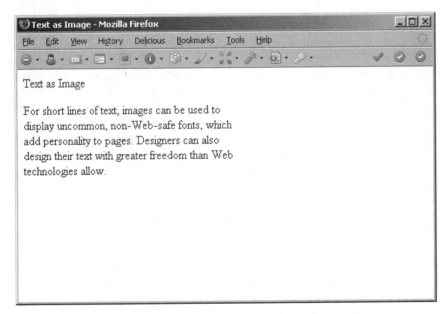

FIGURE 13.5   "Text as Image" alt text displayed with images disabled in Firefox. (Visit www.pearsonhighered.com/riley to view this figure in color.)

Exercise B

Examine the Web-safe fonts at the site maintained by Perez (2008). What anatomical characteristics do the fonts share? How do the fonts differ in their anatomical characteristics? If you have access to different computers, such as Windows and Mac, do any of the fonts seem any more legible than others? What if font smoothing is turned on or off?

COLOR ON THE SCREEN

In the early days of the Web, many computers were limited to displaying 256 colors. Web designers were therefore urged to use a 216-color Web-safe or browser-safe palette. These Web-safe colors displayed reliably on all computers; the 40 colors missing from the Web-safe palette were colors that displayed differently on Mac and Windows computers (Weinman, n.d.)

Now most computers are capable of displaying millions of colors. Some designers still use a 216-color palette, but because it is limited to 6 shades of red, green, and blue, it offers very little subtlety in color. In the worst cases, this palette may lead to pages with distractingly bright-colored backgrounds and text that may cause eye fatigue for page visitors, who do not need bright colors so much as a high contrast between text and background to more quickly scan the contents of Web pages visually (Ling & van Schaik, 2002).

As with fonts, though, computers may display color differently. One important display factor is *gamma correction*, which "controls the overall brightness of an image" (Computer Graphics System Development Corporation [CGSD], 2000) between Windows and Mac computers. Windows uses a gamma correction value of 2.2, whereas Mac uses 1.8. This leads Windows computers to display darker colors closer to black and lighter colors with less brightness. The gamma correction on Mac tends to bleach out lighter colors, significantly increase the brightness of dark colors, and bring darker colors closer to gray.

Web page designers should account for different gamma corrections by being wary of low-contrast color combinations, especially between text and backgrounds: for Mac users, this means being particularly careful with combinations of dark colors, which may appear even darker on a Windows computer. For Windows users, colors that display well on their computers at the brighter end may be washed out to bright white on Macs. And for both Mac and Windows users, it is important to consider that site visitors may have adjusted the settings on their monitors for greater or lesser brightness and contrast. For older adult users, high contrast is especially important because human eyes lose the ability over time to distinguish color and perceive light (Becker, 2004).

For these reasons, it is always safe practice to keep the background of text areas very light and the text itself very dark. Visual interest and color can be used on other areas of the page, as in borders and images that do not require reading, navigation, and other page interaction. Better still, as a UD approach, high-contrast colors will make the page all the more readable for the young and those with normal vision.

One final consideration of color on the screen is color blindness, particularly when designing clickable page elements such as hyperlinks. Depending on a user's type of color blindness, he or she may have difficulty distinguishing between red and green and sometimes yellow and blue colors. There are a number of Web sites that preview live Web pages to reflect how they would be experienced by colorblind users with different color deficits. Colorblind Web Page Filter (http://colorfilter.wickline.org/) is one of the more popular sites that you can use to check Web pages. The colors will appear strikingly different when rendered; that is expected. What is important to look for when using a colorblindness simulator is whether there is perceptible information, such as hyperlinks or color keys on diagrams and illustrations, that is no longer distinguishable when the page is displayed through the colorblindness simulator.

Exercise C

Visit a Web design gallery that can organize sites by color, such as Web Creme (http://www. webcreme.com/). Look at different sites whose colors are bright (yellow, pink) or dark (brown, red). If you look at them on Windows, are there contrasting colors that are too dark to be used comfortably? On a Mac, are there colors that are too bright? Also try running some sites, particularly green and red ones, through the Colorblind Web Page Filter (http://colorfilter.wickline.org/). Is there any perceptible information lost that is based on color alone?

LAYOUTS THAT MAXIMIZE SCREEN SPACE

In addition to different color settings, computers and visual displays (both CRT monitors and the LCD panels that are gradually replacing them) have different capabilities for showing screen space. There are three important factors in screen display: resolution, which is a numerical description of the pixels a display can show; aspect ratio, which is the size of the display's width relative to its height; and the physical size of monitor or LCD panel, in inches, on the diagonal from bottom left to upper right.

In the early days of the Web, there were three basic resolutions available on computers: 640 pixels wide by 480 pixels tall (640 × 480), 800 × 600, and 1024 × 768. Computer monitors also shared a 4:3 aspect ratio common to television screens. Of those three resolutions, only 1024 × 768 is used with any regularity now; and it is becoming more common, for 4:3 monitors, to see resolutions of 1280 × 1024 (Nielsen, 2006). Resolution is controlled by a user's operating system, based on the display capabilities of the user's graphics card and monitor or LCD panel.

It was common to have 4:3 monitors that were sized 13, 15, 17, 19 and 21 inches and up. Regardless of the physical size of the screen, any given monitor might have a resolution of 1024 × 768, meaning that the same amount of screen "real estate" was visible (1024 pixels on the horizontal, 768 on the vertical) on a 13-inch monitor as on a 21-inch monitor. However, just as with television sets, larger screens produced physically larger pictures—not larger fields of vision.

The primary display concerns for Web page designers are the different resolutions and aspect ratios available, not monitor size. While 640 × 480 and 800 × 600 have all but disappeared, many more resolutions have been added, including 1280 × 1024 and 1600 × 1200, both of which have a 4:3 aspect ratio. More recently, 16:9 and 16:10 (sometimes referred to as 8:5) widescreen displays have added widescreen resolutions that are much wider (1280, 1680, and even 1920 pixels wide) but that are comparatively shorter (800, 1050, and 1200 pixels tall). Figure 13.6 shows the White House Web site as it would be viewed at different resolutions on screens with different resolutions and aspect ratios.

As you can see, the visible area of the page is quite different from screen to screen. The widescreens generally offer more horizontal space but are not as tall. The area below the visible portion of a Web page as it loads on screen prior to scrolling is described as the area "below the fold," a term carried over from the horizontal fold on newspapers. The area above the fold is considered prime real estate in Web page design; but it is clear from Figure 13.6 that the area above the fold is relative to display resolution and aspect ratio.

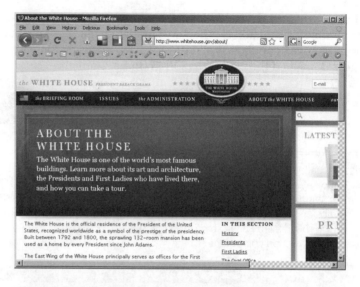

FIGURE 13.6   The White House Web site viewed on screens of different resolutions.
(Visit www.pearsonhighered.com/riley to view this figure in color.)

FIGURE 13.6   (*Continued*)

What helps whitehouse.gov make maximal use of the fold is keeping site-branding art (the White House logo) to a minimum vertical size and also using a horizontal navigation bar. Horizontal navigation not only keeps all the navigation items in view on shorter screens, but it also avoids reducing the available width of the page for content: the main content column on the left and the promotional-type column on the right. A vertical navigation area, in other words, reduces the amount of content that could appear on the page and so must be designed with care so as to not crowd out page content.

The whitehouse.gov site also makes use of what is known as a *fixed layout*: that is, it is horizontally the same size from screen to screen (though the designers have also elected to center its layout horizontally, which is why there are equal amounts of white space to the left and right of the layout from screen to screen). The alternative to a fixed layout is a *liquid layout*, which expands and contracts relative to the width of the screen it is viewed on.

Nielsen (2006) is a vocal proponent of liquid layouts because of their ability to fit onto a range of screen sizes. He also suggests that users with particularly large screens may not maximize their browser windows to fill the entire screen. In other words, even though a user may have a screen resolution of 1680 × 1050, he or she may use only a fraction of that for a browser. Additionally, users may have bookmarks or browsing histories open in their browser, which may take up significant amounts of horizontal space, just as additional toolbars such as the WDA fill the vertical space of the screen.

When deciding to use a fixed or liquid layout, it is important to consider the site's content. While text can easily reflow to fit the screen, images are presented at a fixed size. That means that a photographer preparing a gallery of images might opt for a fixed layout, while a technical communicator preparing text-heavy online documentation might opt for a liquid layout. The photographer, in other words, needs to ensure that all images on the page are properly framed by the layout. The technical communicator might also be concerned that, in the case of software documentation, a user might decrease the browser window to a size small enough to view simultaneously the documentation and the software it documents.

There are two widely used techniques for producing page layouts on the Web. The first and older technique involves using HTML tables, which function much like tables in a word processor, to establish page layout. HTML tables work fairly reliably from browser to browser, but they have two significant disadvantages. The first is that HTML tables present significant accessibility challenges for users of adaptive technology such as screen readers and alternative devices such as mobile phones. (However, see WebAIM's (n.d.) article on improving the accessibility of tables.) HTML tables also lock the content of a page—its content, images, and navigation—into a layout that is harder to revise later.

The more recent and preferable manner to create page layouts is through CSS. CSS layouts have two advantages: First, they keep the page design separate from the page content, which means that CSS is less likely to interfere with adaptive or alternative devices. Second, CSS can be changed and revised without affecting the content of a page. The most famous example of this is the CSS Zen Garden (http://www.csszengarden.com), a gallery of Web page designs done entirely in CSS. The HTML of the pages is the same from page to page.

Unfortunately, CSS design also has a higher learning curve for page designers, particularly those who use WYSIWYG editors. If you are interested in learning more about CSS design, you can read about it in greater depth in Shea & Holzschlag's (2005) *The Zen of CSS Design* (Shea maintains the CSS Zen Garden). Cederholm's (2006) *Bulletproof Web Design* is a good general-purpose text for learning to design page layouts without tables and WYSIWYG editors. Both books also address problems that older browsers have in rendering CSS layouts.

Exercise D

Using KompoZer or another Web editor, try to develop two layouts for a page with tables: a fixed one, specifying widths in pixels, and a liquid one, using percentages. To explore page layout quickly, instead of text content, try coloring your table's cells to represent different page areas: navigation, header art, content, sidebars, and so on. Try viewing your layout on different-sized screens; Pederick's WDA for Firefox has a Resize function that will precisely resize the browser window for you. What types of Web sites or site content would work best in the fixed layout? Which ones would work better in the liquid layout?

PREPARING IMAGES FOR THE WEB

When preparing images for print, the resolution of the file (in dots per inch, DPI) is a very important measure of image quality. However, for the Web, image dimensions and compression are more important. On the Web, images display according to their dimensions in pixels: a 350-pixel by 500-pixel image will appear the same size on screen, regardless of whether its resolution is 300 DPI or 96 DPI.

Also, whereas TIFF tends to be the preferred format for printed images, Web designers should use either JPEG or PNG formats. JPEG is often best for complex images, such as photographs. PNG images, which have largely replaced the older GIF format common on early Web pages, are useful for text images and other design elements with a limited number of colors. PNGs are lossless images, like TIFFs, meaning that their compression rate does not affect image quality. However, because they are lossless, PNG images can result in substantially larger file sizes for complex images such as photographs. Larger file sizes mean longer download times, especially for site visitors on dial-up or mobile Internet connections.

Preparing images for the Web, then, is a balance between quality and file size. As a general rule, higher quality images (that is, those that have the least compression, the most colors, and the largest dimensions in pixels) will be larger in terms of file size, whereas lower quality images (heavy compression, reduced colors, small dimensions) will have a smaller file size.

Most photographic image sources, either photographs from digital cameras or scanned material, tend to be much larger than necessary for the Web. Even on basic digital cameras, images can easily be thousands of pixels wide and tall. Their large size is necessary for print; most laser or ink jet printers can print at 300 or even 600 DPI. On a 600-DPI printer, an image that prints at 4 inches wide would have to be 2400 pixels (600 DPI × 4 inches) wide on screen. Commercial printing presses can print at even higher resolutions.

But screens are low resolution by comparison and display in pixel units, not inches. Digital photographs coming straight from a camera are generally too big to display fully on even the most high-resolution screen displays that were considered previously.

You may have visited Web sites in the past that have tiny images that seem to take forever to load. This is due to the site's designer using a Web editor to resize images, many of which have options such as the ones in KompoZer, shown in Figure 13.7.

It is considered very poor practice to resize images this way. In fact, images "resized" this way are not resized at all, but rather shrunk to fit particular dimensions on the Web page. This means that the full-size image still has to be downloaded, which is why some pages have small images that take a disproportionately long time to load; if you right-click such images in your browser and choose an option such as Open Image in New Tab, you will see that the actual image is considerably larger than it appeared on the Web page itself.

Image-editing programs such as Adobe Photoshop or Fireworks, or a free and open-source alternative such as the GNU Image Manipulation Program (GIMP), are much better suited to resizing images. In addition to resizing the image and, therefore, its file size, most image editors have special algorithms that maintain the visual quality of the image even as its resized. Images resized in a Web editor often appear mildly distorted, or pixelated, whereas images resized in an image editor often look even better than their original, larger version. Note, though, that while images can be reduced without a loss in quality, images that are enlarged are rarely suitable for use on the Web or in print.

Once you have resized your photographic images, they should be saved as JPEGs and compressed (most image editors allow you to specify the file's compression when

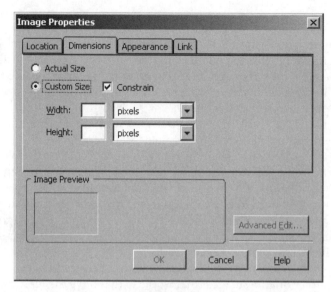

FIGURE 13.7 KompoZer allows adjustment to image sizes, but this is bad practice. (Visit www.pearsonhighered.com/riley to view this figure in color.)

you go to save). However, there is no one best compression rate or file size; experimentation is essential.

For example, consider the text image from the font section given earlier. Figure 13.8 shows both a PNG and JPEG version, with no compression on the JPEG. The PNG in this case is only 7 kilobytes (KB), whereas the JPEG is more than twice that file size at 16 KB. To reduce the JPEG to 7 KB, it has to be compressed by quite a lot. And as you can see in Figure 13.9, that results in *compression artifacts*, or junk pixels generated in the compression process. In the case of this text, the PNG is the better choice: small file size and high quality.

Photographic images, however, are almost always better suited to the JPEG format. But compression works differently and is more or less noticeable, depending on an image's content. Consider Figure 13.10, which has the same image of a house, bare trees, sky, and snow but under three different compressions: none, mild, and high.

FIGURE 13.8 JPEG (top) with no compression and lossless PNG (bottom).

FIGURE 13.9 JPEG image compressed to 7KB to match PNG file size. See Figure 13.8.

The JPEG with no compression is 278 KB—very large for an image whose dimensions are only 500 by 375 pixels. The mild compression image is only 41 KB, or about 15% of the file size as the uncompressed image. The highly compressed image is 31 KB, which is 75% of the size of the mildly compressed image. For that little savings in file size, the image quality has degraded severely.

It is important to notice that not all parts of the image have degraded the same. Consider the branches on the trees, which still look crisp in the mildly compressed image and, to a certain extent, the highly compressed image. There is a noticeable drop in quality in the snow and sky areas, which appear mottled in the mildly compressed image and practically pixilated in the highly compressed image.

An image with more intricate detail (such as tree branches) will usually result in a larger file size, whereas areas of roughly similar color (such as sky) will result in a smaller file size. But rarely is a photographic image all intricate detail or all similar

FIGURE 13.10 Photographic image under three different JPEG compressions. (Visit www.pearsonhighered.com/riley to view this figure in color.)

color: That is why it is essential to experiment with your images until you find an effective compromise between compression, file size, and image quality.

Finally, remember that, as with the image text in the font section, you should always provide descriptive alt text on your images. Pictures may be worth a thousand words, but alt text is limited to 1,024 characters. Be as descriptive as possible: "Photograph of a house surrounded by snow and bare trees at sunset."

Exercise E

Go to the Creative Commons area on the photo-sharing site Flickr (http://www.flickr.com/creativecommons/) and browse the BY: Attribution License photographs, which you are allowed to use and manipulate for your own projects (if you publish them on the Web, though, be sure to give attribution to the original photographer). Try finding images that have large amounts of similar-colored areas, images that are highly detailed, and others that provide a mix. Resize and recompress the images in your image editor. How small can you get the file sizes before their quality is noticeably compromised? How significantly does compression reduce the file size on very small versus very large versions of the images? See if you can develop a set of guidelines for yourself on how to best compress different kinds of images using your image-editing program.

INDICATING ACTIONABLE AREAS

Web site visitors expect to do more with Web pages than read and view images; they also expect to navigate the site, often by clicking on text or images.

Users' expectations about the location and appearance of links come from two sources: the structure of other sites and the structure of pages within a site. The main navigation links for a site commonly appear in one or both of two locations on a page: across the top or to the left of page content. If both locations are used, the top is generally reserved for higher level groupings of information, while the left panel is used for more specific groupings. Not surprisingly, research indicates that users perform better when navigation links are placed consistently within the various pages of site (e.g., the links should not appear in the left panel on the homepage and then move to the right panel on interior pages; Health and Human Services [HHS], 2006, p. 60).

Visual identification of hyperlinks is a strong aid to users, who need visual cues to identify which text constitutes an *actionable area*, an area on which users can click. Common methods of visually identifying hyperlinks are underlining, distinctive color, or both underlining and color. According to Nielsen (2008), links in main navigation bars do not need to be underlined or set in color, since the navigation bar itself clearly indicates an actionable area. Nielsen's investigation of 27 company intranets indicated that 75% of them used a consistent link color (typically blue), regardless of whether the links ran in as part of the surrounding text or were set off in list format. He argues, however, that distinctively colored links that are set off in lists do not also need to be underlined: "In a big list, underlining can decrease readability and—depending on spacing and typeface—it can be cluttered and ugly."

For users interacting with a page with a mouse, the mouse cursor is a clear indicator of whether an item is actionable or not. In Figure 13.11, the mouse cursor changes how we interpret the image; in one case, the image appears to be clickable, due to the finger-pointing icon. In the other, the arrow suggests that the image is not actionable.

FIGURE 13.11   Different mouse cursors over the same image indicate actionable areas. (Visit www.pearsonhighered.com/riley to view this figure in color.)

The goal of designing actionable areas, then, is to correctly cue users as to which items are clickable and which are not. Users who believe an area to be clickable that is not will be frustrated, perhaps suspecting that their browser or your page is malfunctioning. Conversely, users who believe an area is not clickable, when in fact it actually is clickable, may miss important content or functionality that is part of your site.

Cues such as color and underlining indicate actionable areas on text, as can small bits of background color. But it is also important to remember that some users may not use a mouse at all to navigate your site, but instead use a keyboard. Most browsers allow users to use the Tab key to move through links and provide a dotted border around the active link, which can be followed by hitting the Return key (Figure 13.12).

Images are strongly suggestive of actionable elements, particularly if they have any sort of three-dimensionality about them: drop shadows, for example, or bevels. For this reason, it is important to avoid those kinds of effects on elements such as page headings and other areas that actually are not clickable.

Regardless of the visual effect you employ to suggest an element's actionability, it is always good practice to provide a large area that can be clicked on for any given element. In Figure 13.13, the navigation element on the left requires the actual text of "Resume" to be clicked on, whereas the example on the right will activate the link from anywhere within the colored area. UD principles would suggest providing the larger clickable area not only because of the needs of individuals with low motor skills, but because everyone would have an easier, more accurate experience clicking on an item that has a large tolerance for mouse positions and error.

FIGURE 13.12   Keyboard navigation is possible by browsers providing dotted borders on active actionable areas. (Visit www.pearsonhighered.com/riley to view this figure in color.)

FIGURE 13.13   Providing a large actionable area (right) is more universally accessible than a small target area of text (left).

Exercise G

Examine the following collection of screen components with mouse cursors. Which items appear to be clickable but have an arrow cursor? Which items do not appear to be clickable but have a pointer cursor? How would you design these items differently? What is it about the design of each of these items that suggest to you that they are clickable or not?

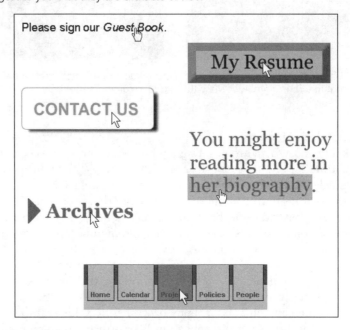

DESIGNING AND TESTING FOR USABILITY

The guidelines presented in this chapter represent *heuristics* (strategies, guidelines, or principles developed or widely accepted by experts, either through empirical research or extensive practice) for resolving design problems and making design decisions. However, you should also become familiar with the concepts of *usability testing* and *iterative design*. Usability testing refers to the process of testing a product or document, such as a Web site, with representative users and observing how accurately and efficiently they can complete desired tasks, such as looking up a name in an employee directory.

Typically, more subjective reactions are also gathered to gauge users' responses to the look and feel of the site. For example, a company might want to know whether its site's green background—chosen to connote ecofriendliness—conjures a sense of ill-health instead. Iterative design refers to the process of incorporating user responses into the design process, refining the design, and retesting. Designers may have users respond to *paper prototypes* (sketches of pages) or to *wireframes*, skeletal layouts (typically without extensive design elements) that suggest how users would move through a site's proposed pages. For more on paper prototyping, see Snyder (2003).

Usability testing is a complex field in and of itself, and even an introductory view of it lies outside the scope of this book. However, good surveys of processes and principles related to usability can be found in Barnum (2002), HHS (2006), and Krug (2005).

Conclusion

Although many of the principles of print design can be carried over to Web design, the ways that fonts and color work on the Web, the size of screens, and the preparation of images all require special care, particularly if they are to indicate, or avoid indicating, actionable areas on a Web site.

Usability testing is an important part of the iterative design process that defines Web design generally. And all aspects of Web design are well served by accounting for UD principles that meet the needs of a range of users, regardless of their technological access or physical abilities.

Summary of Key Concepts and Terms

accessibility
actionable area
alt text
assistive/adaptive
  technology
Cascading Style Sheets
  (CSS)

compression artifacts
fixed layout
gamma correction
heuristics
Hypertext Markup
  Language (HTML)

iterative design
liquid layout
paper prototypes
single sourcing
universal design
usability testing

Web-safe fonts
Web standards
what-you-see-is-what-you-
  get (WYSIWYG)
wireframe

Review Questions

1. What are the seven principles of UD? How do they apply to Web design?
2. Give an example of a Web-safe font. What makes a font Web safe? What alternatives are there for presenting unusual fonts on Web pages?
3. What are the primary display concerns that Web designers have to keep in mind in designing for the screen?
4. What are the different issues in preparing images for the screen versus for print?
5. What are some techniques used to indicate actionable areas on a Web page?

Additional Exercises

1. Go to stumbleupon.com and click the Stumble! button until you find a site that interests you but that you have never visited before.
   a. Analyze the rhetorical situation (i.e., the purpose and audience) for the site: What goals do you think the company is trying to accomplish or should try to accomplish with its Web site? To what audiences should the site communicate? For what purposes would those audiences use the site?
   b. Analyze the homepage for how well it accomplishes the following: (i) effectively uses space on the screen (i.e., screen real estate), (ii) effectively meets expectations for typical navigation and layout, (iii) effectively indicates hypertext, and (iv) effectively uses visual elements, such as fonts, color, and images.
   c. Based on your analysis of the site's purpose and audience and your analysis of its current design, create a paper prototype for a redesigned page.

2. Analyze the audiences and purposes of the following Web sites:
   a. Delicious: http://delicious.com
   b. Newsvine: http://www.newsvine.com
   c. Recovery.gov: http://www.recovery.gov
   Then, for each site, list three tasks that you would ask participants in a usability test to carry out to determine the extent to which users can do want they want to do with the site. For example, you might ask participants testing the Web site of the insurance company Blue Cross/Blue Shield (http://www.bcbs.com) to carry out these tasks:
   • Locate a dermatologist within 5 miles of your home.
   • Find information about using your BlueCard when you are outside the United States.
   • Find the glossary definition of the acronym SCHIP.

Print Objects: Expanding Upon Conventional Print Forms

James Maciukenas

Previous chapters have discussed a range of print and electronic forms: for example, newsletters, flyers, brochures, posters, and Web sites. An article by Brumberger (2007) expands upon strategies for investigating typical print and electronic forms by proposing the introduction of *visual thinking exercises* into visual literacy courses to encourage students of design to explore document elements and structures through sketching.

In the spirit of promoting visual thinking and encouraging exploration, this chapter discusses print objects as a way to further expand your design ideas beyond conventional print forms. By the end of this chapter, you should be able to do the following:

- Understand what a print object is
- Recognize the value of adding print objects to your document design repertoire
- Become familiar with the process of brainstorming, sketching, and prototyping a print object

This chapter illustrates some samples of print objects and takes you through an exercise demonstrating how to conceptualize and produce your own print object. These features are designed to help you better understand the process of implementing novel design strategies for projects with practical requirements.

OVERVIEW OF RELEVANT DESIGN CONCEPTS AND PRINCIPLES

Print objects introduce object-based qualities into conventional print design exercises through the use of three-dimensionality, *trompe l'oeil* (literally, a design that "tricks the eye"), and other techniques. Print objects are a way of exploring physicality and materiality through exercises in three-dimensional and quasi-three-dimensional model making. Print objects expand upon Brumberger's (2007) visual thinking exercises to include the application of activities she observed (and found inspiration in) when visiting an architectural design studio—for example, sketching and model making—while exploring genres familiar to technical and professional communication.

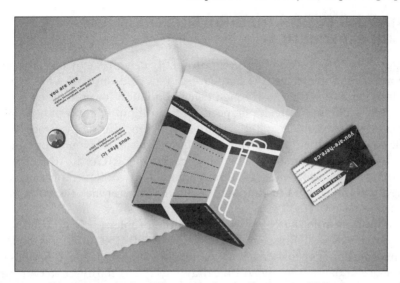

FIGURE 14.1 Press kit with trompe l'oeil illustration box and swim cap. (Visit www.pearsonhighered .com/riley to view this figure in color.)

This chapter shows how you can benefit from the challenge of *novel design*, in particular, the creation of print objects that convey their message through the medium of a conceptually related object. Common uses of print objects include invitations, press kits, and promotional items—all cases where a message must stand out from many others competing for an audience's attention. For example, when design students held their end-of-year art show in a natatorium, their press kit included a swim cap (Figure 14.1). Similarly, a university's luncheon invitation to area schoolteachers was printed on small brown paper bags like those traditionally used to carry lunch to school. Each of these examples illustrates novel design strategies, such as the use of metaphor and three-dimensionality, to create a print object.

WHY THESE PRINCIPLES ARE IMPORTANT

Exploring novel design has practical benefits for future designers, since research indicates that novel designs enhance audience interest (Abed, 1994; Berlyne, 1960, 1971; Berlyne, Graw, Salapatek, & Lewis, 1963; Phillips & McQuarrie, 2002). Yet, print objects and their ability to convey a message through novel design have not found much of a foothold outside of specialty advertising and promotional materials and certainly not as a core exercise in visual literacy courses. The limited use of print objects for professional communication purposes may stem from the extra cost involved in producing intricate packaging. However, this limitation should not outweigh the benefits that print objects can provide in situations when large production runs and the generous budgets necessary to facilitate them are not an immediate concern.

Ignoring these immediate concerns, exploring novel design through print objects will challenge you to layer conceptual, visual, and physical design elements onto your projects. This challenge will further develop your ability to creatively solve design problems for document types you may already be familiar with, such as the press kit, the trifold brochure, and the poster (among other possible document types).

DEMYSTIFYING DESIGN THROUGH SKETCHING AND HANDS-ON EXPLORATION

Brumberger (2007) proposes a method to "demystify design . . . by teaching students to see the normal—the mundane, the familiar—in new and unusual ways" (p. 384). She clarifies designer and writer Marty Neumeier's equation for generating a visual concept, namely, "problem + (fresh perspective × intuition) = concept" (p. 385). Brumberger stresses the importance of the activity of sketching during the process of arriving at possible concepts rather than relying on a computer-based layout program where the final product will be assembled, whether it be Microsoft Word, Adobe InDesign, or other document-layout software. It is through the activity of sketching that a design can be explored without constraints imposed by knowledge (or lack thereof) of a software program's features or tools.

The important role sketching can play in the problem-solving process has been stressed by others as well. Brasseur (1993), Goldschmidt (1994), and Laseau (1986) each identify drawing as a way to access imagination. Maciukenas (2006) describes sketching as "the practice of using brief illustrative drawings . . . to clarify interconnected ideas" used to communicate ideas to others (p. 331). Fish and Scrivener (1990) propose that sketching leads to the clarification of "confused things [which] rouse the mind to new inventions" (p. 120). Brumberger (2007) builds on this work by proposing visual thinking exercises, a problem-solving process using sketching as a foundation. Her exercises are based partly on the work of psychologist Vera John-Steiner. John-Steiner (1997) describes visual thinking as "the representation of knowledge in the form of structures in motion; it is the flow of images as pictures, diagrams, explanatory models, orchestrated paintings of immense ideas, and simple gestures" (p. 109).

This chapter contends that print objects provide a practical, model-making and paper-prototyping exercise to fulfill the explanatory model aspect of John-Steiner's work and offer students of visual literacy yet another strategy to turn to when tasked with designing a document. Like sketching, working with print objects requires (and allows) designers to break free of software tools and take, literally, a hands-on approach to creating a novel design.

THE VALUE OF MAKING PRINT OBJECTS

Making print objects encourages problem-solving strategies through exercises that develop your ability to not only show your ideas, but to make and demonstrate your ideas through direct application in "documents" that might take three-dimensional form, such as those seen in Figures 14.1, 14.3, and 14.4. Print objects can help you develop the ability to "infuse the act of making with the act of thinking" described by Lupton (1998, p. 161) as a goal of visual literacy courses. Brumberger (2007) also makes a similar statement that "visual thinking entails much more than visualization" (p. 381).

Print objects require you to grapple with the complexity of layering conceptual, visual, and physical design elements to further develop your problem-solving abilities, yet they remain relevant because of their positioning within the field that is already being explored: technical and professional communication. Examples can be found in advertising, corporate communication, and packaging design (among others) and allow you to participate not only in the act of visualization but also in the act of object making.

CONNECTING NOVELTY AND PROFESSIONAL COMMUNICATION

Creative experimentation certainly would not be considered a novel concept to professional communicators, yet when designing documents to communicate messages to specific audiences, novelty most likely would not be listed as a design requirement.

FIGURE 14.2   Contract highlighted with Post-it Arrow Flags for easily locating where signatures are required. (Visit www.pearsonhighered.com/riley to view this figure in color.)

Often in professional communication, an effective document is a standard familiar form such as a contract, a poster, or invitation. Paradoxically, the familiarity of these forms may also open the door to novelty in professional communication.

Example 1: Arrow Flags

A simple and familiar example of three-dimensionality being used in workplace settings is the variety of Post-it Brand products used to note and mark documents for future reference by their users. One product, Post-it Arrow Flags (see Figure 14.2), might be encountered during the closing of the purchase of a home.

The seemingly endless pages of a variety of agreements to sign within a contract are often printed black and white on 8.5 × 11-inch paper in 10 point, Times New Roman type, with consistent headers and footers. The format of the documents allows the user to understand that an important and singularly purposed transaction is taking place, such as the purchase of a home. Yet, if left to navigate through this process by only the documents themselves, the user might quickly become overwhelmed when attempting to locate where signatures are required. The novel Arrow Flags (a simple print object applied to the document, providing contrast lacking in the original document) quickly identify where action is required. Therefore, the novelty of the Arrow Flags enhances the clarity of the document, allowing the user to more effectively complete the actions requested by the document due to the addition of a visual layer to the document. Print objects, therefore, can be seen as a useful addition of novelty to one genre of professional communication, the contract.

Example 2: The Poster

The poster is a professional communication genre that can take advantage of the novelty of print objects. The example in Figure 14.3 uses trompe l'oeil techniques to give the flat plane of the poster the appearance of three-dimensionality through the use of realistic photography, presenting a scene to capture the attention of an audience.

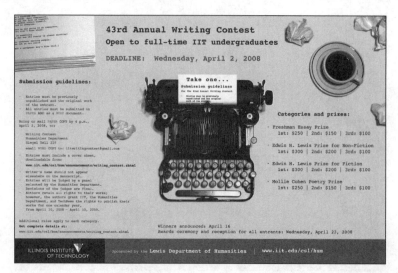

FIGURE 14.3 Poster advertising and encouraging participation in a writing contest using trompe l'oeil photography and takeaway flyers dispensed by the typewriter. Designed by James Maciukenas. Used by permission. (Visit www.pearsonhighered.com/riley to view this figure in color.)

The poster in Figure 14.3 adds another layer of interest and usefulness to its audience by offering take-away flyers from a pocket accessed through a cut through the poster where paper would normally be fed through a typewriter when in use. This pocket holds a number of the "Take one . . ." flyers, which serve as reminders to potential entrants of where they can access more information about the contest, how to enter, and when to submit their entries.

Example 3: The Invitation

The invitation is another professional communication genre that can take advantage of the novelty of print objects. The example of student work in Figure 14.4, which illustrates a print object used to invite viewers to a new coffee shop, uses three-dimensionality to add objectlike qualities to the flatness of a conventional invitation in order to capture the audience's attention. Three-dimensionality is achieved by using the coffee cup and a commonplace hot beverage sleeve in combination to create the invitation rather than relying on a more conventional card or flyer format.

In addition to three-dimensionality, the invitation in Figure 14.4 adds layers of interest and usefulness for its audience by offering information about the business in a novel way. Usually, check boxes on the side of a to-go coffee cup hot beverage sleeve are used by coffee shop employees to identify the drink ordered by the client. In the invitation shown in Figure 14.4, the check boxes provide information to the client about the business: conveniences, including a drive-through and comfy sofas, and products offered by the business, such as tasty coffee and pastries. The coffee cup also serves as a delivery mechanism for flyers stored in the cup and accessed through the lid. The cup holds a number of the "Please TAKE ONE!" flyers, serving as reminders to visit the coffee shop again.

Each of the examples just illustrated uses three-dimensionality to create atypical forms for typical print forms. Each uses print objects to solve common design problems, resulting in novel designs, and each was arrived at through a process of layering conceptual, visual, and physical design elements to create an effectively designed document.

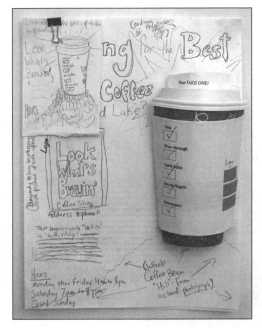

FIGURE 14.4 Prototype of an invitation advertising the grand opening of a coffee shop. Conveniences are listed in checkboxes on the hot beverage sleeve, and take-away flyers are dispensed through the lid of the cup. Designed by Patricia Nowacki. Used by permission. (Visit www. pearsonhighered.com/riley to view this figure in color.)

CONCEPTUALIZING AND CREATING A PRINT OBJECT

This section discusses some strategies for conceptualizing and creating a print object to enhance or replace a document that is conventionally delivered through a two-dimensional design on paper.

A print object introduces object-based qualities into a conventional print design through the use of actual or perceived three-dimensionality. Most importantly, a print object uses actual or perceived three-dimensionality as added value for the document in a way that a conventional print design does not. For example, the graphic design featured on a cereal box is not considered a print object because three-dimensionality is provided by the cardboard box the design is printed on, not by design itself.

The student work example in Figure 14.5, a poster advertising flu shots for faculty, staff, and students, uses photography and familiar objects to create a scene the intended audience might be familiar with and wants to avoid: catching the flu and the need for tissues. Value is added to the design through the perceived three-dimensionalities of the trompe l'oeil nature of the photographic image of the tissue box and of the physical presence of tissues. The tissue is actually one of many takeaway flyers the audience can remove from the poster to serve as a reminder to get their flu shot. The tissues not only add visual interest to the poster, but they also add the experience of needing to use tissues, reinforcing the experience the audience wants to avoid, catching the flu.

In order to begin your print object exercise, first select a document type and specific use that will form the basis for the print object that you will conceptualize. Some suggested document types and events are listed in Table 14.1; however, your instructor may provide additional suggestions.

Next, brainstorm physical objects that may be associated with the event you choose and that would provide added value to the document type through the

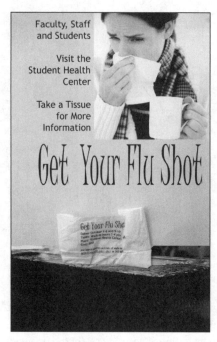

FIGURE 14.5 Paper prototype of a print object announcement for the availability of flu shots for faculty, staff, and students. Designed by Kelly Schaefer. Used by permission. (Visit www.pearsonhighered .com/riley to view this figure in color.)

production of a print object. For example, for the poster in Figure 14.5, possible physical objects that could be associated with flu shots include the needle used to administer the flu shot, a box of tissues, and the tissue itself. For the event that you choose, think about the event and make a list of all the objects you can think of that are required to hold the event and to participate in the event. The essence of finding suitable object(s) to use in the document is to identify an object that viewers themselves will immediately associate with the event and that might also be used to convey visual or verbal information.

Then, choose two or three of the physical objects associated with your event and sketch three possible arrangements of the objects with textual content about the event. The student work example in Figure 14.6 illustrates using sketching to combine possible physical objects and text content for a flu shot–announcement poster.

TABLE 14.1 Suggested document types and events for a print object exercise.

Document Type	Associated Event
Invitation/Announcement	Pet store opening
	Coffee shop opening
	Record-release party
	Theater opening
	Kite-flying lessons
Contest/Event Poster	Early voting
	5K charity run
	Speaker about "Green" architecture
	Flu shots available

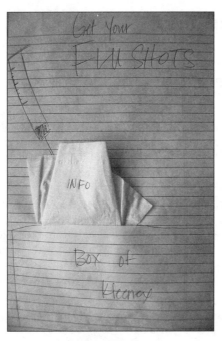

FIGURE 14.6 Concept sketch produced during the brainstorming of a print object. Designed by Kelly Schaefer. Used by permission. (Visit www.pearsonhighered.com/riley to view this figure in color.)

Lastly, produce a *paper prototype* of your print object in order to experience the physicality of the print object conceptualized. The paper prototype does not need to be of the same quality that a final finished product would be. However, it should show the basic proportions of the design in something close to its actual size, and it should demonstrate how any actual or trompe l'oeil objects will figure into the document design. Figures 14.4 and 14.5 illustrate paper prototypes at varying degrees of completion.

Conclusion

In this chapter, examples of print objects are demonstrated to be novel approaches to design problems. Print objects further reinforce the physicality of Brumberger's (2007) visual thinking exercises that can help you develop flexible problem-solving strategies that are becoming more and more important for professional communicators as the field "transcends the border between print and digital texts" (p. 398).

As you continue to explore the relationships between print and digital design tasks, it is important for you to have a better understanding of the qualities that make print and digital texts different. One way to do this is to experience a multilayered design approach combining conception, visualization, and physicality. Print object exercises encourage you, early on in the process, to leave the computer screen and enter the physicality of the world in which the work will exist as an object.

Summary of Key Concepts and Terms

novel design	print object	visual thinking exercise
paper prototype	trompe l'oeil	

GLOSSARY

alignment Design attribute that no item should be placed on the page arbitrarily; every item should have a visual connection with something else on the page.

all caps In typography, text set in all uppercase characters. Type in ALL CAPS creates too much **white space** within and between letterforms to be comfortably read over long stretches of text.

analogous colors Colors such as yellow, yellow-orange, and light orange next to each other on a color wheel. Analogous colors are similar; they harmonize and are attractive together.

anatomical feature A detail in letterforms that contributes to the tone of particular typefaces.

ascender The part of the tall lowercase letters, such as *b* and *d*, that extends above the *x*-**height**.

aspect ratio In typography, the ratio of a typeface's average height to its width. In graphs, the ratio of the *y*-**axis** to the *x*-**axis**; research shows using an aspect ratio of about 2:3 helps show data objectively. In digital photography, the ratio of an image's height to its width; resizing an image without maintaining its aspect ratio causes image distortion. In Web design, the height to width ratio of a Web page's resolution, such as 1280×1024 and 1600×1200, which both have a 4:3 aspect ratio.

assistive/adaptive technology Devices and computer applications that help people with disabilities perform tasks that they would have difficulty doing otherwise. For example, screen readers help people with vision impairments use the Web.

balance A sense of equilibrium created by the arrangement of items with similar weight on opposing parts of the page; one of the central tenets of **Gestalt Theory** related to the use of **grids** states that humans tend to feel more comfortable with a sense of equilibrium. See also **symmetry**.

baseline The invisible line on which letters sit.

bleed tabs Page organizers with color that run to the edge of the page so that the color is visible on the fore edge of the document; useful for organizing and demarcating sections of a document and enhancing searchability.

blue phenomenon The finding and apparent fact that the color blue is well liked universally and cross-culturally.

bold In typography, a typeface style of greater **weight** than the regular font.

bouma The outline shape of a word made by its letters.

broken construction An **anatomical feature** of a typeface that contributes to a friendly tone by displaying imperfection in the letterforms.

bullet list A series of vertically stacked textual items, each set off by a bullet: a typographic symbol, often a dot resembling a bullet hole.

cap-height The height of uppercase letterforms in a typeface.

caption One of several concise verbal components that identify and explain visual elements of a graph or chart. Also, a short piece of text, usually placed under a photograph, which helps the reader interpret the photograph and relate it to the surrounding story; also known as a **cutline**.

Cascading Style Sheets (CSS) A **Web standard** for producing Web page layouts. Cascading Style Sheets disassociate page design from the page content and, thus, can be changed and revised without affecting a page's content.

categorical data A type of **quantitative data** in a chart or graph that compares some property of discrete, nonoverlapping categories; also known as **nominal data.**

category label On a graph, a label for a **tick mark** on the *x*-**axis**.

cell The intersection of a **row** and a **column** in a table.

centered A position of text that is aligned symmetrically around a point equidistant from the left and right margins.

c-fold brochure *See* **trifold brochure**.

chart area The larger area of a graph that contains all the verbal and visual elements related to the graph.

chroma One of three main properties of color, also called **saturation**. The degree to which a **hue** is present, usually measured as a color's purity in relation to gray.

CMYK A color system based on the light that cyan, magenta, yellow, and black absorb. In this system, adding one **hue** to the other makes a darker hue.

color scheme A planned combination of colors for a document, such as colors for the document's background, **headings**, subheadings, and graphs. Some classic color schemes stem from colors' relationships to each other on a color wheel, such as **analogous** and **complementary color** schemes.

column Vertically arranged portions of tables.

column head A label that identifies the content of one individual **column**.

column spanner A **heading** that associates a set of two or more **columns**, usually by using a solid line (i.e., a *rule*) under the spanner.

complementary colors Colors across from each other on a color wheel. Two complementary colors contrast, making each other look brighter and, thus, more aesthetically pleasing.

complementary relationship A relationship between prose and image in which the verbal and visual modes each provide different information about a concept or object, together conveying the concept or object more comprehensively than either could individually.

compression artifacts In digital photography, junk **pixels** generated in the compression process.

conclusion slide The last slide of a presentation, which summarizes the presentation's main points. It also cues audience members about the end of the presentation, giving them a moment to gather their thoughts and prepare questions or comments.

continuation One of the central tenets of **Gestalt Theory** related to the use of **grids,** which states that elements will be grouped together if a continuous pattern can be interpreted, and this pattern will be assumed to continue even if some parts are hidden.

contrast A design strategy that creates visual interest by using elements with noticeably different features; for example, typefaces that differ in the presence or absence of **serifs** or that have substantially different **point** sizes. Williams (2008) suggests that designers should use contrast dramatically, making contrasting items very different from each other.

counter The enclosed space within letterforms such as *o* and *d*.

CPL Characters per line, a commonplace term to describe line length.

cropping In photography, removing part of the image, usually but not necessarily from the edges.

crossbar In typography, a horizontal stroke on a letterform that connects to another stroke (or two) but does not cross the other stroke(s). An uppercase *H* displays a crossbar.

cutline *See* **caption**.

daguerreotype An early form of photography with a distinctive **sepia** tone, developed in the 19th century.

data line A visual representation of the relationship between two or among three or more units of information in a graph.

data point A visual representation of one unit of information in a graph.

data series Each line and its data points in a graph.

decimal numbering The organization of a document's sections with integers and decimal places, such as 3.2.2. Decimal numbering is precise, so readers can easily understand the level within the organizational hierarchy of the section they are reading at any given moment.

decorative visual One of three photographic categories into which visual elements arguably fall; designed to generate feeling in the viewer.

dependent variable In an experiment or study, the observed items that change depending on a change in one or more **independent variables**. For example, in a study of how different line lengths affect reading accuracy, reading accuracy is the dependent variable. In graphs, the dependent variable is plotted along the *y*-axis.

descender The portion of some lowercase letters, such as *g* and *y*, that extends below the **baseline** (the invisible line on which letters sit).

digital printing A printing process that involves layering toner on the surface of the paper; toner, digital printing's "ink," is not absorbed by the paper. With digital printing, only **process color** is possible.

direct labeling The placement of verbal and numerical elements on, or very close to, the associated visual element.

display typeface In typography, typefaces that are designed to be printed in large sizes and used only in short stretches of text. A typical use for a display typeface is a magazine ad or a billboard.

documentary photography A type of photography that often favors wide fields of view, where realism is used to present a scene or person in their natural state.

document set A group of visually related documents; for example, a business card, letterhead stationery, sales brochure, and Web site for the same company would constitute a document set and would ideally be unified by their use of similar visual elements such as color scheme, logo, and so forth.

dots per inch (DPI) A measurement of the output generated by a printer or similar device. A dot is the smallest unit of color that can be generated by the device. The higher the DPI count of the printer, the better document quality the printer can produce.

double-numeration A system of numbering tables and figures in large documents that have formal subparts such as chapters. For example, "Table 2.4" would indicate the fourth table in the second chapter of the document.

double-story Letterform construction consisting of two **counters** joined by a stem or a counter and a nearly enclosed bowl. The lowercase *g* and *a* in some typefaces are double-story (instead of **single-story**).

drop cap A capital letter that is larger than the surrounding text and whose **baseline** is typically lower, or "dropped," relative to the surrounding text; sometimes used informally to describe any large initial letter that begins a text unit.

dual coding theory The research-driven claim that people process words and images through two different cognitive subsystems: one specialized for nonverbal objects and events and the other for language. Dual coding theory suggests that integrating visual and verbal elements in a document or presentation gives the reader/audience two ways to process the message, which in turn fosters comprehension and recall.

empty third dimension A use of 3-D illustration in bar and line graphs that does not represent a real variable.

eyetracking A method of measuring the length of a reader's gaze (**fixations**), as well as the paths of the reader's eye movements (**saccades**) through a document.

file size In digital photography, the number of bytes—a series of data made up of ones and zeros—required to store information about the image and to display the image on a camera or computer. A small image might use 100,000 bytes to store the necessary information, while a large image might use 30,000,000 bytes or more to store the necessary information.

fixation The length of a reader's gaze.

fixed layout A Web page design that displays in the same horizontal size from screen to screen, regardless of a screen's width. The alternative is a **liquid layout**, which expands and contracts relative to a screen's width.

fixed pitch A characteristic of typeface in which the width of letterforms and spaces between letterforms do not vary. In a fixed-pitch typeface, a wide letterform such as *m* and a thin letterform such as *i* are assigned the same amount of space in a line of text.

flush left A position of text that falls at a consistent point with respect to the left **margin**.

flush right A position of text that falls at a consistent point with respect to the right **margin**.

footer A text item that runs across the bottom of a page and is repeated from page to page throughout at least one section of a document in order to help orient readers to their location in the document.

F-shaped pattern A pattern often attributed to readers of Web pages, measured with **heat maps** showing points of longer eye **fixations** throughout a document.

fully justified In typesetting, alignment of text and images within a **column** to align on the right and left margins. Newspaper **columns** are fully justified.

gamma correction An operation that adjusts an image file's brightness and intensity when it is displayed on a screen.

gamut The range of colors that a printer or monitor can produce. The gamut of the **RGB** colors is broader than that of **CMYK** colors.

Gestalt Theory A set of principles having to do with how humans perceive and organize information automatically on an unconscious level.

GIF A file format for images. Graphics Interchange Format (GIF) is often used for graphics or illustrations to be delivered and displayed on Web pages. GIF files use a type of compression with up to 256 colors for the display of an image or graphic.

graph schema One of the steps in the graph-comprehension process, influenced by the viewer's experience with graphs.

graph title One of the typical verbal components found in line and bar graphs; it should concisely and coherently describe the content of the graph (or chart).

grid A tool for managing complexity and for achieving a unified look throughout a document.

gridlines Lines on a graph that start at and are perpendicular to the axes.

gutter The inside (bound) **margin**, automatically larger than the outside (unbound) margin and used in documents that are to be printed double-sided and bound.

halftone In process printing, the technique of layering tiny dots of cyan, magenta, yellow, and black that combine to create the appearance of other colors; the term also refers to an image produced by this technique.

Handout Master A feature of Microsoft PowerPoint that allows users to create handouts from presentation slides easily; however, the handouts generated simply copy the presentation slides in groups of 3, 6, 9, or 12 onto a printed page and thus fail to take advantage of print's ability to display greater detail than slides.

header A text item that runs across the top of a page and is repeated from page to page throughout at least one section of a document in order to help orient readers as to location in the document.

heading A usually short line of text that appears at the top of a section of text. Usually, headings organize documents into a hierarchy of generality. They can be first-level, second-level, or third-level (typically not fourth-level or more). Headings that signal the most general level, the first-level headings, are heavier in **weight** and/or larger in size than other headings.

headline style Capitalizing the first letter of main words in titles of tables and figures, for example, "Number of Uninsured Alabama Motorists by Age Group."

heat map A color representation of the values of a variable, such as the duration of **fixations** throughout a document.

heuristics Strategies, guidelines, and principles developed or widely accepted by experts, either through empirical research or extensive practice, such as in Web design.

horizontal list A list set in the same format as a regular paragraph of text, also known as a **run-in list.**

horizontal rule A left-to-right line used to separate content in a document or in a table. For example, horizontal rules are often used under the table title, under the **column** heads, and at the bottom of the table to separate it from the text that follows it.

hue One of three main properties of color, the one determined by a color's dominant light wavelength. Also called *pigment.*

Hypertext Markup Language (HTML) A **Web standard** for creating structured documents with codes for items such as headings, lists, and hyperlinks.

icon A symbol with a form that suggests its meaning, such as ☼.

image bank An archive of photographs that can be licensed for use in specific document design projects; also known as **stock photo services**.

independent variable In an experiment or study, a variable whose values are independent of (i.e., not affected by) changes in the values of other variables. When independent variables are manipulated, they affect dependent variables. For example, in a study of how different line lengths affect reading accuracy, line length is the independent variable. The independent variable is plotted along the *x*-axis.

indicative visual One of three photographic categories into which visual elements arguably fall; designed to provoke action from the viewer.

informative visual One of three photographic categories into which visual elements arguably fall; designed to promote understanding of an idea.

interval data A type of **quantitative data** in a graph that compares some property at points along a continuum.

interval label On a graph, a label for a **tick mark** on the *y*-axis.

italics A font style that modifies the shape of a typeface, typically by slanting it to the right and giving it a more cursive look.

iterative design In Web site **usability testing**, the process of incorporating user responses into the design process, refining the design, and retesting.

JPEG The most commonly used image file format for image display on the Internet because it can render millions of colors. The Joint Photographic Experts Group (JPEG) format is widely supported by Web browsers.

justification The placement of text relative to the left and right **margins** of a page, **column**, or other design unit.

justified A shorter form of **fully justified.**

juxtapositional A relationship between image and prose in which the verbal and visual modes are at odds with one another.

kerning (noun) The amount of **white space** between letters, adjusted in a way that enhances **legibility** and **readability**; (verb) adjusting space for legibility, readability, or aesthetics.

key In process printing, black ink or toner. Designated with a *K* in **CMYK**. Also, in graphs and charts, a list of a graph's symbols and their meanings, also called a **legend**.

keyword A term that can be used to classify and search for an image.

label Explanatory material for elements in tables; also, one of the typical verbal components found in line and bar graphs to display measurements in the **plot area.**

landscape orientation Referring to an image whose horizontal dimension is greater than its vertical dimension.

landscape photography A type of photography that often favors wide fields of view, where realism is used to present a scene or person in a natural state.

leading White space between lines, needed to distinguish between two lines of text. Measured as the distance (in points) between the **baseline** of one line of type and the baseline of the line of type below it.

left aligned A position of text that falls at a consistent point with respect to the left margin. The right-hand side of the text varies. Also called **flush left** and **left justified**.

left justified A position of text that falls at a consistent point with respect to the left margin. The right-hand side of the text varies. Also called **flush left** and **left aligned**.

legend A list of a graph's symbols and their meanings, also called a **key.**

legibility The ease with which the letterforms in a particular typeface can be processed by a reader.

letterfold brochure *See* **trifold brochure**.

lightbox A device used by photographers that contains a surface of frosted glass lit from underneath, allowing the photographer to view and sort slides. In photography Web sites, a location within the site where images can be stored for future reference or viewing by others.

lightness Also called **value** and **luminance**, one of the three main properties of color, referring to the amount of light a color reflects. Low-value colors are more blackish, and high-value colors are more whitish. Pastels are high-value colors.

Likert scale A series of numbers (usually between 4 and 7) in which lower values are usually associated with lower agreement with a statement, and higher values are associated with higher agreement; often used to measure subjective reactions of research participants.

line spacing The distance (in **points**) between the **baseline** of one line of type and the baseline of the line of type below it.

liquid layout A Web page design that expands and contracts relative to a screen's width. The alternative is a **fixed layout**, which displays in the same horizontal size from screen to screen.

luminance *See* **lightness**.

margin The **white space** between the printed area of a page and the edge of the page.

megapixel One million **pixels**. In digital photography, an image sensor captures millions of pixels, so its ability to capture images is measured in megapixels.

mirror margin A margin that automatically shifts to allow for binding in a document that is to be printed double-sided and bound; also known as **offset margin**.

monoweight Typefaces that have no **thick-thin transition**.

negative polarity In figure-ground configurations, light figures (often text) on a dark background. In studies of Web pages, light text on a dark background is less readable than a **positive polarity** design (i.e., dark text on a light background).

negative space **White space** in a document.

nominal data Data that fit into discrete and distinct categories, such as "Catholic," "Muslim," "Buddhist." It is possible to count the number of items in each category, but there is no one item that is more "Catholic" than another. That is, there is no rank within the categories. Nominal data are also called **categorical data**.

notes Used at the bottom of a table to serve one of several purposes: to identify the source of data or to identify the level of significance if the table reports statistical information.

novel design Strategies for document design that involve metaphor and three-dimensionality. Novel design can be used to create **print objects** that convey their message through the medium of a conceptually related object.

offset margin *See* **mirror margin**.

offset printing A printing technique in which an image or text is inked onto a printing plate, transferred (offset) to a rubber blanket, then transferred to the printing surface.

optimize In digital photography, to reduce **file size** while maintaining sufficient document quality. Optimizing images for the Web allows pages to load faster.

orientation midangle The average slope of all of the lines in a graph. When the orientation midangle is 45°, the viewer's ability to make accurate readings and comparisons is enhanced.

overview slide A slide shown at the beginning of a presentation that signals the presentation's organization. Overview slides make the presentation's main point and its structure clear and thus facilitate comprehension.

Pantone® Matching System A color-matching system that is widely used in the printing industry. This system that allows designers to specify colors by a name or number (e.g., Pantone 3258, a shade of green).

paper prototype A sketch on paper of a document's design, the features of a digital interface, or the features of a device under development. A paper prototype shows the basic proportions of the design in something close to its actual size.

parallel structure Use of similar types of grammatical patterns in similar types of document elements (e.g., using simple present-tense verbs for labels of a Gantt chart).

photo shoot An event at which a photographer takes a requested photograph.

pitch The horizontal space used for each character; usually used in relation to monospace, or **fixed-pitch**, typefaces.

pixel A unit of measurement of a digital image on computer screen or other electronic display.

pixels per inch (PPI) A measurement of the number of **pixels** in one inch of a computer monitor's display. The greater the number of pixels displayed in 1 inch, the higher the image or display quality experienced by the viewer.

plot area The area on a graph defined by its axes.

PNG Portable Network Graphic; a file format for images that is replacing the **GIF** format. The PNG format is non-proprietary, i.e., developers of image-editing software or Internet browsers do not need to pay for a license in order to support this type of compression.

point A measurement of type size, with one point equal to 1/72 inch.

portrait orientation Referring to an image with a vertical dimension greater than its horizontal dimension.

portrait photography A type of photography focusing on an individual's face and expression, often captured during a deliberate pose by the subject.

positive polarity In figure-ground configurations, dark figures (often text) on a light background. In studies of Web pages, dark text on a light background is more readable than a **negative polarity** design (i.e., light text on a dark background).

prepress In traditional printing, preparation of a document up to the printing stage, including typesetting. In **digital printing**, the process of preparing digital files for printing, including checking that fonts are embedded in files and preparing camera-ready artwork.

Presenter View A feature of Microsoft PowerPoint that allows users to view presentation notes and presentation slides simultaneously while the audience sees only the presentation slides.

print object A document with three-dimensional or pseudo-three-dimensional characteristics. Print objects employ physical three-dimensionality, **trompe l'oeil**, and other techniques to make a document's physicality particularly salient.

print run Multiple copies in a document reproduction.

process color In printing, the process of combining cyan, magenta, yellow, and black together to create a color image. In this process, **halftones** of ink or toner for cyan, magenta, yellow, and black layer on paper to create the appearance of other colors.

proportion The ratio of a typeface's **x-height** (the height of its x letterform) to **cap height** (the height of its uppercase letterforms); a variable that contributes to a professional persona.

proximity Design guideline that states that related items should be grouped together so the related items are seen as one cohesive group rather than as unrelated items.

pull quote A short excerpt from a text that is copied in an enlarged format and inserted as a visual element into the page layout.

quantitative data Data that can be counted or expressed numerically. In contrast, qualitative data consist of descriptions of a studied item's properties.

ragged right Text that aligns at the left-hand side, so that right-hand text falls at inconsistent points.

readability Quality of giving "visual comfort" in long stretches of text; also used to refer to the ease with which readers process a body of text.

readability formula An index that takes into account linguistic variables such as word length and sentence length.

redundant relationship A relationship between image and prose in which the verbal and visual modes repeat or paraphrase one another.

register Degree of formality, such as the level of formality that a typeface lends to a document.

release form A document used to receive permission from subjects in a photograph before using the image in a publication or other public display.

repetition A design strategy in which a particular visual element is used at multiple points in a document, thereby creating consistency and unity of design. For example, the same color and font might be used for all headlines in a newsletter, enabling easy identification of them by readers.

resolution Pixels or **dots per inch** in a digital photograph.

RGB The system of colors used for computers and other electronic devices, based on the primaries of red, green, and blue. Also called the *direct color system* because it is based on the **hues** (red, green, blue) that humans perceive directly and that added together create white.

rhetoric The study of using visual or verbal language effectively for a particular purpose and with a particular audience in mind.

right aligned A position of text that falls at a consistent point with respect to the right margin. The left-hand side of the text varies. Also called **flush right** and **right justified**.

right justified A position of text that falls at a consistent point with respect to the right margin. The left-hand side of the text varies. Also called **flush right** and **right aligned**.

rights-managed photo One type of price structure for purchasing the use of a photograph, determined by a number of variables such as the type of document, number of copies, location of use, length of use, and nature of use.

row Horizontally arranged portions of tables.

row head In a table, a label that identifies the content of one individual **row**.

royalty-free photo One type of price structure for purchasing the use of a photograph, by which an individual pays a one-time flat fee (typically determined by size, file type, and **resolution**) for the right to use the image.

run-in list A **horizontal list**, that is, one set in the same format as a regular paragraph of text.

saccade A reader's eye movements. The movements occur when the eyes fix on one point and then move rapidly to another.

sans serif A broad category of typeface. Sans serif typefaces do not have "feet," horizontal lines, at the ends of their letterform strokes. Contrast Times New Roman with Helvetica. Helvetica is a commonly used sans serif typeface; its *x* letterform of does not have feet at the ends of its strokes.

saturation One of three main properties of color, also called **chroma**. The degree to which a **hue** is present, usually measured as a color's purity in relation to gray.

schema A framework for organizing knowledge about some aspect of the world. A professional communicator can employ a schema to facilitate users' understanding of a document by preparing them mentally or psychologically for the subsequent material.

schema theory The proposition that readers understand text better when they are able to integrate the text into pre-existing knowledge (represented in the **schema**, a framework for organizing knowledge about the world).

script One type of **schema** that is a mental representation of the prototypical sequence of events in a familiar situation.

sentence heading (headline) In presentation slides, complete sentences, as opposed to phrases, used as the titles of individual slides. So, instead of writing a phrase such as "The Danger of Explosion Fragments," a presenter looking to use a sentence heading might write "Explosion fragments outpace the blast and become the primary threat." Sentence headlines may facilitate comprehension and recall.

sentence style Capitalizing only the first letter of the first word in titles of tables and figures, for example, "Number of uninsured Alabama motorists by age group."

sepia A tone of warm brown colors used to make a recent photograph seem to have been taken in the distant past, as the tone mimics the color tone of **tintypes** and **daguerreotypes**, early forms of photography developed in the 19th century.

serif A broad category of typefaces. Serif typefaces, such as Times New Roman, have short, mainly horizontal lines (or "feet") at the ends of the main strokes of their letterforms.

similarity One of the central tenets of **Gestalt Theory**. This tenet states that design elements with like attributes will be perceived as related and as a group.

single-sourcing Creating one document that serves multiple media (e.g., screen viewing and printing) and multiple audiences or groups of users.

single-story Letterform construction consisting of one **counter**, as opposed to two counters (making it **double-story**). Some lowercase letterforms, such as lowercase *a*, switch from double-story in regular type to single-story in **italics**.

six-by-six rule A commonly stated guideline aimed at keeping presenters from creating text-heavy slides. The rule says no more than six words per line and no more than six lines per slide. The rule's intent is to keep audience attention on the oral presentation rather than on the written text on the slides.

Slide Master A feature of Microsoft PowerPoint that allows users to create and modify design defaults, such as font size for **headings** and layout of verbal and visual elements. Using the Slide Master avoids tedious and unnecessary work, such as replacing and resizing slide content on each individual slide.

Slide Sorter A feature of Microsoft PowerPoint that allows users to see a reduced-sized view of all slides in a presentation at once, which can be useful for organizing a presentation, checking the amount of text in the slides, and checking for visual consistency.

small caps A typeface style in which all letterforms are displayed in uppercase characters, but those characters are smaller than the normal style of uppercase characters in the same font. Small caps create rectangular-shaped text and can be used to differentiate textual elements.

spot color Ink colors mixed prior to the printing run, also called *custom colors*.

stacked list A **vertical list** that helps readers locate and process information more easily than text without this feature.

stage-setting relationship A relationship between image and prose in which the verbal and visual modes interact in such a way that one contextualizes and forecasts the content of the other.

stock photo An existing photo used for a document design project, rather than a custom-created image.

stock photo service An archive of photographs that can be licensed for use in specific document design projects; also called an **image bank**.

straddle rule In tables, a line that runs across several **columns**, usually under a **column spanner**.

stub In a table, the leftmost **column**. The stub typically identifies the information found in each row. In other words, the stub consists of a series of **row heads**.

stub head Identifies the category that the items in the stub (the leftmost **column**) have in common.

style guides A manual (either online or print) that specifies standards about how a document is to be prepared, especially with respect to details that come up during the writing and editing process—for example, format, punctuation, and usage.

supplementary relationship A relationship between image and prose in which one mode—visual or verbal—is dominant; the other mode elaborates on the dominant mode's message.

symmetry A technique for conveying **balance** in which visual elements are placed as mirror images of each other; related to the tenet of **Gestalt Theory** that states that humans tend to feel more comfortable with a sense of equilibrium.

table body All the **cells** that form the intersection of a **column heading** and a **row heading**.

table spanner In tables, a line (i.e., a *rule*) that divides the table's data horizontally so that two sets of data can share **column** headings.

table title The main **label** of a table that takes the form of a noun phrase; should mention the units of measurement, the variable being measured, and the entities of interest.

terminals The ends of the strokes of a letterform.

text typefaces Typefaces that are designed to be legible in smaller sizes and readable over stretches of text. Times New Roman and Helvetica are common examples.

thick-to-thin transition Also called *modeling*, the variation in a letterform stroke's thickness from one end of the stroke to the other end.

tick mark Indications on a graph to designate categories or intervals of data on each axis.

TIFF The most commonly used file format for print documents. The Tagged Image File Format (TIFF) file format is uncompressed and retains all information and image detail that the original image file contained.

tintype An early form of photography, often having a distinctive **sepia** tone, developed in the 19th century.

title slide The first slide of a presentation should include some basic information to orient the audience to the speaker and the topic: the title, date, and place of the presentation; the speaker's name and affiliation; and the organization's logo.

trifold brochure A brochure based on a piece of paper (usually 8.5 × 11) folded twice (like a business letter) to create a brochure with a total of six panels: three on the outside and three on the inside; also known as a **c-fold** or **letterfold brochure**.

trompe l'oeil In French, literally, "fool (or trick) the eye"; a technique that causes the viewer to perceive three-dimensionality in what is actually a two-dimensional design.

Trumatch® A color-matching system that allows designers to specify colors by a numbering code. The code consists of a number (1–50) for **hue** family, a letter (a–h) for **saturation**, and a number (1–7) for amount of black.

type family A group of related typefaces that have the same basic design; the typefaces may differ in **weight**, orientation, width, and so on, but not design. Such typefaces are designed carefully for letterform **proportion** and spacing between letterforms.

universal design An approach that enhances accessibility and **single-sourcing** for the Web, outlined in seven principles: equitable use, flexibility in use, simplicity and intuitiveness, perceptible information, tolerance for error, low physical effort, and appropriate size and space.

usability testing Testing a product or document, such as a Web site, with representative users and observing how accurately and efficiently they can complete desired tasks, such as looking up a name in an employee directory.

value *See* **lightness**.

variable pitch A characteristic of typeface letterforms in which different letterforms take up varying amounts of space; for example, wide letterforms such as *m* take up more space than thin letterforms such as *i*. Compare **fixed pitch**.

vertical list *See* **stacked list**.

visual thinking exercise A problem-solving process for document design that uses sketching on paper and by-passes software tools.

Web-safe fonts Fonts that are commonly available (especially in Windows and Mac operating systems) and likely to be installed on end users' computers. Thus, using a Web-safe font increases the likelihood that the designer's intended font will display as planned.

Web standards Formal technical specifications that define and describe the use of certain aspects of Web design, for example, **HTML**.

weight The width of the strokes that make up the letter-forms of a typeface.

what-you-see-is-what-you-get (WYSIWYG) A design interface, such as a Web design interface, that allows the designer to see the document as it will appear to its audience. The designer can manipulate a document without remembering codes or even knowing how to work with them.

white space Space in a document with no visual or verbal elements (i.e., unmarked space). It helps readers locate and group information on a page; also called **negative space**.

wire frame In Web design, skeletal layouts (typically without extensive design elements) that suggest how users would move through a site's proposed pages.

x-axis Horizontal axis of a graph.

x-axis label One of the typical verbal components found in line and bar graphs. It should concisely and coherently identify the variable plotted along the *x*-axis. In graphs, that variable will typically be the **independent variable**.

x-height The height of a typeface's *x* letterform.

y-axis The vertical axis of a graph.

y-axis label One of the typical verbal components found in line and bar graphs. It should concisely and coherently identify the variable plotted along the *y*-axis. In graphs, that variable will typically be the **dependent variable**.

REFERENCES

Aaronson, B. (1970). Some affective stereotypes of color. *International Journal of Symbology, 2*, 15–27.

Abed, F. (1994). Visual puns as interactive illustrations: Their effects on recognition memory. *Metaphor and Symbol, 9*, 45–60.

Adams, F. M., & Osgood, C. E. (1973). A cross-cultural study of the affective meaning of color. *Journal of Cross-Cultural Psychology, 4*, 135–157.

Adams, M. J. (1979). Models of word recognition. *Cognitive Psychology, 11*, 133–176.

Alley, M., & Neeley, K. A. (2005). A case for sentence headlines and visual evidence. *Technical Communication, 52*, 417–426.

Alley, M., Schreiber, M., Ramsdell, K., & Muffo, J. (2006). How the design of headlines in presentation slides affects audience retention. *Technical Communication, 53*, 225–234.

American Psychological Association. (2001). *Publication manual of the American Psychological Association* (5th ed.). Washington, DC: Author.

Arditi, A. (2005). Effective color contrast. *Lighthouse International*. Retrieved August 24, 2007, from http://www.lighthouse.org/color_contrast.htm

Arntson, A. E. (2007). *Graphic design basics* (5th ed.). Belmont, CA: Thomson Wadsworth.

Ashcraft, M. H. (1998). *Fundamentals of cognition*. New York: Addison-Wesley.

Aslam, M. M. (2006). Are you selling the right colour? A cross-cultural review of colour as a marketing cue. *Journal of Marketing Communications, 12*, 15–30.

Baker, R. (2005). Is multiple-column online text better? It depends! *Usability News 7.2*. Retrieved April 7, 2010, from http://psychology.wichita.edu/surl/usabilitynews/72/columns.asp

Barnum, C. (2002). *Usability testing and research*. New York: Longman.

Bartell, A. L., Schultz, L. D., & Spryidakis, J. H. (2006). The effect of heading frequency on comprehension of print versus online information. *Technical Communication, 53*, 416–426.

Becker, S. A. (2004). E-government visual accessibility for older adult users. *Social Science Computer Review, 22*, 11–23.

Bellizzi, J. A., & Hite, R. E. (1992). Environmental color, consumer feelings, and purchase likelihood. *Psychology and Marketing, 9*, 347–363.

Berlyne, D. (1960). *Conflict, arousal, and curiosity*. New York: McGraw-Hill.

Berlyne, D. (1971). *Aesthetics and psychobiology*. New York: Appleton-Century-Crofts.

Berlyne, D., Graw, M., Salapatek, P., & Lewis, J. (1963). Novelty, complexity, incongruity, extrinsic motivation, and the GSR. *Journal of Experimental Psychology, 66*, 560–567.

Bernard, M., Chaparro, B., & Thomasson, R. (2000). Finding information on the Web: Does the amount of whitespace really matter? *Usability News 2.1*. Retrieved January 12, 2010, from http://www.surl.org/usabilitynews/21/whitespace.asp

Bernard, M., Liao, C., & Mills, M. (2001). Determining the best online font for older adults. *Usability News 3.1*. Retrieved April 7, 2010, from http://www.surl.org/usabilitynews/31/fontSR.asp

Bernard, M., & Mills, M. (2000). So, what size and type of font should I use on my Website? *Usability News, 2.2*. Retrieved January 4, 2010, from http://www.surl.org/usabilitynews/22/font.asp

Bernard, M., Mills, M., Frank, T., & McKown, J. (2001). Which fonts do children prefer to read online? *Usability News 2.1*. Retrieved April 7, 2010, from http://www.surl.org/usabilitynews/31/fontJR.asp

Bernard, M., Mills, M., Peterson, M., & Storrer, K. (2000). A comparison of popular online fonts: Which is best and when? *Usability News, 3.2*. Retrieved January 4, 2010, from http://www.surl.org/usabilitynews/32/font.asp

Bertin, J. (1983). *Semiology of graphics: Diagrams, networks, maps*. Madison: University of Wisconsin Press.

Birdsell, D. S., & Groarke, L. (1996). Toward a theory of visual argument. *Argumentation and Advocacy, 33*, 1–10.

Blair, J. A. (1996). The possibility and actuality of visual arguments. *Argumentation and Advocacy, 33*, 23–39.

Blokzijl, W., & Naeff, R. (2004). The instructor as stagehand: Dutch student responses to PowerPoint. *Business Communication Quarterly, 67*, 70–77.

Brasseur, L. (1993). Visual thinking in the English department. *Journal of Aesthetic Education, 27*, 129–141.

Bruce, M., & Foster, J. J. (1982). The visibility of colored characters on colored backgrounds in viewdata displays. *Visible Language, 16,* 382–390.

Brumberger, E. R. (2003a). The rhetoric of typography: The persona of typeface and text. *Technical Communication, 50,* 206–223.

Brumberger, E. R. (2003b). The rhetoric of typography: The awareness and impact of typeface appropriateness. *Technical Communication, 50,* 224–231.

Brumberger, E. R. (2007). Making the strange familiar: A pedagogical exploration of visual thinking. *Journal of Business and Technical Communication, 21,* 376–401.

Burmark, L. (2002). *Visual literacy: Learn to see, see to learn.* Alexandria, VA: Association for Supervision and Curriculum Development.

Burton, G. E. (1991). The readability of consumer-oriented bank brochures: An empirical investigation. *Business & Society, 30,* 21–25.

Cahoon, R. L. (1969). Physiological arousal and time estimation. *Perceptual and Motor Skills, 28,* 259–268.

Caldwell, B., Cooper, M., Reid, L. G., & Vanderheiden, G. (2007). Understanding WCAG 2.0: A guide to understanding and implementing WCAG 2.0, World Wide Web Consortium, Retrieved April 7, 2010, from http://www.w3.org/TR/UNDERSTANDING-WCAG20/

Carney, R. N., & Levin, J. R. (2002). Pictorial illustrations still improve students' learning from text. *Educational Psychology Review, 14,* 5–26.

Carpenter, P. A., & Shah, P. (1998). A model of the perceptual and conceptual processes in graph comprehension. *Journal of Experimental Psychology: Applied, 4,* 75–100.

Carswell, C. M., Emery, E., & Lonon, A. M. (1993). Stimulus complexity and information integration in the spontaneous interpretation of line graphs. *Applied Cognitive Psychology, 7,* 341–357.

Carswell, C. M., & Wickens, C. D. (1987). Information integration and the object display: An interaction of task demands and display superiority. *Ergonomics, 30,* 511–527.

Cederholm, D. (2006). *Bulletproof Web design.* Berkeley, CA: New Riders.

Center for Universal Design. (1997). Universal design principles. Retrieved April 30, 2009, from http://www.design.ncsu.edu/cud/about_ud/udprincipleshtmlformat.html

Center for Universal Design. (2008). About UD. Retrieved April 30, 2009, from http://www.design.ncsu.edu/cud/about_ud/about_ud.htm

Chang, D., & Nesbitt, K. V. (2006). Developing Gestalt-based design guidelines for multi-sensory displays. *Proceedings of the 2005 NICTA-HCSNet Multimodal User Interaction Workshop,* Sydney, Australia (pp. 9–16). Darlinghurst, Australia: Australian Computer Society.

Chaparro, B., Baker, J. R., Shaikh, A. D., Hull, S., & Brady, L. (2004). Reading online text: A comparison of four white space layouts. *Usability News* 6.2. Retrieved April 7, 2010, from http://www.surl.org/usabilitynews/62/whitespace.asp

Choungourian, A. (1968). Color preference and cultural variation. *Perceptual and Motor Skills, 26,* 1203–1206.

Clark, J. (2002). The image problem. *Building accessible Websites.* Retrieved April 30, 2009, from http://joeclark.org/book/sashay/serialization/Chapter06.html

Clark, J. M., & Paivio, A. (1991). Dual coding theory and education. *Educational Psychology Review, 71,* 64–73.

Cleveland, W. S., McGill, M. E., & McGill, R. (1988). The shape parameter of a two-variable graph. *Journal of the American Statistical Association, 83,* 289–300.

Clynes, M. (1977). *Sentics: The touch of emotions.* Garden City, NY: Anchor Press.

Computer Graphics System Development Corporation (CGSD). (2000). Gamma. Retrieved April 30, 2009, from http://www.cgsd.com/papers/gamma.html

Craig, J., & Bevington, W. (1999). *Designing with type: A basic course in typography* (4th ed.). New York: Watson-Guptill.

Danger, E. (1969). *How to use color to sell.* Boston: Cahners.

David, C. (2001). Mythmaking in annual reports. *Journal of Business and Technical Communication, 15,* 195–222.

Decrop, A. (2007). The influence of message format on the effectiveness of print advertisements for tourism destinations. *International Journal of Advertising, 26,* 505–525.

Doumont, J. (2005). The cognitive style of PowerPoint: Slides are not all evil. *Technical Communication, 52,* 64–70.

Dragga, S., & Voss, D. (2001). Cruel pies: The inhumanity of technical illustrations. *Technical Communication, 48,* 265–274.

Duin, A. (1989). Factors that influence how readers learn from text: Guidelines for structuring technical documents. *Technical Communication, 36,* 97–101.

D'Zmura, M. (1991). Color in visual research. *Vision Research, 31,* 951–966.

Farkas, D. (2005). The explicit structure of print and on-screen documents. *Technical Communication Quarterly, 14,* 9–30.

Finkelstein, E. (2003). *How to do everything with Microsoft Office PowerPoint 2003*. New York: McGraw-Hill.

Fish, J., & Scrivener, S. (1990). Amplifying the mind's eye: Sketching and visual cognition. *Leonardo, 23,* 117–126.

Flanders, V., & Peters, D. (2002). *Son of Web pages that suck: Learn good design by looking at bad design*. Alameda, CA: Sybex.

Flanders, V., & Willis, M. (1998). *Web pages that suck: Learn good design by looking at bad design*. Alameda, CA: Sybex.

Fonts.com. (2010). Retrieved November 26, 2008, from Monotype Imaging Web site: http://www.fonts.com

Fraser, B., Murphy, C., & Bunting, F. (2003). *Real world color management*. Berkeley: Peachpit Press.

Gage, J. (1999). *Color and meaning: Art, science, and symbolism*. Berkeley, CA: University of California Press.

Gerard, R. M. (1957). *Differential effects of colored lights on psychophysiological functions*. Unpublished doctoral dissertation, University of California, Los Angeles.

Gerard, R. M. (1958). Color and emotional arousal [Abstract]. *American Psychologist, 13,* 340.

Goldschmidt, G. (1994). On visual design thinking: The vis kids of architecture. *Design Studies, 15,* 158–174.

Gorn, G. J., Chattopadhyay, A., Sengupta, J., & Tripathi, S. (2004). Waiting for the Web: How screen color affects time perception. *Journal of Marketing Research, 41,* 215–225.

Gregory, J. (2002/2003). Social issues infotainment: Using emotion and entertainment to attract readers' attention to social issues leaflets. *Information Design Journal, 11,* 67–81.

Guilford, J. P., & Smith, P. C. (1959). A system of color-preferences. *American Journal of Psychology, 72,* 487–502.

Guthrie, J. T., Weber, S., & Kimmerly, N. (1993). Searching documents: Cognitive processes and deficits in understanding graphs, tables, and illustrations. *Contemporary Educational Psychology, 18,* 186–221.

Hall, R. H., & Hanna, P. (2004). The impact of Web page text-background colour combinations on readability, retention, aesthetics and behavioural intention. *Behaviour & Information, 23,* 183–195.

Harris, C. R. (1991). Digitization and manipulation of news photographs. *Journal of Mass Media Ethics, 6,* 164–174.

Health and Human Services (HHS). (2006). Research-based Web design & usability guidelines. Retrieved January 15, 2008, from http://www.usability.gov/guidelines/index.html

Hill, A. L., & Scharff, L. V. (1999). Legibility of computer displays as a function of colour, saturation, and texture backgrounds. In D. Harris (Ed.), *Engineering psychology and cognitive ergonomics* (pp. 123–130). Sydney: Ashgate.

History of Gantts. Retrieved March 24, 2006, from the Gantt Charts site: http://www.ganttchart.com/History1.html

Hodgson, P. (1991). Qualitative research and tour brochure design. *Journal of the Market Research Society, 33,* 51–55.

Hodgson, P. (1993). Tour operator brochure design research revisited. *Journal of Travel Research, 32,* 50–52.

Hyönä, J., & Lorch, R. F. (2004). Effects of topic headings on text processing: Evidence from adult readers' eye fixation patterns. *Learning and Instruction, 14,* 131–152.

Irby, K. (2000). Hot tips for writing captions. Accessed January 20, 2008, from http://poynter.org/content/content_view.asp?id=4355

Itten, J. (1997). *The art of color: The subjective experience and objective rationale of color*. New York: Wiley.

Jacobs, K. W., & Suess, J. F. (1975). Effects of four psychological primary colors on anxiety state. *Perceptual and Motor Skills, 41,* 207–210.

Jansson, C., Marlow, N., & Bristow, M. (2004). The influence of colour on visual search times in cluttered environments. *Journal of Marketing Communications, 10,* 183–193.

John-Steiner, V. (1997). *Notebooks of the mind: Explorations of thinking*. New York: Oxford University Press.

Jones, S. L. (1997). A guide to using color effectively in business communication. *Business Communication Quarterly, 60*(2), 76–88.

Karpowicz Lazreg, C. K., & Mullet, E. (2001). Judging the pleasantness of form-color combinations. *American Journal of Psychology, 114,* 511–533.

Kaufman, K. A., & Tebelak, R. M. (1993). Skimmers—How to reach our new audience? *Proceedings of the International Professional Communication Conference '93* (pp. 335–339). New York: IEEE.

Kelly, D. (2007). 10 tips to improve color management. *Publishing Executive*. Retrieved January 18, 2010, from http://www.pubexec.com/article/10-tips-improve-color-management-66060/1

Kosslyn, S. M. (1989). Understanding charts and graphs. *Applied Cognitive Psychology, 3,* 185–226.

Kosslyn, S. M. (1994). *Elements of graph design*. New York: W. H. Freeman.

Kostelnick, C., & Roberts, D. D. (1998). *Designing visual language: Strategies for professional communicators*, Boston: Allyn & Bacon.

Krug, S. (2005). *Don't make me think: A common sense approach to Web usability* (2nd ed.). Berkeley, CA: New Riders.

Larson, K. (2004, July). The science of word recognition, or how I learned to stop worrying and love the bouma. Retrieved September 1, 2005, from Microsoft Corporation Web site: http://www.microsoft.com/typography/ctfonts/WordRecognition.aspx

Laseau, P. (1986). *Graphic problem solving for architects and designers.* New York: Van Nostrand Reinhold.

Lewandowsky, S., & Spence, I. (1989). Discriminating strata in scatterplots. *Journal of American Statistical Association, 84,* 682–688.

Lin, C. (2003). Effects of contrast ratio and text color on visual performance with TFT-LCD. *International Journal of Industrial Ergonomics, 31,* 65–72.

Ling, J., & van Schaik, P. (2002). The effect of text and background colour on visual search of Web pages. *Displays, 23,* 223–230.

Lorch, R. F., Jr., & Chen, A. H. (1968). Effect of number signals on reading and recall. *Journal of Educational Psychology, 76,* 263–270.

Lorch, R. F., Jr., & Lorch, E. P. (1995). Effects of organizational signals on text-processing strategies. *Journal of Educational Psychology, 87,* 537–544.

Lorch, R. F., Jr., & Lorch, E. P. (1996). Effects of headings on text recall and summarization. *Contemporary Educational Psychology, 21,* 261–278.

Lowrey, W. (2003). Normative conflict in the newsroom: The case of digital photo manipulation. *Journal of Mass Media Ethics, 18,* pp. 123–142.

Lupton, E. (1998). The designer as producer. In S. Heller (Ed.), *The education of a graphic designer* (pp. 159–162). New York: Allworth Press.

Maciukenas, J. (2006). Sketching a grand order: A link between conceptualizing and realizing Internet structure. *Proceedings of the International Professional Communication Conference 2006* (pp. 328–334). New York: IEEE.

Mackiewicz, J. (2005). How to use five letterforms to gauge a typeface's personality: A research-driven method. *Journal of Technical Writing And Communication, 35,* 291–315.

Madden, T. J., Hewett, K., & Roth, M. S. (2000). Managing images in different cultures: A cross-national study of color meanings and preferences. *Journal of International Marketing, 8,* 90–107.

Manning, A. D. (1998). Scott McCloud: *Understanding comics: The invisible art. IEEE Transactions on Professional Communication, 41,* 66–69.

Manning, A., & Amare, N. (2006). Visual-rhetoric ethics: Beyond accuracy and injury. *Technical Communication, 53,* 195–211.

Manning, A., & Amare, N. (2007). The language of visuals: Text + graphics = visual rhetoric. *IEEE Transactions on Professional Communication, 50,* 57–70.

Mayer, R. E. (1989). Systematic thinking fostered by illustrations in scientific text. *Journal of Educational Psychology, 81,* 240–246.

Mayer, R. E., Bove, W., Bryman, A., Mars, R., & Tapangco, L. (1996). When less is more: Meaningful learning from visual and verbal summaries of science textbook lessons. *Journal of Educational Psychology, 88,* 64–73.

Mayer, R. E., Dyck, J. L., & Cook, L. K. (1984). Techniques that help readers build mental models from scientific text: Definitions pretraining and signaling. *Journal of Educational Psychology, 76,* 1089–1105.

Mayer, R. E., & Gallini, J. (1990). When is a picture worth ten thousand words? *Journal of Educational Psychology, 82,* 715–727.

Mayer, R. E., & Moreno, R. (2003). Nine ways to reduce cognitive load in multimedia learning. *Educational Psychologist, 38,* 43–52.

Mayer, R. E., Steinhoff, K., Bower, G., & Mars, R. (1995). A generative theory of textbook design: Using annotated illustrations to foster meaningful learning of science text. *Educational Technology Research and Development, 43,* 31–43.

McWade, J. (2003). *Before & after page design.* Berkeley, CA: Peachpit Press.

Meyer, J., Shamo, K., & Gopher, D. (1999). Information structure and the relative efficacy of tables and graphs. *Human Factors, 41,* 570–587.

Miller, J. (2004). *The Chicago guide to writing about numbers.* Chicago: University of Chicago Press.

Nakshian, J. S. (1964). The effects of red and green surroundings on behavior. *Journal of General Psychology, 70,* 143–161.

Neal, C. M., Quester, P. G., & Hawkins, D. I. (2002). *Consumer behaviour: Implications for marketing strategy* (3rd ed.). Roseville, NSW: McGraw-Hill.

Nes, F. L. V., Juola, J. F., & Moonen, R. J. A. M. (1987). Attraction and distraction by text colors on displays. In J. J. Bullinger & B. Shackel (Eds.), *Human-computer interaction—INTERACT'87* (pp. 625–630). Amsterdam: Elsevier Science, North-Holland Publishing.

Nielsen, J. (2006). F-shaped pattern for reading Web content. Retrieved October 1, 2007, from http://www.useit.com/alertbox/reading_pattern.html

Nielsen, J. (2006). Screen resolution and page layout. Retrieved April 30, 2009, from http://www.useit.com/alertbox/screen_resolution.html

Nielsen, J. (2008, May 13). Link list color on intranets. Retrieved June 6, 2008, from http://www.useit.com/alertbox/link-list-color.html

Padgett, J. B. (2000). William Faulkner anecdotes and trivia. *William Faulkner on the Web.* Retrieved April 26, 2009, from http://www.mcsr.olemiss.edu/~egjbp/faulkner/trivia.html#wl3

Paivio, A. (1986). *Mental representations: A dual coding approach.* New York: Oxford University Press.

Perez, A. M. (2008). Common fonts to all versions of Windows & Mac equivalents. Retrieved April 30, 2009, from http://www.ampsoft.net/webdesign-l/WindowsMacFonts.html

Perloff, R. M., & Ray, G. B. (1991). An analysis of AIDS brochures directed at intravenous drug users. *Health Communication, 3,* 113–125.

Phillips, B. J., & McQuarrie, E. F. (2002). The development, change, and transformation of rhetorical style in magazine advertisements 1954–1999. *Journal of Advertising, 31,* 1–13.

Pinker, S. (1990). A theory of graph comprehension. In R. Freedle (Ed.), *Artificial intelligence and the future of testing* (pp. 73–126). Hillsdale, NJ: Lawrence Erlbaum Associates.

Poynter Institute. (2004). Online images: Faces, size attract. Retrieved Dec. 19, 2007, from http://www.poynterextra.org:80/eyetrack2004/photos.htm

Pracejus, J. W., Olsen, G. D., & O'Guinn, T. C. (2006). How nothing became something: White space, rhetoric, history, and meaning. *Journal of Consumer Research, 33,* 82–90.

Profusek, P. J., & Rainey, D. W. (1987). Effects of Baker-Miller pink and red on state anxiety, grip strength, and motor precision. *Perceptual and Motor Skills, 65,* 941–942.

Radl, G. W. (1980). Experimental investigations for optimal presentation-mode and colours of symbols on the CRT-screen. In E. Grandjean & E. Vigliani (Eds.), *Ergonomic aspects of visual display terminals* (pp. 127–136). London: Taylor and Francis.

Rayner, K. (1975). The perceptual span and peripheral cues in reading. *Cognitive Psychology, 7,* 65–81.

Reichert, T., Heckler, S. E., & Jackson, S. (2001). The effects of sexual social marketing appeals on cognitive processing and persuasion. *Journal of Advertising, 30,* 13–27.

Resnick, M. L., & Sanchez, J. (2004). Effects of organizational scheme and labeling on task performance in product-centered and user-centered retail Web sites. *Human Factors, 46,* 104–117.

Richards, A. R. (2003). Argument and authority in the visual representations of science. *Technical Communication Quarterly, 12,* 183–206.

Richards, A. R., & David, C. (2005). Decorative color as a rhetorical enhancement on the World Wide Web. *Technical Communication Quarterly, 14,* 31–38.

Riley, K., & Parker, F. (1998). Parallels between visual and textual processing. *IEEE Transactions on Professional Communication, 41,* 175–185.

Robbins, N. B. (2005). *Creating more effective graphs.* Hoboken, NJ: Wiley Interscience.

Rutter, R. R. (2007). How to size text in CSS. *A List Apart: For People Who Make Websites, no. 249.* Retrieved April 30, 2009, from http://www.alistapart.com/articles/howtosizetextincss

Samara, T. (2005). *Making and breaking the grid: A graphic design layout workshop.* Beverly, MA: Rockport.

Schellens, P. J., & de Jong, M. (2004). Argumentation schemes in persuasive brochures. *Argumentation, 18,* 295–323.

Schmitt, B. H. (1995). Language and visual imagery: Issues in corporate identities in East Asia. *Columbia Journal of World Business, 30,* 28–36.

Schriver, K. A. (1997). *Dynamics in document design: Creating texts for readers.* New York: Wiley.

Schultz, L. D., & Spyridakis, J. H. (2004). The effect of heading frequency on comprehension of online information: A study of two populations. *Technical Communication, 51,* 504–516.

Shah, P., & Hoeffner, J. (2002). Review of graph comprehension research: Implications for instruction. *Educational Psychology Review, 14,* 47–69.

Shah, P., Mayer, R. E., & Hegarty, M. (1999). Graphs as aids to knowledge construction: Signaling techniques for guiding the process of graph comprehension. *Journal of Ethical Psychology, 91,* 690–702.

Shah, P., & Shellhammer, D. (1999, July). *The role of domain knowledge and graph reading skills in graph comprehension.* Paper presented at the 1999 meeting of the Society for Applied Research in Memory and Cognition, Boulder, CO.

Shaikh, A. D. (2005). The effects of line length on reading online news. *Usability News 7.2.* Retrieved April 8, 2010, from http://psychology.wichita.edu/surl/usabilitynews/72/LineLength.asp

Sharpe, D. T. (1974). *The psychology of color and design.* Chicago: Nelson-Hall.

Shea, D., & Holzschlag, M. (2005). *The Zen of CSS design: Visual enlightenment for the Web.* Berkeley, CA: Peachpit Press.

Shieh, K., & Lin, C. (2000). Effects of screen type, ambient illumination, and color combination on VDT visual performance and subjective preference. *International Journal of Industrial Ergonomics, 26,* 527–536.

Simon, W. E. (1971). Number and color responses of some college students: Preliminary evidence for a blue seven phenomenon. *Perceptual and Motor Skills, 33,* 373–374.

Snyder, C. (2003). *Paper prototyping: The fast and easy way to design and refine interfaces.* San Francisco: Morgan Kaufmann.

Springston, J. K., & Champion, V. L. (2004). Public relations and cultural aesthetics: Designing health brochures. *Public Relations Review, 30,* 483–491.

Spyridakis, J. H. (2000). Guidelines for authoring comprehensible Web pages and evaluating their success. *Technical Communication, 47,* 359–382.

Strizver, I. (2001). *Type rules!* Cincinnati, OH: North Light Books.

Sutherland, R., & Karg, B. (2003). *Graphic designer's color handbook: Choosing and using color from concept to final output.* Gloucester, MA: Rockport.

Text Matters. (n.d.) Typography for visually impaired users. Retrieved September 1, 2005, from Text Matters Web site: http://www.textmatters.com/our_interests/guidelines/typog_visual_impaired

Tracy, W. (1995). Legibility and readability. In R. McLean (Ed.), *Typographers on type* (pp. 170–172). New York: Norton. (Original work published 1955)

Tufte, E. R. (1983). *The visual display of quantitative information.* Cheshire, CT: Graphics Press.

Tufte, E. R. (2003). *The cognitive style of PowerPoint.* Cheshire, CT: Graphics Press.

Tversky, B. (2002). Some ways that graphics communicate. In N. Allen (Ed.), *Working with words and images: New steps in an old dance* (pp. 57–74). Westport, CT: Ablex

Valdez, P., & Mehrabian, A. (1995). Effects of color on emotions. *Journal of Experimental Psychology, 123,* 394–409.

Walker, P., Smith, S., & Livingston, A. (1986). Predicting the appropriateness of a typeface on the basis of its multi-modal features. *Information Design Journal, 5,* 29–42.

Walker, S. (2001). *Typography and language in everyday life: Prescriptions and practices.* Essex, England: Pearson Education.

Walsh, T. (1998). Illustrations in oral presentations: Photographs. *IEEE Transactions on Professional Communication, 41,* 209–212.

Wang, A., Fang, J., & Chen, C. (2003). Effects of VDT leading-display design on visual performance of users in handling static and dynamic display information dual-tasks. *International Journal of Industrial Ergonomics, 32,* 93–104.

Warde, B. (1995). The crystal goblet or printing should be invisible. In R. McLean (Ed.), *Typographers on type* (pp. 73–78). New York: Norton. (Original work published 1955)

WebAIM. (n.d.). Creating accessible tables. Retrieved April 30, 2009, from http://www.webaim.org/techniques/tables/

Web Content Accessibility Guidelines 2.0. (2007). In B. Caldwell, M. Cooper, L. G. Reid, & G. Vanderheiden (Eds.), *W3C.* Retrieved August 28, 2007, from http://www.w3.org/TR/WCAG20

Weinman, L. (n.d.). The browser-safe Web palette. Retrieved April 30, 2009, from http://www.lynda.com/resources/webpalette.aspx

Weller, D. (2004). The effects of contrast and density on visual Web search. *Usability News 6.2.* Retrieved January 12, 2010, from http://www.surl.org/usabilitynews/62/density.asp

White, J. V. (1990). *Color for the electronic age.* New York: Watson-Guptill.

White, J. V. (2003). Color: The newest tool for technical communicators. *Technical Communication, 50,* 485–491. (Reprinted from *Technical Communication, 38* (1991): 346–351)

Wickens, C. D., & Hollands, J. G. (2000). *Engineering psychology and human performance* (3rd ed.). Upper Saddle River, NJ: Prentice Hall.

Wierzbicka, A. (1990). The meaning of colour terms: Semantics, culture, and cognition. *Cognitive Linguistics, 1,* 99–150.

Wilkinson, L. (1999). Graphs for research in counseling psychology. *The Counseling Psychologist, 27,* 384–407.

Williams, R. (2003). *The non-designer's design book* (2nd ed.). Berkeley, CA: Peachpit Press.

Williams, R. (2008). *The non-designer's design and type books: Design and typographic principles for the visual novice.* Berkeley, CA: Peachpit Press.

Williams, T. R. (2000). Guidelines for designing and evaluating the display of information on the Web. *Technical Communication, 47,* 383–396.

Williams, T. R., & Spyridakis, J. H. (1992). Visual discriminability of headings in text. *IEEE Transactions on Professional Communication, 35,* 64–70.

Wilson, G. D. (1966). Arousal properties of red versus green. *Perceptual and Motor Skills, 23,* 942–949.

Winn, W. (1991). Color in document design. *IEEE Transactions on Professional Communication, 34,* 180–185.

Zacks, J. & Tversky, B. (1999). Bars and lines: A study of graphic communication. *Memory and Cognition, 27,* 1073–1079.

INDEX